Praise for Dr. William R

When a Parent Is Depressed

How to Protect Your Children from the Effects of Depression in the Family

"A reader-friendly book for parents. . . . The fact that depression often runs in families is well established. But landmark research, which focuses on prevention, now shows what can break the cycle and help protect youngsters from future illness. Child psychiatrist William Beardslee has run two major studies involving hundreds of children. . . . Beardslee's team found one type of intervention in families with a depressed parent to be particularly helpful: a brief series of meetings with a clinician, some for parents alone and children alone, plus family sessions together. Importantly the child learned he was not responsible for his parent's sadness. Communication in the family improved. Beardslee believes that open family discussions lead to understanding the illness and help protect the next generation."
— Karen S. Peterson, *USA Today*

"An excellent book. . . . William Beardslee, M.D., wisely notes that you should talk to your children only 'when you can recognize depression as an unwelcome illness rather than a shameful secret.' He urges depressed parents to stay involved in their children's lives. Any small act of caring — reading a bedtime story, say — will convey the message, *I'm getting better and I'm still here for you.*"
— Ann Pleshette Murphy, *Family Circle*

"Can a mother or father struggling with depression still raise well-adjusted, healthy kids? Absolutely, says Dr. William Beardslee. . . . His book is full of helpful clinical information, practical advice, and, most important, hope. *When a Parent Is Depressed* is a reassuring resource for families burdened by depression."

— Vinca LaFleur, *Washington Post*

"Here is clinical knowledge become publicly available wisdom. William Beardslee's book will be of great help to many American families. He addresses the melancholy that weighs heavily on some parents — impairs their home life as mothers and fathers — and for so doing will surely earn the gratitude of his many readers, indeed, of all who wish the best for children."

— Robert Coles, M.D.

"In this day and age, there are so many forces that conspire to pull families apart. Dr. Beardslee's strategy in which all family members touched by depression are brought together to 'break the silence' is simple but full of wisdom. It is the psychiatric version of the old family doctor house call. One cannot help but be uplifted by these stories of struggle and recovery."

— Rosalynn Carter

"This book is a remarkable resource for any family struggling with depression. Taking a preventive and therapeutic approach, Dr. William Beardslee shows what parents and caretakers can do to not only lessen the impact of depression on children's lives, but also give them the tools to cope."

— T. Berry Brazelton, M.D.

"Depression is a common condition that will rupture emotional connections with the people we love. *When a Parent Is Depressed* addresses the needs of those who are affected the most, our families and especially our children. Dr. Beardslee draws on decades of clinical experience to bring us inspirational examples of how families heal."

— Dr. Drew Pinsky

"Dr. William Beardslee presents a groundbreaking step-by-step approach to treating depression as it is experienced within families when one caregiver is depressed. In this book you will meet many families and read the case histories of families who worked together to beat the odds of this devastating disease."

— Marc Musacchio, *San Diego Union-Tribune*

"A useful and accessible resource. . . . Beardslee takes a preventive approach to help families recognize depression, develop resiliency, and reduce the risks. Profiles of families who have coped well with a range of challenges, from divorce, death, job loss, and other life woes, show the characteristics associated with triumphing over adversity and avoiding depression." — Vanessa Bush, *Booklist*

"Written with a keen mind and a knowing heart. Dr. Beardslee offers enabling insights for those suffering from depression and for their loved ones."

— Jerome Groopman, M.D., Professor of Medicine
at Harvard University and staff writer at *The New Yorker*

"Twenty percent of Americans suffer from depression at some point. In *When a Parent Is Depressed*, veteran psychiatrist William Beardslee explores this disease and gives great hope to families affected."

— Beth Stein, *Nashville Tennessean*

"In *When a Parent Is Depressed*, we see the work of a discerning researcher, a compassionate clinician, and an impassioned activist. In a voice that is both provocative and reassuring, William Beardslee challenges our prejudices and distortions about depression, a common and misunderstood illness that is shrouded in mystery and silence. Beardslee teaches us that returning from depression is a long journey and a family affair that requires honesty, courage, and ongoing dialogue. Throughout this illuminating text, Beardslee speaks of his patients and their families with empathy and the deepest respect, and looks to the healer within each of them."

— Sara Lawrence-Lightfoot, Emily Hargroves Fisher
Professor of Education at Harvard University,
author of *Respect: An Exploration*

"Maternal depression (it's twice as likely for a mother to get depressed than for a father) is a triple whammy for children. First, there's typically an event — a death, change of family economic status, a divorce — that precipitates the depression in the parent but also, obviously, affects children, too. Then there's the depression itself. It changes dynamics in a family, in the way a person parents: Mom not only may spend a lot of time in her bedroom, but when she comes out, she's irritable and mopey. . . . And there's the secrecy. In most families where a parent is depressed, there's a lot of shushing. . . . Dr. Beardslee pioneered the practice of discussing depression with children, just as you would if the parent were diagnosed with diabetes. Why is this so important? Children who grow up with parental depression that is kept secret are two to four times more likely to develop depression themselves by age fifteen than if their parent had no illness. Long before fifteen, however, other problems can surface, depending on how old a child is when a parent's depression begins and how long it goes untreated and untalked about."

— Barbara F. Meltz, *Boston Globe*

When a Parent Is Depressed

How to Protect Your Children

from the Effects of Depression

in the Family

William R. Beardslee, M.D.

Little, Brown and Company   Boston · New York · London

Originally published in hardcover under the title *Out of the Darkened
Room* by Little, Brown and Company, June 2002
First paperback edition, December 2003

The author is grateful for permission to include the following previously copyrighted material: Excerpt from *Let Us Now Praise Famous
Men*. Copyright © 1941 by James Agee and Walker Evans. Copyright ©
renewed 1969 by Mia Fritsch Agee and Walker Evans. Reprinted by permission of Houghton Mifflin Company. All rights reserved; "The Fury
of Rain Storms" from *The Death Notebooks* by Anne Sexton. Copyright
© 1974 by Anne Sexton. Reprinted by permission of Houghton Mifflin
Company. All rights reserved; Excerpt from "The Writer" from *The
Mind Reader* by Richard Wilbur. Copyright © 1971 by Richard Wilbur.
Reprinted by permission of Harcourt, Inc., and Faber and Faber Ltd.

ISBN 0-316-73889-1
LCCN 2003109475

10   9   8   7   6   5   4   3   2   1

Designed by Chris Welch

Q-MB

Printed in the United States of America

For my father, my mother,
and my sister

"The light still shines in the darkness,
and the darkness has never put it out."
— JOHN I:5, J. B. PHILLIPS TRANSLATION
OF THE NEW TESTAMENT

"The child is the bearer of whatever the future
shall be. . . . At this center . . . his incomparable tenderness
to experience, his malleability, the almost unimaginable
nakedness and defenselessness of this wondrous
five-windowed nerve and core."
— JAMES AGEE, *LET US NOW PRAISE FAMOUS MEN*

Contents

When a Parent
Is Depressed

Introduction
A New Way of Helping Families

When parents become depressed, they bear a double burden. Even as they wrestle with the darkness that clouds their lives, they must struggle to maintain their role as guardians of their children's future. Making matters worse, depression is often completely mystifying both to the sufferers and to those around them.

The key point in understanding depression is to recognize that it is in part a biological illness, although it profoundly affects feelings and relationships. Depression is just as much a medical condition as heart disease or diabetes. For many depressed people, hope can begin there too, because we now know that depression is not only an illness, but also a highly treatable one.

For some, however, awareness of the biological aspect of the disease actually compounds their suffering, because many depressed parents fear that, through their genes, they will pass along this illness to their children. Many parents likewise believe they have harmed their kids by being withdrawn or angry, or because they are overwhelmed at times when trying to care for them. Parents are often ashamed of having the illness and live alone with their fears. They feel they cannot discuss what they are going through with family members, and they fear prejudice from outside the family against those with mental illnesses. Other parents impose their own rule of silence because they do not want to confirm their worst fear — that they have damaged their children.

Unfortunately, fear, shame, and confusion about depression often prevent families from getting help until the problem becomes quite severe. All too often, parents shut themselves in and weep for days, lose their jobs, or are hospitalized without ever talking to their spouses or children. Families coping silently with depression often live through events so painful that they color every aspect of their lives. These events are so disruptive that they become the central component of the family's collective experience, yet often each member of the family is forced to suffer alone. As a result, children are witnesses to mothers or fathers being completely overwhelmed (even leaving home in ambulances), yet this is never discussed with them. Spouses see the person they married change before their eyes, yet never consider that a medical illness is the cause.

Through a series of long-term studies beginning in 1979, my colleagues and I discovered in family after family that the fear and shame that cause people to suffer in silence are simply not justified. Many children raised in the most challenging of circumstances overcome their difficulties and become remarkably healthy and happy adults. Parents put under extreme pressure by depression have demonstrated time and again that there are specific actions and strategies that they can employ to promote healthy development in their children.

In this book, I hope to explain these possibilities to a wide audience and to help families affected by depression learn to use these strategies.

Twenty percent of Americans will suffer depression sometime in their lifetimes. Not only is depression common, it is becoming increasingly common. Those born in the sixties and seventies have proportionally higher rates of depression than do those born in earlier generations. Depression strikes rich and poor alike, and it can show up as an underlying cause whenever people don't do well wrestling with life's other adversities. Unrecognized and untreated depression is a problem not just in this country. Worldwide, depression is the fourth most important cause of impairment in work and home life, and by the year 2020 it will be the second leading cause. Depression can also compound other problems. Those with heart disease who also suffer from depression are far less likely to fully recover. In studies of mothers living in poverty, those with depression failed to take advantage of programs directly designed to help them; they did not even make effective use of help offered by friends and neighbors.[1]

Certain illnesses such as schizophrenia can create adversity, causing people to be unable to manage life tasks, even something as fundamental as holding down a job. Depression, on the other hand, often begins with a loss or other adversity, and then in turn leads people further downward on the socioeconomic scale. Unrecognized and untreated, depression is the mental illness most frequently associated with suicide, both in adults and in children.[2]

Offsetting these disturbing statistics is the fact that excellent treatments have become available for the majority of cases of depression. Treatments can involve effective medications, such as sertraline, as well as systematic approaches to talking through and making sense of the illness. These "talk therapies" — in particular, cognitive, behavioral, and interpersonal therapy — can make a significant difference in sufferers' lives.[3]

Yet depression remains constantly underrecognized and undertreated. In many studies, only about a quarter of adults with depression received adequate treatment; for children, the percentage was even worse.[4]

Treatment begins with recognition. Likewise, in the prevention approach I describe here, we could only help families after affected parents acknowledged their depression, recognized that help was available, and availed themselves of that help.

In dozens of families that we have worked with over the years, we have seen that no matter what difficulties parents face, the central concern of their lives is not themselves but how to raise their children. Accordingly, our fundamental approach is to align resources and strategies with this concern. We try to help families find new ways of interacting and reconnecting to the larger world in which their children live. Over time, our aim is to prevent depression by helping families identify and build on their strengths and resources.

Because depression is not just a biological illness but affects relationships — it touches the entire community of those committed to raising a child — we address the parents' illness within the context of the whole family: children, grandparents, aunts and uncles, and friends.

Parents need many different resources to heal themselves and to help their children. They need good information about what depression is and how to recognize it. They need ways to combat misunderstanding and to focus on their children. They also need to know about emerging research on what happens to families when parents are depressed, both about the difficulties families encounter and how some families have overcome them. More specifically, they need to know what they can do to prevent difficulties before their children become ill. If their children do show signs of distress, parents need to know how to get help quickly. These are the resources we provide in our work with families. They are the same ones I will provide in the chapters that follow.[5]

Information only brings change when families can talk openly about depression. Our task at Children's Hospital Boston and at Judge Baker Children's Center in Boston has been to get families to do this, together, often for the first time. Our work began by listening to parents' fears, and then moved forward through a program of helping families make the undiscussable — the silence and shame of depression — discussable, allowing them to tie these discussions to the specific actions they can take. You will see an example of this process at work with one particular family in chapter 1.

The centerpiece of our approach, to help families be able to talk together and understand depression together, is a meeting in which all family members touched by the illness are included. We call this "breaking the silence." Parents need to be able to voice their concerns and have their questions answered. Children have to be able to talk about their experiences, to have their voices heard, their fears addressed. Obviously, this can only happen as a dialogue within the family; it cannot be imposed by someone from the outside. To be able to reach one another, family members have to begin to understand themselves and depression in a new way. Equally important, they need to recognize and employ the full range of resources they can muster.

Families can, and do, change. But the action required is not a one-time event. Families must keep talking together over the years that follow the initial conversation as their children grow and change.

Fran O'Connor, whose family will be described in more detail in chapter 7, summed up the opening of a family dialogue this way: "Before, I was just fatalistic about the depression. I thought it would get worse or go on forever. But this has really helped; talking about it, going through the process, has made it more manageable. Even though I know I may get depressed again, I have an attitude about being able to get through it rather than sink into it, whereas before I couldn't get beyond it. It brought us much closer together as a family."

For families, this new way of viewing depression involves not just learning new strategies but uncovering unknown strengths. Another of the parents we worked with described our approach in these words: "It affects the way I think about our family. It made us realize what a good relationship we have, how good we are at taking care of each other and our children. It gave us an increased sense of respect for each other, a whole new paradigm shift, a look at what we are doing that's positive, not just what we're not doing."

Often, direct and powerful conversations take place between parents and children as they deal with depression. Meg Smith, whose alcoholic and abusive husband put her through an acrimonious divorce, said this of her eight-year-old son. "He was speculating about what was going on or who was wrong. He thought that I thought he was causing all the troubles between his father and me, and we began to talk. He said to me right in the office once, 'I ruined your life.' And I said, 'Quite the contrary. You saved my life. Had it not been for you, my life would have gone down the tubes.'" Her reflections about how she changed appear in chapter 13.

What is essential for parents is being on track with their children's lives. Depression and its attendant difficulties can disrupt that track, but we know from experience that families can get back on it. The key is the parents' essential commitment to their children, which, with the kind of help I offer here, can reemerge and become even stronger.

When a Parent Is Depressed offers a new perspective, one very different from the usual concerns of traditional psychiatry. It focuses on prevention, not only of possible recurrence of depression in parents, but of any resultant or future episodes in their children. Like other empirical prevention approaches, it is based on the new and rapidly expanding knowledge of how children mature successfully at different stages in the face of adversity. The aim of prevention programs is to use this knowledge to intervene at appropriate points along the path of a child's growth before any illness is evident. Our objective is to help children develop strength and resilience, to steel themselves against adversity wherever possible. When difficulties develop, it also means seeing that children and their parents get help quickly and effectively.[6]

In the past, the medical community sometimes compounded the problems of depressed parents by understanding the illness only insofar as it affected the individual. Health care providers would try to treat the parents' illness, but for the most part, they never inquired about the kids. No one considered the family as a whole. But depression is a family illness.

Most clinicians still see families only when they are in crisis and in pain. At best, that kind of contact gives a snapshot of the moment, enabling immediate care in that moment. My own practice began this way, which is the experience that led me to the idea of prevention.

Since my days as a resident in training, I have been on call in the emergency room at Children's Hospital in Boston on a monthly basis, and I have consulted with those caring for children hospitalized in acute crisis. In the emergency room, children often appear with their lives wracked by depression, compounded sometimes by substance abuse, sometimes by family violence, often after suicide attempts. Not only are these children desperate, but the systems that care for them, their families, schools, and other providers, are exhausted. To wait until the depression has reached this crisis point is to wait too long to give the best possible care to children.

In contrast, our program for preventive intervention involves reaching children before they are in crisis and trying to increase the positive or protective influences in their lives. Beginning in 1979, we studied 275 youngsters from 143 families, looking in detail at parental depression, divorce, disruptive life events, and other factors to see what effects they had on children. We followed most of the families for four years, and many for far longer than that. This led us to formulate an adversity index as a way to sum up all the forces that conspire to bring on depression in children.

We also followed the public-health model in understanding the relationship between risks and resilience. Risks are conditions that increase the rate of depression within a group of individuals or families when compared to groups without those conditions. Often, of course, several of these risk factors can batter a family all at once. Divorce often comes together with depression, at times complicated by alcoholism or by the loss of job or home, often in someone who has many relatives with depression, and it is these things coming together simultaneously that creates the greatest burden for children.

From this group of 275 youngsters, some emerged as powerfully resilient. We selected 18 of these youngsters, from 14 different families, for follow-up study to better understand the specific characteristics associated with their triumph over adversity. Good relationships with others, the capacity to get tasks accomplished, and self-understanding characterized these young people. In addition, we did another study of young women from the inner city who were at high risk for depression because of adolescent pregnancy. Even here, amid very high rates of depression, we found individuals who were exemplars of resilience, and from whom we learned much.

We put what we learned into a prevention program for families. From those youngsters who, in our early work, manifested extraordinary resilience, we were provided with vital clues about what all children need. While our objective may be to *prevent* depression, our method is to *promote* resilience. Our object was to build strength and resilience in every child and in every family under our care. We started with the idea that the problem of depression was so widespread that we needed an approach that could be used not only by physicians but also by clergy, teachers, educational counselors, psychologists, social workers, and families themselves. We tried different forms of preventive intervention to get the message across, using both lectures and clinician sessions with families. By repeated evaluations of more than one hundred families over many years, we learned what families believed helped them best.[7]

What we discovered was that the part of family life most disrupted by depression is the gift of being able to construct a meaningful story together. Families need to believe that a past was shared, that a present is being shared, and that a future can be shared; and that all this shared experience takes place within the larger context of a community, a religious faith, and a culture. Depression erodes that sense of continuity. Children are at the center of families' stories and represent their hopes for the future. To make matters worse, the combined difficulties that depression poses for families — the loss of energy, the withdrawal, and the disruptions in relationships — impair the family's capacity to talk, understand, and make plans for dealing with the adversity together. Breaking that silence, learning to talk together and make sense of the illness together, reknitting the sense of continuity, emerged as the heart of our approach to preventing depression in children.[8]

Prevention also involves assessing the needs of the child over the next one to five years and positioning resources to answer those needs. It requires a long-term commitment to parents and to what their children need. Developing this approach meant departing from standard treatments. It meant going against the grain. I was constantly advised by others in my field not to consider prevention because it was too difficult and because it took too long to evaluate.

Families were uncertain too at first. But then we realized that thinking about the long-term development of children is what parents do naturally, and our preventive approach made a great deal of sense to them when presented in that light. In essence, our approach found common ground with parents simply by thinking about children the way parents always have.

I am happy to report that over time, our own anxieties, as well as the anxieties of the families and of other clinicians we worked with, proved groundless. The families have responded with enthusiasm to our approach, and it has done an amazing amount of good, a benefit I hope to extend to you with this book.

When a Parent Is Depressed draws on the many different experiences I have had over the last twenty-five years as a doctor working with families with depression. I have had the privilege of studying both what happens over time in families where depression occurs and what the effects of a systematic prevention approach can be. I have tried this approach in an inner-city neighborhood and in new clinics we have started at Children's Hospital. I have taken care of families directly and trained other people to take care of them. As the chairman of psychiatry at Children's Hospital, I have grappled with how to develop programs and render the best possible care in a climate that is increasingly unfriendly to those with mental illness and has virtually no interest in prevention.

For me, the work is deeply personal. Long before I went to medical school, I was interested in the connection between the way people tell their stories, how they understand themselves, and how they can survive and indeed prosper. I first learned about the qualities of resilience by listening to the stories of civil rights workers who stayed in the movement for more than fifteen years. Later, I learned more from dealing with survivors of childhood cancer.[9] Moreover, during the last twenty-five years, my wife and I have been deeply committed to raising four children. Raising a family while trying to help other people raise children taught me a great deal about what it takes to be a good parent and tempered any ideas I had about quick and simple answers. This work also brings back memories of my older sister, whom I admired greatly, and who was stricken with a profound depression in her mid-twenties. Just as I was beginning both my married life and my professional study of resilience, she committed suicide. As I have struggled to help families make sense of their experience, I have also struggled to make sense of my own.

I hope you will find what follows both reassuring and useful in your own life, no matter how trying your circumstances may be.

One

Beginning the Journey
Framework for Change

Breaking the silence as a family represents a commitment to doing things differently. In this chapter, I want to share with you the pathway to better family health we most often observe, and which we recommend.

Getting started on this path means first recognizing depression as an illness and getting the treatment you need, then staying with that treatment, often for a long time. Naturally, getting started is a time of self-doubt, of asking questions like "Will my child be all right?" and "Will my marriage survive?" But the more fundamental question to ask is "Am I ready to change? Am I ready to think about talking to my family in a new way?"

This new way of communicating means confronting straight-on fears about having harmed your child. Of course, it also means entertaining the possibility that you have *not* harmed your child. It even means recognizing that children can be strengthened against the possibility of harm. That strengthening, which we call developing resilience, is the fundamental promise of this book. Developing resilience is one of the many ways in which breaking the silence means gradually rediscovering hope.

Families begin at different places on this road to understanding. Some, the veterans of many treatments, start already knowing a great deal about depression; others, even those who've suffered for many years, are just becoming aware of depression as an illness. Some are reeling from a series of losses, while others are emerging from personal depths unrelated to life events. Wherever a family starts, the more fully it can articulate what its worries are and where it needs help, the better these can be addressed.

Regardless of where it begins, change comes slowly and in uncertain fits and starts, and the way ahead often seems very unclear. Once families have recognized the illness and begun treatment, though, they generally make sense of depression by moving through the following six steps:

1. Sharing a history together
2. Bringing knowledge about depression and resilience to bear on their own unique circumstances
3. Addressing the needs of the children
4. Planning how to talk to the children
5. Breaking the silence together as a family
6. Continuing the family dialogue

These stages can vary and sometimes they are not obvious. Still, I offer this basic sequence of events as a framework for getting started. It's the sequence we've used in working with many, many families. As you'll discover in the pages ahead, I've also used this same six-step framework to guide you through the first half of this book.

These stages first became apparent to me as I observed the journey of Katherine and Dan Petrocelli and their children.[1] They came to us for help with their children having heard of our new program from the therapist treating Katherine, and they were among the very first families I worked with. From the beginning, I made certain to work collaboratively with those caring for Katherine's depression to coordinate our care for the family.[2]

Every family's story has unique characteristics, but the Petrocellis' story is unusual in that her depression was closely tied in Katherine's mind to a specific and terrible family secret. Their story is also unusual in the depth of the depression she suffered. Even so, there are aspects that are typical: not just the gradual progression of stages, but the profound and deep uncertainty, the gnawing doubts that families live through and are able to get beyond.

Sharing a History Together

Katherine and Dan Petrocelli first came to see me one December when Katherine was in the throes of an acute depression. Her face was etched with suffering, gaunt and drawn, and she lived with daily thoughts of suicide. When she talked about herself and her recent hospitalizations, her speech was painfully slow, as if each word were wrung from her at great cost. But when Katherine spoke of her three children, her face lit up with pleasure.

Katherine was determined to make a family Christmas as wonderful as the ones she remembered from the early years of her marriage, when her children were young and when she had felt better. Katherine was determined "this time" to stay out of the hospital, against her psychiatrist's advice. She revealed the stubborn will and determination that often led her into struggles with her caregivers but that also kept her reaching out for and holding on fiercely to her husband and children.

So strong was her desire to make things better for her family that in spite of her pain, Katherine insisted we plan a family meeting. Katherine's commitment to being the best parent possible despite the ravages of her illness was a source of enormous strength for the family. The same was true of her husband, Dan. He stepped in repeatedly when Katherine wasn't able to function or care for their children, chauffeuring the kids, preparing meals, supporting her even when she stayed in bed, unable to face the demands and darkness of winter.

Katherine recalled her first recognized episode of depression, which had occurred two and a half years before our first meeting. Her youngest daughter had just been stung by a bee at the beach and had broken out all over, and Katherine was driving her to the hospital. The trauma of her daughter's pain, combined with her awareness of salt breezes and of sand squeaking under the tires, stirred memories. She saw herself riding with her grandfather down the same beach roads many years earlier, but it was not a pleasant recollection. What it brought to mind was the fact that she'd been molested. Not only had Katherine been violated by her grandfather that day long ago, she had felt obligated to keep silent about it, and had done so for years at terrible cost.

In talking both to me and to her therapist, sometimes as often as three times a week, Katherine began to explore how painful that silence had been. She also became aware that there had been several other times when she'd been depressed: following the births of her two older children, and once when she'd been hospitalized for a bladder infection.

Katherine's illness was shaped by her experience with her wealthy and powerful family. Just as this family seemed to tower haughtily over the rest of the community — a town fading away after the loss of a once-thriving fishing industry — so the family looked down on her. She had been labeled the "family problem." Despite being the oldest, and despite laboring constantly to win the family's love, she felt herself to be her mother's least-favorite child, blamed for everything but expected to wait on the other members of the family hand and foot.

In many ways, Katherine's brothers and sisters repeatedly undermined her attempts to get better, particularly during periods of acute depression. She told me about one example: "Dan was out, and I felt really terrible, really scared. So did the kids. Scared enough that I called my brother and told him I was afraid to be alone. Two hours went by before he turned up, and when he did, he paraded around the house in front of the kids, proclaiming himself my savior. He talked about me to the children and to Dan. 'Will she be safe going upstairs by herself?' as though I were invisible, or stupid. My kids freaked out seeing him take control that way." She felt her brothers had tried to take charge of her treatment and hadn't helped her recover from the devastation of sexual abuse, and the kids were right in the middle of it.

When I began with the Petrocellis, Katherine did not yet understand the reason for her feelings about her place in the family, and she struggled with them. When Katherine became depressed, she lost all her energy, all her concentration, and all interest in the world around her. She couldn't sleep. She couldn't manage. A nurse by profession, she blamed herself for not being able to cure her own illness. She even thought of suicide, which was the reason for her first and a subsequent psychiatric hospitalization during the previous two and a half years.

Katherine, Dan, and I agreed early on that I should keep in touch with her doctors. It was especially important that I work closely with Katherine's psychotherapist and psychopharmacologist in light of the potential for a suicide attempt or for more hospitalizations.

Knowledge About Depression and Resilience

Although Katherine was a medical professional, she and Dan still had some misconceptions about her disease. We talked about how depression was no one's fault, no more than any other biological illness such as a heart attack or chronic condition such as diabetes. After all, I pointed out, if no one expects a person who's had a heart attack to jump right back into full swing, then why should a depressed person be expected to? Katherine laughed grimly. "So depression's legitimate, like a heart attack. You should tell my parents that."

When the discussion turned to their children, Katherine and Dan spoke with warmth, humor, and great enthusiasm about each child. Their oldest, Thomas, was nineteen, hard-driving, pragmatic, and athletic. Thirteen-year-old Lisa was a nonstop talker with a "ton of friends." The youngest child, eight-year-old Mary, was quiet and shy but sometimes exploded into anger. After she once screamed at her parents that she wished she were dead, Katherine and Dan worried that Mary might be depressed. But I could hear no major symptoms of depression in their descriptions of the three children. In fact, the family continued to function remarkably well in the face of Katherine's illness. The kids felt close to one another and carried on at school as they had always done. They were even able to eat meals together on occasion. The vital patterns of their lives had been preserved.

Having listened to Katherine and Dan describe their children, I began to introduce the general idea of resilience. This notion — that in the midst of the family's devastation, the children could be strong — was completely new to Katherine and Dan.

Dan and Katherine supported my meeting individually with each child. My goals for the conversations with Thomas, Lisa, and Mary were to evaluate their general state of mind, their potential risk for childhood depression, and signs of their resilience. I also wanted to give them the opportunity to have their questions answered and to help them speak up for themselves.

We've found that parents who've learned how depression affects children are more open to having someone outside the family meet with their kids, though they may do so with great anxiety. Before reaching this point, parents may be afraid that a clinician will prove them bad parents. They also worry that the children will tell a woeful tale of a family without hope. Their willingness to let children speak, and to ask them about what's going well and whether they have worries or concerns, represents a significant first step in resolving the dilemma of depression in families.

Addressing the Needs of Children

I met first with nineteen-year-old Thomas — forceful, clearthinking, and laconic. I came to this meeting prepared for a dramatic encounter full of meaningful, if unpracticed, discussion of family events. Thomas, however, immediately made it clear that he'd much rather have been with his friends than talking with his parents' well-meaning doctor. On the one hand, Thomas denied that he was worried about his mother's illness and seemed to minimize the situation. "Mom went in the hospital," he said. "She told us it was because she was depressed. Mom thought her mother didn't like her or something. I don't see why she can't just pull herself together if she really wants to." On the other hand, Thomas was concerned about how hard things had been on his father, and he feared that his parents might get divorced.

I next met with Lisa, who was obviously more comfortable talking about her mother's illness and its impact on her and the rest of the family. Right away, she told me of the time she'd found what seemed to be a suicide note written by her mother. Katherine drove long distances along the shore to see her therapist and sometimes stopped the car by the side of the road, overcome by thoughts that everyone would be better off without her. Lisa had found the note stuffed under the car seat. She had confronted her mother, who then confessed that she couldn't promise she wouldn't carry out the suicide. After this episode, Lisa had desperately wanted to talk to her mother about her fears, but she was afraid that the conversation itself might trigger a suicide attempt. Lisa told me that she was constantly worried that the holiday season would be too much for her mother. Lisa, more than anyone else in her family, remembered that it had been the stress of Christmas a few years earlier that had brought on signs of depression, including irritability, sleeplessness, and fatigue.

In spite of the pain her mother's illness caused everyone in the family, Lisa found many positives in her life, including her friendships and activities — being captain of the ice hockey team, cheerleading, and jazz dancing. There was even a lot to appreciate within the family, she told me, especially when her mother wasn't feeling so irritable and unhappy. In fact, Lisa's version of family life corresponded closely to the way Katherine and Dan told the story.

Eight-year-old Mary didn't ask as many questions as her two older and more sophisticated siblings. But she made it clear that she was frightened and wanted her mother to be better.

Did I learn anything awful about the family? Not at all. I felt comfortable that none of the children was depressed. The patterns of their lives — the rhythms of going to school, hanging out with other kids, drawing, dancing, playing sports — were intact. Yet, despite the children's apparent ability to "get on with their lives," they clearly misunderstood their mother's illness and were very disturbed by it. They were baffled by Katherine's disruptive actions toward them, her erratic behavior, including sudden departures or bursts of temper interspersed with periods of calm.

Although each child spoke about different things, their comments were consistent enough to affirm that they shared a common experience of their mother's depression. Each recognized the depression in terms of Katherine's hospitalizations, her irritability, and her withdrawal. I hoped that because of their common perceptions, eventually they would be able to talk about the experience.

Planning How to Talk to the Children

Our original plan for the family meeting coincided with the Christmas holidays, but by that time Katherine's depression had worsened. The family decided that the meeting was so important they wanted to delay it until Katherine felt ready. I agreed with them, and I had a long conversation with her psychotherapist, who also agreed.

During the following months, with Dan's support and with her therapist's help, Katherine came to a new understanding of herself and her illness. This self-understanding became the bedrock on which the Petrocellis would build a different way of being a family.

It represented both her coming to grips with the dark specters of how she had been raised and her own fears that she was repeating it. As she tried to think about a new way to talk to her children, Katherine began to reach through the shame and the depression to reexamine the sexual abuse and her troubled relationship with her family, especially her mother. She began to see how her self-blaming and perfectionism were a legacy from her mother, for whom Katherine could never do anything right. Her mother was obsessively neat, and Katherine, who had picked up this trait, worried that she might be perpetuating her past. "I remember my mother viciously dumping my clothes all over the floor because I hadn't cleaned up my room properly. I was so miserable, but the awful thing is that I've done the same thing to my own children. I once saw Mary standing in the driveway, so bewildered and forlorn. I saw myself as a child in her. I would have done anything for my mother, anything at all. I would have swept the garage floor with my own body if it would have pleased her. I'm so afraid that my children will have a childhood like mine and think of me as the ogre."

As she recalled more details from her childhood, Katherine began to wonder if her own mother had struggled with depression. Then again, she began to see the ways in which she was very different from her mother. Likewise, she recognized that the childhood experiences of Thomas, Lisa, and Mary were very different from hers. Katherine began to separate her past from her present, to accept her childhood, and to feel new confidence in herself. She put it this way: "I know my kids have gone through some rough times. And I used to think that they'd completely stopped respecting me as a parent and as a person. I was so sure that they couldn't possibly love me anymore. I guess I just can't jump to that conclusion anymore."

Katherine also needed to make another journey, reliving the great difficulties she had had when, after one of her hospitalizations, she tried to talk about her abuse with her family. No sooner had she shared her story with her brothers and sisters than they picked up the phone and repeated the story to their mother, whose response was, "I'll take it to my grave that this disgusting thing ever happened." Imagine, then, Katherine's courage in seeking another family conversation with her own children.

Katherine, Dan, and I now began to plan for the family meeting. What should Katherine tell her children about her grandfather's abuse? About her thoughts of suicide? About her unhappy relationship with their grandmother, who lived only ten miles away? What did the children need to know? Katherine and Dan wanted to make sure that whatever they said would make things better for the family, not worse.

At first, we decided together that they needed to discuss what the children had actually witnessed and were worried about. These included Katherine's outbursts and her thoughts of suicide, but not things that had happened long ago.

For the Petrocellis, then, there was clear agreement to talk about Katherine's depression and the family dynamics around her symptoms, such as irritability, unpredictable behavior, and withdrawal. Katherine was willing to talk about her thoughts of suicide but feared that talking about the abuse would ruin her children's relationship with their grandparents, aunts, and uncles. Dan wanted to talk about the sexual abuse lest the children someday hear about it from someone in Katherine's family. Eventually, after much discussion, Katherine and Dan chose together to talk about the abuse.

Breaking the Silence Together

We decided to meet in the Petrocelli home, so the children would feel comfortable and see that their parents — rather than their parents' doctor — were leading the way. It was a beautiful early spring day when Thomas, Lisa, and Mary filed into the living room, each clearly wishing to be somewhere else.

This meeting represented months of planning on Katherine and Dan's part. It had been a long journey to understanding before she was ready to talk with her loved ones about her hospitalization and what they'd been through together, the many arguments and the daily agony of not being able to regain who she'd been earlier in her life. But through it all, as we will see time and again, her paramount concern was to be able to take care of her children.

Katherine spoke first, reassuring them that she was all right, that she could handle the meeting without getting upset. Dan joined in, supporting her, letting the kids know that everyone would get a chance to speak, then and in future conversations. I shared with the whole family how much respect I had for their courage and willingness to talk.

Hesitant but composed, Katherine looked directly into the faces of her children and began to address one of the most painful aspects of her depression — her thoughts of suicide. "Weren't you really concerned?" she asked them. "What about the time I left at night? Did you think I was never going to come back?"

Thomas responded boldly, voicing what so many family members feel. "Why are you asking that? All you're doing is refreshing the memory of what happened. I just don't understand why you're doing it."

Then her youngest daughter, hoping to smooth things over, said, "You're doing so well. Why risk talking about this in this meeting? There are no problems."

Dan calmly insisted that this had to be done and that they were going to do it together.

Softly, Katherine responded, "I feel comfortable enough about the way things are going that I don't feel talking will make things worse. I think it's another step forward. I love you very much. I'm going to tell you something I have thought about for a long time. Because you're my children, I'm going to share it with you. I want you to understand it and to know it so you're not going to be afraid of it and think it could happen to you. I think it's going to clarify a whole lot of things."

Since this information had been helpful to the two of them, Katherine and Dan had asked me to talk first to the whole family about the basic facts of depression. We started by addressing some of the children's misconceptions. Thomas told us that he thought Katherine's depression was caused by how she'd been treated as a child. Katherine gently replied, "There's a lot more to it than just that. Really bad things happened to me when I was a little child. In those days, we just didn't talk about bad things, but if you don't talk about things, they come back to haunt you. I kept things inside for too long. And I'd like to change that now."

The room was tense; the children's frightened eyes fixed on Katherine as she told them about how she came to recall her grandfather's abuse. She told them about her unhappy place in her family. She also made it clear that she had begun to accept these events. She couldn't change the past, but perhaps she could learn to deal with her feelings.

Katherine began a frank discussion about her treatment, including the setbacks and problems she'd experienced over the years. Often, Dan would step in with a comment or question, showing a comfortable and loving rapport with his wife. Dan described the onset of Katherine's depression as he'd heard it from a doctor: "It's like what you've heard about Vietnam veterans and posttraumatic stress. Years later, the stress and pain come back to them."

Thomas began to cry when he heard Dan's explanation. He no longer had trouble understanding why his mother just couldn't will herself back to health.

Katherine reiterated how important it was that their family try to talk about things openly from now on. Even Thomas eventually agreed. Katherine continued, "I'm sorry that we have to talk about all these sad things. I'm sorry, but I know it's the right thing for your father and me and especially for you children. I love you so much. My love for you leads me to tell you so you'll understand for yourselves. Maybe you'll be able to understand how bad I've sometimes felt, how sometimes I've wondered if it would be easier if I just went away. I know that I would hurt you much more by leaving. Even when I thought about leaving, during the worst days of my illness, it never was to leave you forever. I really wanted to see if I could leave myself, if I could run away from myself for a while. But I love you so much I don't want you to be afraid for me or for yourselves. And I know you'll be okay, yourselves. You didn't have my childhood, so you won't have to go through what I've gone through with depression. I love you so much."

The family talked on and on, clearly shaken by Katherine's story, but also somewhat relieved.

Continuing the Family Dialogue

When I met Katherine and Dan a week later, they were glad to have held the session. All of us had been quite concerned about Thomas: his anger and his wish to deny his mother's illness. But the family had continued to talk even in the few days since I'd met with them, and he and the rest of the family were fine.

We made plans that I would be available to them whenever they needed it and that they would keep talking to one another. We set a time when I would see them again. We kept that date, and I stayed in touch with them throughout the years that followed.

In later chapters, I will come back to the idea of a family meeting and explore it from other perspectives. But having provided this overview of the six steps, I now need to back up and, just as we do with the families in our care, discuss in greater depth the basic information families need, providing a more detailed view of the essential facts of depression and resilience.

Two

Sharing a History Together

Depression attacks the soul," said a mother struggling to raise her three children. It robs sufferers of the certainty of the present and casts a heavy pall over the future. Feelings of guilt and shame and worries about missed opportunities and lost chances are constant companions. Memories of those who have passed away and of what has been lost become inescapable preoccupations. Being depressed means it takes far more time than usual to accomplish tasks and starting anything seems almost insurmountable. As another mother said, it is "circles within circles, a sadness out of control."

One of the objectives in getting families to talk together is to create a common understanding of the illness. In this chapter, you will hear many voices sharing different perspectives on depression. If you suffer from the illness, some of these descriptions may confirm your own experiences and thus provide assurance that you're not alone. If you are the spouse or child or other relative of a depressed person, here too you will see people just like yourself struggling to make sense of it.

"Imagine that you are standing on a sidewalk," another woman said, "and you see your child get run over by a bus. Now imagine that you can't tell anybody, you can't scream, you can't cry out, you can do nothing that will relieve the intensity as the pain fills your entire consciousness. When I'm depressed, that pain is what I wake up with in the middle of the night and then stare at the ceiling in the dark until morning comes, completely alone . . .

"The pain usually ebbs some during the day, although any glitch or difficulty, real or imagined errors or slights, will bring it flying back to slam me in the face and make my heart stop. My thoughts are consumed in an endless litany of why and how I should die, while I am drowning in an enormous sadness that this is what my life is."

Because the signs of depression start as extensions of normal feelings — despair, guilt, and hopelessness: feelings many people experience in times of great adversity — there can be at first a confusing blur between normal emotional upheaval and true depression. The symptoms of depression also tend to appear gradually, not all at once.

Most of us have difficulty talking about emotional experiences as symptoms of illness. We often get through adversity by simply putting our feelings aside and focusing on the task ahead. Such a strategy doesn't work for depression, but it often takes a long time for a sufferer to realize this.

It is also true that as the symptoms of depression become more severe, we may wish to deny them entirely. Because depression continues to be so misunderstood, there is a stigma that lingers. Those who sufferer from depression are often victims of prejudice and discrimination, so even when they are aware of the illness they may try to hide it. Sadly, sometimes the sufferers turn such prejudice against themselves, believing they are to blame for their own illness.

For these reasons, depression often goes unrecognized or unacknowledged. However, even when it is suspected, most people, either those who are suffering or their families, do not know where to turn for help.

Families need to share the knowledge that depression is not "having a bad day" or feeling the normal pain of losing a job or a relationship. It is a diagnosis in which a set constellation of symptoms comes together and is accompanied by an underlying biological disorder. The core symptoms are:

1. A persistent sadness, manifested by feeling down and blue and crying almost every day and/or
2. A persistent loss of pleasure in almost all activities

One of these must persist for two weeks or more to meet the formal diagnostic definition of depression, but they often last far longer and they often occur together.

Beyond one or both of these symptoms, depression is an associated set of changes in seven additional areas. These are:

3. Loss of energy and fatigue
4. Diminished appetite or increased appetite accompanied by weight gain or loss of ten pounds or more
5. Changes in sleeping with either excessive sleeping or sleeplessness, often with early-morning awakening
6. Periods of agitation or of being slowed down in speech and action
7. Feelings of worthlessness, self-reproach, or excessive guilt
8. Indecisiveness and inability to make decisions
9. Recurrent thoughts of death, suicidal ideas, wishes to be dead, or an actual suicide attempt

Altogether, to have what the medical profession calls a major depression means to have at least one core symptom and five of the seven associated symptoms at the same time for two weeks or more. If the symptoms are due to some other medical illness, or due to abuse of alcohol or drugs, depression is not the diagnosis. If the symptoms occur in the first few months after a serious loss, they are described as a bereavement reaction.[1]

Knowing these symptoms can help your entire family recognize the difference between a normal reaction to adversity and a persistent depression. By sharing the knowledge in the family, each member can begin to see and help whenever someone who has recovered from a depression may be entering another episode. The same symptoms are used to diagnose depression in adolescents and even younger children, so knowing them can help you decide whether you need to seek help for your children.

Of course, people suffering from depression don't experience and categorize the symptoms in the bland, objective language of clinicians. One sufferer described symptoms of loss of energy and feelings of worthlessness much more vividly: "It was like a blackness that takes over my brain. I couldn't do anything. I would sit in a chair forever. My view of myself is so bleak. I thought people who looked at me would throw up. I was always blaming myself."

And more to the point of our discussion, people don't experience depression in isolation. The illness can be all consuming and can profoundly alter family life. As one of the mothers we worked with said, "Depression is dragging, feeling worthless, and that affected all my relationships. I don't cook. My sexual relationship with my husband is nil. I nag my children. I look at the negative, pessimistic side of things. I take no pleasure in things, and I do think about suicide — not dying, but I just don't see the sense in living."

Another put it this way: "The more depressed I am, the more I want to sit and read the paper and drink coffee and just be alone in the morning. I resented the children for being there. In order to deal with it, I stopped getting the morning paper. Now I don't even get coffee anymore. I get up a half an hour early so I can get organized. When you're depressed you have this time element. You have to do so much for your kids or so little, just to get them out the door. I resent my husband for not helping out more in the morning. When I was depressed, we had a lot more take-out meals, though my children don't usually eat what I cook anyway."

Being tired and losing sleep for no apparent reason is almost always part of depression, but the objective, albeit necessary, description of a change in sleep pattern does not begin to capture what happens as a parent becomes more and more tired. The changes compound and complicate the sufferer's sense of self; of pride, self-confidence, and initiative; and daily and hourly they disrupt the essential tasks of managing a family.

"Difficulty getting to sleep is why I initially went on the Ativan [an anti-anxiety drug]," one mother said, "but when it got worse, I felt very agitated. I'd go to the grocery store and forget what

I went for. One day I went specifically because I needed mayonnaise. I drove all the way to the store. Then I got there and I didn't know why I was there, and I didn't get the mayonnaise. I remember talking to my psychiatrist and saying, 'I know I need to do this before this and finish that before I do the other thing, but I just sit there and try to do it and I find myself spacing, spending more time spacing out, and I burst into tears.'"

Depression can also force us to dwell in the past. As one mother said, "Depression brought up lots of feelings for me. My inability to say no, my sexuality, my religious inhibitions, my inability to take pleasure in things. My family was very rule bound."

In depression, there is constant self-criticism and second-guessing of one's parenting. "I worry that I'm not as patient with my son as I should be," another woman said. "The sixth time you have to tell him to do something is the problem with being a single mom. It's just you; there's not somebody to step in and say, 'Why don't you go out and get a cup of coffee and I'll take it from here?' I worry that my patience won't hold out. I won't know what the boundaries are and what I should be saying to him."

"It's hard for my son," another mom said. "Sometimes I'm afraid he's afraid to ask me questions. I'm concerned that my son will have the same ill feelings toward me that I have toward my mother."

Another described how the onset of her depression changed her kids. "They think it's a real drag. They feel the anger. They wish I could get it together. Sometimes they despair. It's happened so many times. They worry I won't be able to function or pull things off the way I used to. They think I'm very scared and very angry. They think I don't love them. Sometimes they don't want to have anything to do with me."

Anger and irritability are frequently part of the experience of depression in families, an aspect that is hard to deal with because it is so difficult for spouses and children to understand. "My sons know I get cranky and yell when I do not feel good," one mother told us. "I feel like I should snap out of it. I feel guilty that I can't make myself come out of it. I'm worried about my children. Whether they will get it is my biggest worry. They sense something is wrong, but they do not know what. If I were my son, I would always want to be told the truth, so I want to tell them, but right now it's just hard."

Spouses and children are often deeply aware of the changes brought on by depression and are quite bewildered. As one husband said of his wife, "There's a lack of ability to enjoy things. She's always enjoyed being busy, takes pride in accomplishments, keeping things in order, a fantastic organizer. But those behaviors just began to not be there. She spent more time in front of the TV than doing things like knitting and reading. She said she felt tired and couldn't put in the usual amount of time."

Another husband said, "I think it's the impact of expectations and reality not met. I didn't want to be married to a depressed person. I didn't expect it. She'll withdraw more, go into her room, become less involved."

Children for the most part are left out of any explanation of what depression is, but they live through all the disruptions that their parents undergo. Children naturally blame themselves and search for reasons. As one boy of twelve said, "I get kind of mad because I don't know what's going on. It's like she's mad, but she's not. It's weird; she won't answer me. Sometimes she cries, and I just leave her alone, I leave the room and don't let it bother me." Later he said, "I get mad because I need to talk to her and she won't. I want to help her, but she won't let me. She just pushes me away like there's nothing I can do." He echoed the confusion of most children when he added, "Why does she suddenly feel that way with no cause?" Interestingly, this same boy later expressed the belief that his mother was depressed because all of her relatives were dead.

Another child, struggling to make sense of the illness, said, "I don't know. . . . It could be physical, like a physical imbalance of the brain, or it could be just the environment. She has to take care of us alone. She has to do things alone."

Another summed it up by saying simply, "I don't think she had a great childhood."

In short, children struggle to make sense of what is a part of their daily lives, and mostly on their own. Universally, children feel guilty, and many believe that they've caused their parents' illness.

Depression affects families in multiple different ways. In straightforward terms, there's less energy to do tasks, so fewer tasks get done. There's also much less confidence on the part of the sufferer. So particularly those tasks that are difficult and challenging, and those involving other persons, such as setting limits for children and sticking to them, are threatening. Interactions, the ways people talk and respond to one another, are profoundly changed. Also, the factors associated with depression, such as heavy drinking or severe anxiety, take a heavy toll.[2]

Study after study has documented that couples with untreated depression have lower levels of satisfaction and sense of well-being. Depression leads to higher rates of divorce, compounding the problem of depression both for the sufferer and the children.[3] Above all, in far too many families, depression is neither recognized as a serious illness nor understood, and many of the misunderstandings are compounded by guilt and blame, by trying to make sense of the sufferer's behavior and not knowing how to.

What I have just described is the "shared history" that millions of families know all too well. They may be going through it unconsciously. They may be unable to talk about it, and they may have no awareness of how other family members experience the same events, but they are, in fact, going through it together. It may be familiar to you as well.

Breaking the silence together allows for the expression of feelings like those just described, but in a way that is not disruptive. The kind of family meeting we advocate allows for an exchange of points of view to let family members get inside one another's experience.

Depression especially disrupts the memory of what's been positive and what's been accomplished in the past for the sufferer and the family, just as in the present it profoundly disrupts a person's ability to take pleasure in children, relationships, and most anything else. Breaking the silence together also means learning to recognize and speak about many of the positive accomplishments and activities shared within a family, positives easily obscured by depression. Also, among family members, depression assails the idea that there is a predictability about their lives together, a continuity between past, present, and future. In essence, depression distorts the very idea that a family can make sense of things together and that parents can raise their children successfully. The telling of a family story restores that continuity, especially stories that span generations, stories about those who've gone before — parents, grandparents, great-grandparents — and how the past points to the future. Children are at the center of a family's commitments and represent the family's connection to the future. Also, part of the story is how a family fits into the larger frameworks of their faith, the culture they are part of, and the community they live in, as they celebrate the events that affirm their connections to these frameworks and to one another. Breaking the silence allows families to recover and affirm the strengths in their histories, to rediscover those connections.

Experiences with depression almost always start as a series of disjointed incidents in the life of the individual sufferer, experiences that cause the sufferer to feel alone. The process of breaking the silence starts by talking together about these disjointed experiences.

To start talking at all involves a risk; it means finding time and space, and, above all, being willing to see whether there is a new way to understand depression. This only occurs when there's planning and commitment. If there are two parents, couples need to be sure that they want to do it together before talking to their children. They need to feel safe, that it is okay to begin talking. They need to acknowledge aloud and to each other that they are trying something new and that they will help each other. Both members of the couple may want to read about how to break the silence before trying it themselves. For those raising children alone, it's often helpful to talk this over with someone who understands depression, like a close friend. I want to share some of the questions families have found helpful in getting started, with the hope that they will be helpful to you as well.

Beginning to talk means considering that it is possible to have a history that can be discussed together. Perhaps more important, it means considering the whole of the family's story. We ask families what they've been through together, encouraging them to put into words what their histories have been and what their lives are in the present.

Stories are not continuous but broken by seminal events: the birth of a child, the entry into school, the passing of a loved one. These are linchpins around which families remember and orient their experiences. A shared history, then, is not just about depression, although that is an important part of it, but also about births and deaths, new jobs and jobs lost, good times and bad.

Everyone's voice and everyone's memories are important. If there's a history of an event such as a hospitalization, we ask one spouse, "What was it like for you?" and then, "What was this like for your partner?" then turn to the partner and ask the same questions. Again and again, we find that couples have talked little or not at all about what they've been through together. I hope you and your partner will be able to ask these kinds of questions of each other.

Families organize their hopes and dreams for themselves and for their futures through their children. If the future of the children is threatened, then the whole structure of family life is disrupted. We hope to help families return the children to the forefront of the family's concern.

Just as we ask parents what it has been like to endure the depression, we also ask them what they believe it is like for their children, so from the beginning the children have a place in the story. Parents also reflect on how, in one way or another, the story eventually will be shared with their children. Thus, the children start as a silent presence, then move toward being active speakers.

By coming together and talking, families can gradually begin to understand that their histories and stories are about much more than just depression, and to identify resources they can build on for the future.

General information about depression and resilience only comes alive when it directly addresses deep-seated concerns. Above all, we ask families what their worries are. We then try to answer as directly as possible their specific concerns about themselves, their treatments, their marriages, and whatever else, tailoring the information to their unique circumstances. As further chapters unfold, I will again and again ask you to consider what it is you want help with most.

Three

Knowledge of Depression
Biological Basis and Cause

D epression is no more anyone's fault than diabetes. In some people, it occurs only once and in others it comes again and again. This chapter will explain the basic facts, as we know them, about what depression is and what causes it. In so doing, it also makes clear that "cause" is never simple to pin down and that many complex factors flow into it.

A chronic, recurrent medical illness such as rheumatoid arthritis can be managed through a combination of medication, stress reduction, and close interaction with a doctor who is flexible in employing different treatments as needed over time. The same is true of depression.

Depressed individuals and their families are often dismayed when their recoveries aren't instantaneous or permanent, but it's more reasonable, just as with rheumatoid arthritis, to expect a slow recovery period with occasional setbacks. Most people understand that a heart attack requires a period of rest and recovery, but we also know that a great many sufferers recover fully; this analogy is helpful in understanding depression as well.

Families have many questions about depression — some about the genetics of the illness, others about some new treatment they've read about in the media, and others about the particular illness of a parent. I will address general information about depression in what follows, but I urge you to seek additional information and a consultation with your doctor if there is a particular question that isn't adequately covered here.

Those with many relatives with severe depressive or bipolar illness across several generations may benefit from a more extensive exploration of the family history with regard to the illness and more detailed information about the degree of familial risk through review with a specialist. Those facing more than one illness at once, such as depression and anxiety or depression and drug abuse in a family member, also need detailed information about how these different illnesses come together, how each one is treated, and how the treatments are coordinated.

But once again, I want to emphasize that depression is not anyone's fault. I hope this brief review of the scientific findings about this illness will demonstrate that nothing could be further from the truth.[1]

Perhaps the clearest evidence of the biological nature of depression comes from sleep studies. Depressed individuals show profound disturbances in the fundamental rhythms shown on electrical recordings, called electroencephalograms, or EEGs, that track sleep patterns. There is less of the usual restorative sleep that provides a balance for normal life and much more excited rapid-eye-movement sleep. When someone recovers from a depression, this pattern reverses.

Depression also disturbs hormone balances and energy levels, and even affects the transmission of impulses from nerve cell to nerve cell in the brain. These physical disturbances accompany the symptoms that we experience as changes in mood and behavior.

The bedrock of what we know about the physiology of depression involves chemical messengers in the brain. In depressed individuals, nerve cells have a decreased ability to transmit impulses across the gaps between them, tiny spaces called synaptic junctions. The chemical messengers used to cross these gaps are called neurotransmitters. The three most important of these chemical messengers are epinephrine, dopamine, and serotonin.

Epinephrine is associated with the part of the brain and the nervous system that rouses the body to action. Dopamine operates in areas focused on arousal and goal-directed activity. Serotonin is located primarily in the midbrain and upper pons, areas that govern the unconscious rhythms of the body. These rhythms include going to sleep and awakening, as well as normal changes in body temperature over twenty-four hours. This region also regulates appetite, as well as sexual and aggressive behavior.

Knowledge of these neurotransmitters has allowed us to find medications to treat depression. These antidepressant drugs target one of the chemical messengers and increase its transmission across the synaptic junctions. They work either by decreasing enzymes that break down the neurotransmitters, or by preventing the neurotransmitters from being reabsorbed. Either way, they help to restore normal function.

The different systems in the brain rely on different neurotransmitters, but they also are intricately intertwined. The different systems mutually regulate one another, so medications that affect one system influence others. No single abnormality in serotonin or dopamine is responsible for all forms of depression. It's more complicated than that.

New ways of making images of the brain suggest that blood flow is diminished and that functioning decreases in certain areas during depression. These areas recover normal blood flow when the depression has passed and the individual recovers.

Many depressions also involve the profound disturbance of a mechanism within the body called the "fight or flight response." This mechanism arose far back in our evolutionary history to help us respond to sudden threats to our survival. It involves sensory awareness of the threat and a response to that threat in the cerebral cortex that kick starts further responses throughout the body.

From the cerebral cortex, the threat signal goes to the brain's hypothalamus, and from there, on through central neural hormones to the pituitary gland in the base of the brain. When the signal is received, the pituitary releases its hormones into the blood to the adrenal glands, which in turn release hormones to prepare the entire body — skin, muscles, heart — for immediate lifesaving action. Again, there is extensive connectedness among the different parts of these hormonal systems, with multiple ways in which changes in one area influence other areas.

Dr. Charles Nemeroff and colleagues at Emory University demonstrated in studies of women severely abused in childhood that such severe trauma causes a kind of constant state of arousal for "fight or flight." This arousal takes the form of an oversecretion of hormones from the hypothalamic pituitary system, which makes the individual prone to later depression. This has been confirmed using studies in which animals subjected to severe stress also develop this hormone secretion that gets stuck in the "on" position.[2]

The same kind of interweaving of hormonal imbalance and mood changes can arise from the use of certain medications, particularly those used for inflammation and infection. Likewise, a malfunction of the adrenal glands can lead to excessive secretion of hormones called corticosteroids, which results in Cushing's syndrome. A deficiency of this same hormone causes a condition called Addison's disease, and both conditions are associated with depression.

Decreased secretions of thyroid and growth hormones also disturb mood. Individuals with too little thyroid (hypothyroidism) are prone to depression, while those with too much thyroid (hyperthyroidism) are prone to the excited and uncontrollable state we call mania.

For all these reasons, a complete medical history and physical should be part of any diagnosis of depression.

Biology Is Not Destiny

Families often experience depression as a catastrophe coming out of the blue. At other times, the disorder seems linked to specific life events. Depression has long been associated with the death of a close loved one as well as other losses. Certainly, depression can result solely from bereavement, undergoing a difficult divorce, losing a job, or moving to a new community without support.

However, if you have many first-degree relatives — parents, aunts, uncles, brothers, sisters, and grandparents — with clear-cut, well-diagnosed depression or mania, it does increase the likelihood that you too will experience these difficulties. Genetics can be a factor, but it is by no means the whole story. Part of the hopeful message of this book is that biology is *not* destiny. Instead, we speak of the entire set of an individual's adversities as "risk factors." Offsetting these risk factors, individuals also have resources and strengths. Depression occurs when risk factors overwhelm resources and strengths. The objective of this book is to help families tip the balance toward strength.

Risk factors are clearly identifiable forces that occur well before the beginning of a disorder and increase the likelihood that an individual who has one or more of these factors, as compared to those who do not, will become ill. The presence of a risk factor for depression does not mean that everyone who has it will become depressed. In fact, in many instances the majority of people with the risk factor do not succumb.

Risk factors simply provide a broad set of categories that helps make depression understandable. They show that the illness does not occur at random. The concept of risk factors can help you assess some of the forces that, if present, might predispose you or your loved ones toward the illness, or make existing depressions worse. The hope embedded in risk factors, of course, is that knowing them allows you to take appropriate action.

The well-established risk factors for depression include:

1. Having a parent or other close biological relative with a mood disorder
2. Losing someone close to you through death, divorce, or separation; becoming unemployed; being in a chronically dissatisfying situation such as an unsatisfying job, or being in a chronically unfulfilling relationship full of conflict
3. Having a chronic medical disorder
4. Witnessing violence or being the victim of violence — especially physical or sexual abuse, rape, or violent crime
5. Having had a depression before in your life
6. Having a tendency to brood or ruminate and to be unable to let go of things and move on
7. Experiencing a recurrent sense of helplessness and hopelessness, or a sense that no matter what you do the world is not at all under your control; this places an individual at risk and also may be a first sign of depression
8. Being female
9. Living in poverty[3]

What does it mean to say that "being female" is a risk factor for depression? It does not mean that women get depressed and men don't. What it means is simply that if one looks at a group of adults and asks them questions about depression, on average twice as many women will report either being depressed or having been depressed. Nor does this risk factor tell us what it is about being female that leads to this difference. The most likely explanation is the difficult role that women have in our culture: maintaining relationships for families, taking care of children, and struggling with multiple other demands, often without enough support.

Having a parent or other relative with depression may indicate a genetic risk, because a child may share genes with the parent that predispose to depression. It is also true that a parent with depression may be less able to provide for the child, thus tipping the balance toward depression in that child, but not because of genes. Of course, the onset of depression may result from a combination of these two factors, or because of a third risk factor, such as bereavement or exposure to violence. Just because a parent and a child in the same family become depressed, it does not necessarily mean that one causes the other.

How much does any one risk factor increase the rate of depression? In the absence of all other factors, not a great deal.

In one study, living in poverty increased the chances that someone would become depressed in the year following the initial assessment by about 10 percent. That is significant, but still not overwhelming.

Although the rate of depression is higher in women than in men, the majority of women in any large study do not and have never experienced depression.

Sadly, we are increasingly aware of the terrible toll that being a victim of violence, witnessing violence, or suffering sexual or physical abuse in childhood or adolescence takes. These are very powerful risk factors for later depression in both children and adults.[4]

The more risk factors occur together, the greater the risk for depression. If you don't have to face such risk factors as loss of house and income, your overall risk is substantially lower than if those disruptions are present. It is the chronic adversities — being unemployed for years, or having several loved ones die, or leaving a community of support and not finding another — that are most impairing.

Affluence provides no magic shield against depression: It strikes people from all cultural, racial, ethnic, and religious groups, and at all economic levels. Still, there is no denying the strong link with socioeconomic disadvantage. Those with fewest resources, when faced with multiple adversities, are at highest risk for depression.[5]

Two stories show the range of these socioeconomic adversities.

One mother began working with us a few days after the breakup of her marriage. "I'd married an Italian prince who had a palatial home on the shore," she told us. "He was drinking constantly and was physically abusive. I just couldn't manage it. At night, I'd drink a whole bottle of wine and wake up the next morning and the bottle would be empty. I'd say, 'How did I do that and I'm still up and functioning?'

"It took me a while to figure out I was depressed. I even argued with my psychiatrist about it. Looking back, I see I was waking up in the middle of the night. I was crying constantly. I was always in tears in my car. I would cry at the drop of a hat and I was nuts, angry, lashing out. I had friends calling me up every day saying, 'Promise me you won't do anything crazy. . . .'

"I just saw the worst in everything. My life was spinning out of control."

With her marriage torn apart, she lost her home and the community she'd become a member of, and suddenly she had to find a job, all the while managing the care of her son. But as we've seen with so many parents, through all her turmoil, concern for her little boy was her primary focus. This helped her gain some important perspective.

"Depression also teaches you a lot about what's important in life," she said. "In the last year I was with my husband, we gave a party for five hundred and fifty people. The next year, when we were separated, not one of those people spoke to me. I'm told people don't know what to say in these situations."

Another story of a young woman from very different circumstances has haunted me since the early 1980s.

Joanna was born and raised in South America and had moved to Boston with her husband two years before she was interviewed. She was nearly nineteen, and she'd been separated from her husband for a year and a half. She lived alone in a small fourth-floor apartment with her son, aged twenty months, and her daughter, three months. By her account, her early life had been difficult. Her parents divorced when she was three, and she had gone back and forth between her father and her grandmother on the one hand, and her highly promiscuous mother on the other. "My mother has always been a problem for me," she said. "I did not approve of the life she led."

From age seven on, Joanna went to live with her father and his mother. At thirteen, she went back to live with her mother because her father's life changed and he could no longer keep her. Unfortunately, her mother just wasn't able to be a parent for her, and Joanna experienced her first, and quite severe, depression.

Despite the fact that she met all the medical criteria for a major depressive disorder, no one recognized Joanna as depressed and she got no treatment. Two years later, falling in love with an older man alleviated her sadness but unfortunately led her into a relationship that didn't work. She became pregnant at sixteen, married, and moved to the United States, putting distance between herself and her family. Shortly after her son was born, her husband had an affair and she left him. This started another bout of depression for Joanna, which continued unabated for months.

A year later, she reconciled briefly with her husband and became pregnant. Then he left and never saw her or the second child again. When we interviewed Joanna, her second child was still an infant, and she spoke of how tired she was all the time. It took her three to four hours to fall asleep at night, and she was simply dragging through each day on public assistance with two small children.

Joanna had many risk factors: the loss of a stable community in which to live, a relationship that wasn't working and that led to regular separations, no economic support, and, above all, extreme isolation. There also appeared to have been depression in several of her relatives. This is what we mean when we say that various risk factors can compound one another. Sadly, it was Joanna's very attempt to find a way out of her unhappy childhood, falling in love, that led to depression. Her isolation led to a poor choice of husband, which led to further isolation. Saddest of all, such factors can combine in ways to keep people from getting the help they need for themselves and for their children.

Genetic Influences in Some Depressions

When you think of risk factors for depression, it may be genetics that first leaps to mind. The fact remains, however, that there is no strict genetic determinant for the vast majority of depressions.

To date, no single gene has been identified for the transmission of depression. In those instances in which there is a genetic component, several different genes are responsible, operating either in relationship to one another or separately.[6]

Genes are most likely to be involved in families in which there is an extensive, well-described, detailed history of a severe mood disorder, especially mania, in a large number of first-degree relatives — parents, grandparents, aunts, and uncles — across several generations. Genetics is also more likely to be involved in such families when there are long-standing episodes of depression or mania in the absence of any severe environmental adversities such as job loss or exposure to violence. But still, it is the assembly of events over time, rather than any one risk factor, that determines outcome.

The strongest evidence of genetic influence on depression comes from twin studies. Researchers look at individuals with identical genetic makeup but different environments, namely twins from the same egg who have been reared apart from each other. In such unusual pairs, when one of the twins develops manic-depressive disorder, the other does about 70 percent of the time. This indicates a strong genetic predisposition. On the other hand, this also means that even with an identical genetic makeup, 30 percent of the time the other twin did not become ill. Looking at severe, recurrent, long-standing depression without mania, the same kind of studies show that 50 percent of the time the other twin does not become ill.

Once again, biology is not destiny.

The most we can say is that when there is no set of adversities associated, depressions do cluster in some families — but even for those with such histories, this does not mean that all members will become depressed. Rather, it means that the chance of becoming depressed increases by 5 to 20 percent compared to those with no family history.

The most comprehensive of the recent genetic studies, conducted by Dr. Kenneth Kendler, affirmed again the balance of genetics and adversities in depression. He and his colleagues followed groups of young women, some of whom were related to one another genetically (e.g., identical twins, fraternal twins, and siblings), and some not. He also looked at the adversities they'd undergone, such as suffering traumatic loss as well as prior depression. All of the known influences taken together could explain only about half the cases of depression. The work also confirmed both the importance of recent traumatic events and genetic factors. Kendler himself emphasizes that although studies can demonstrate broad categories of influence, it is not possible to estimate with certainty how to apply this to the risk in any given individual's life — an important caution that again emphasizes that depression is not inevitable.[7]

Childhood depression has been recognized as a distinct illness only recently, and how genes figure in it is still almost unknown. Studies of families of children who have experienced long-standing depression do show that there is more of a family history of depression than in families where there is no childhood depression. But even so, most families in which childhood depression occurs do not have an extensive history of depression, so it's simply not correct to draw conclusions about genetic influence.

Focusing on genetics tends to obscure other essential truths for those worried about depression in their families. Once again, just as there are risk factors, there are protective factors, the resources and strengths that make depression less likely, or at least less severe.

Early treatment can be one such protective factor. So can having close, intimate, confiding relationships, whether it is a marriage, a friendship, or a bond with a sister or brother.[8]

Just as being in a difficult job can predispose you toward depression, so being able to work and get pleasure and satisfaction from a job can protect you.

Because depression is influenced by so many factors — losses and adversity, a family history of the disease, a tendency to fixate on the negative — the best models for understanding the cause of the illness are interactive, meaning they take into account different factors, how they balance one another, and how they affect one another over time.

Whenever there is a risk, both protective forces and adversities have much to say about who gets depressed and who doesn't. The same is true for genetic and social risks. Studies by the sociologist Dr. George Brown have shown, for example, that a risk factor such as the death of a parent in childhood leads to depression in adulthood only when the individual lacks the protective resources of close friendships and/or a satisfying work situation, and faces a stress in adulthood.[9]

Bottom line: The best we can say is that it is the assembly of events over time rather than any one risk factor that determines outcome.

Or, put another way, we can say that:

1. In the psychological sense, depression is being overwhelmed and coming to feel helpless and hopeless, almost always because of certain events.

2. In the social sense, depression is both an interpersonal disorder and a family illness.

3. In the biological sense, depression represents a profound change in usual functioning, a change that is somewhat more likely in some families than others.

All three perspectives concur in emphasizing that depression, once it occurs, is a devastating illness, and that the presence of depression itself will further complicate the lives of those who suffer from it. Having one depression may even change the underlying biology of the brain to increase the vulnerability to later depression, in a process called "kindling."[10]

We can draw two important conclusions: First, once again, that biology is not destiny,[11] and second, that it is vital to build the positive resources of children and families so as to try to prevent depression in children, or, when that is not possible, to intervene very intensely early in its course.

As you will see throughout the rest of this book, the single most important area to focus on in protecting you, your spouse, and your children is promoting healthy and open relationships within the family and among extended family, friends, and the larger community.

In the next chapter, I address treatment interventions. Then I will turn to promoting the open communication described above, as well as other steps you can take to minimize the risk of depression occurring in those you love.

Four

Knowledge of Depression
Diagnosis and Treatment

G etting treatment for depression for yourself, your spouse, or your child can be lifesaving. It is the first essential action to take in breaking the silence with your children. Sadly, far too many people struggle for years before getting help.

In this chapter, I provide an overview of the different kinds of depression and their treatment. I also describe the battle that getting treatment involves. Finding treatment often begins with a difficult journey toward admitting the need for help. Then the struggle shifts to overcoming insurance barriers, then to staying with the process through ups and downs. As adults, we are proud of being able to manage on our own. For many, getting treatment, especially for mental illness, feels like giving up. But it is exactly the opposite. Getting treatment is precisely what you need to restore your capacity to be independent and manage on your own.

There are four key elements to getting treatment:

1. Getting help means first realizing that something is wrong, that there are nagging thoughts and feelings and sleep disturbances that won't go away. It means considering the possibility that depression is present.
2. Getting help also means recognizing that help is available and that treatment works.
3. Obtaining treatment means finding someone who is skilled and experienced in treating depression and who will work with you over time. Such caregivers are often found through the assistance of friends who have wrestled with depression, through family

members, or through your trusted physician. This caregiver must be able to explain in language you can understand the nature of your specific depression, and what the range of appropriate treatments is (the same information I will provide in a general way in the pages that follow). And then it means that you and this person make a choice. You try an approach and then follow it through to make sure it is working. Unfortunately, it may also mean battling with insurance companies to make sure they pay for the coverage you require.

4. Obtaining help means staying in treatment until the signs and symptoms recede, often a period of months. Sometimes one approach doesn't work completely and you need to try another one.

Getting treatment also means being willing to deal with the life-threatening emergencies that may come along: thoughts of suicide, planning for suicide, and moments when you are out of control and unable to calm down. These constitute genuine emergencies in either an adult or a child, and require immediate evaluation by a skilled caregiver — a pediatrician, family practitioner, or someone whose primary work is dealing with mental illness. They are just as urgent as other emergencies in medical practice. If these issues arise, see a professional right away.

You should feel confident knowing that depression is among the most treatable of the major mental illnesses.[1] Treatment involving the two main approaches, medication and talking therapies, has shown dramatic improvement in the past twenty-five years. Both approaches have proven effective for mild to moderate depression when compared to each other. There is some evidence that for depressions involving profound disturbances of eating, sleeping, and energy, medication may be the more effective of the two. There is increasing evidence that for the more severe depressions, or those associated with other problems, combinations of the two are likely to prove most effective.[2] Over time, many families find that combinations of approaches are helpful for all kinds of depression, and almost all the families we worked with received combined treatments.

For a treatment to be deemed successful by the rigorous standards of medical evaluation — and both talk therapy and medication have passed this test with flying colors — a number of the symptoms of depression must remit, the impairments must become much less severe, and the sufferer and the family must be able to see improvement. Ideally, the depression will disappear entirely. Thus, it is important that you go over with your caregiver what it is you both think will change and then gradually evaluate whether these areas, such as difficulty sleeping or concentrating, or feeling sad all the time, are improving.

Both talk therapy and medication aim to address the core disturbances that depression brings — changes in ways of thinking, changes in how the sufferer acts toward others, changes in underlying biological processes. Because depressions differ so much from one another, the more a clinician understands and the more you understand the different types of depression, the more precise the diagnosis will be and the easier it will be to choose the right treatment.

The treatment of depression is more complicated when other diagnoses — alcoholism, for example — are present. Physical illnesses such as hypothyroidism, and certain medications such as steroids or birth control pills can cause depression, so your doctor will ask about these. Feeling depressed can also be the beginning sign of a wide variety of other medical illnesses, including other psychiatric illnesses. That's why a full medical exam and family history are so important.

In chapter 2, I described the nine criteria for a diagnosis of major depression. But there are two other main types of depression: dysthymia and mania/bipolar disorder.

Dysthymia

Dysthymia is a chronic wearing away of energy and a loss of sense of self. Often when we ask depressed parents when their depression started, at first they say, "It's been there ever since I was a child." "I've always been moody," said one father whose dysthymia eventually gave way to major depression. "I've had fears of being paralyzed by a sense of despair. It took me a long while to put this together as depression. I've been this way all my life, and there were spells that were much worse, like in college. I've always been able to function day to day, but the trigger for me is missing deadlines. Pressure would snowball, deadlines would pile up, and finally I took a year off. I felt like a failure and I had a sense I was never going to do anything more than menial work, and I really touched bottom a year in college."

Depression often goes unrecognized, and it often begins with the symptoms we call dysthymia. In formal terms, this set of symptoms overlaps with those for major depression, but only two or three of the nine will be present. The symptoms of dysthymia in formal diagnostic terms also must be present much longer than the two weeks required for the diagnosis of depression — a minimum of two years. But the persistence of these symptoms even for a few months should cause you to seek an evaluation. Untreated, dysthymia not only wears away at the fabric of life, but very often leads to full-blown depression. Once again, you need to get help before a much more severe depression develops.

My colleague Martin Keller coined the phrase "double depression" to describe the plight of sufferers who have both dysthymia and recurrent major depression, a particularly devastating combination.[3]

Mania and Bipolar Disorder

Mania represents the antithesis of depression. Sufferers from mania act high, talk rapidly, and do odd things, but they are often unaware that this is different from their normal behavior until they recover, at which time they are often tormented by feelings of guilt and shame. In formal terms, mania means that at least three of the following symptoms are present for more than a week: being increasingly active, talking nonstop, feeling that one's thoughts are racing and out of control, having delusions of grandeur, or an exaggerated sense of one's own abilities, and being easily distracted. Difficulty sleeping is almost always a component. Sometimes, mania leads the sufferer to spend a great deal of money, or to undertake wild sexual escapades. These behaviors generally are of much shorter duration than the symptoms of depression, and not on the continuum of usual experience, either for the sufferer or for those around him or her. Often, they involve a break with reality, imagining voices, or believing that one possesses superhuman powers. Frequently, episodes of mania alternate with depression, which is called bipolar disorder, and very often a period of depression is a precursor to an episode of mania in people with bipolar disorder.

Irritability and anger, which often accompany mania, can also accompany depression. Recognizing mania is somewhat easier because the sufferer's functioning is so disrupted. Approaches to treating mania are quite different from those applied to depression, both in terms of providing support for the sufferer and in the use of medications to try to prevent recurrence.

Related Diagnoses

Families also need to know that depression, at least half the time, comes along with another illness, and that both need active treatment.

Difficulties with alcohol or drugs, and severe anxiety are the most common.

Drinking alcohol is never a treatment for depression. In fact, alcohol is itself a depressant and in many ways profoundly compounds the problem. For many alcoholics, an underlying depression has preceded the drinking and the drinking represents a misguided attempt to try to relieve the pain. This pattern is so common that a third of those with depression develop alcoholism. The same is true of other substances that are abused: cocaine, marijuana, and hallucinogens for example. They only make the problem worse.

Many of those who are depressed have suffered abuse or have been traumatized by violence or assault. Reaction to the trauma, separate from depression, is called "posttraumatic stress disorder." The term was originally used to describe the flashback experiences of war veterans. Often, depression occurs with eating disorders, in particular anorexia nervosa or bulimia, both disorders in which the sufferer has a terrible self-image and goes to excessive lengths to lose weight or to avoid gaining weight.

Each diagnosis requires a somewhat different approach, and when there are two problems, for example, eating disorders and depression, the clinician and the family must formulate a plan to deal with both.

Timing of Depression

Depressions differ from one another, but studies of the course of depressions show that about half the time, a major depression recurs, often more than once.

Depressions, above all, are not constant, often varying with the seasons. Winter is in general a particularly hard time for people with depression because of the lack of daylight, and because we often get less exercise in cold weather. In Christian, Jewish, and Muslim traditions, winter is also the time of holidays that celebrate children, hope, and light in the midst of darkness. This can be particularly difficult for people with depression because of the heightened contrast between the inner agony and the outer expectations of holiday cheer.

Anniversaries of deaths, birthdays, and other important family events can have the same effect. So as we work with families, and as you think about your own family, it is important to know that certain times of year should be approached cautiously. You need to plan ahead of time how to get through them.

Life also has key moments associated with markedly increased rates of depression. For children, there's a substantial increase in rates of depression during and just after puberty. Depressions occur often in women raising young children, especially when they are alone without adequate support. Depression is common after divorce, and isolation makes depression a special concern for the elderly.

Childhood Depression

Of course, the kind of depression of greatest concern to parents is childhood depression. This was not even recognized as a diagnostic category until the 1970s. As we've noted so often, depressed parents feel guilty about the effect of their illness on their children and fearful that the illness will be passed on. Addressing these fears begins with knowing what childhood depression is and what it is not.[4]

Caregivers recognize depression in children by systematically asking about the same set of changes that I described as the symptoms of depression in chapter 2, but couched in the language of children. With children under fourteen, clinicians will ask the parents the same set of questions and put the two sets of answers together. Often clinicians will do this with older children as well. Also, those who work with children recognize that children often do not put their feelings into words, but instead show their feelings through their actions.

Because children change dramatically from toddlerhood to adolescence, the questions a clinician will ask a sixteen-year-old are quite different from those he or she will ask a six-year-old, but the symptoms — changes in sleeping, eating, energy, and thoughts of feeling hopeless, helpless, overwhelmed, and even suicidal — are the same at any age. In fact, they occur with increasing frequency as children grow older. Suicide is one of the leading causes of death in adolescence. Many youngsters experience suicidal thoughts, and it is important that these receive immediate evaluation by a professional. Preventing suicide is not something you want to trust to a home remedy. Just as with adults, one core symptom and at least five associated symptoms are required for a caregiver to make a formal diagnosis of major depression, but even one or two symptoms, if they interfere with how a child is doing, are cause for concern.

If you are worried about depression in your child, it's important to ask directly about his or her feelings. It is also important to look at what has been happening in the child's life, in particular, losses, setbacks, or times when the child is negative about him- or herself.

Major changes in the routine of children are significant indicators — not going to school, losing interest in friends, becoming irritable, being preoccupied, and not paying attention to hygiene. Withdrawing or crying all the time are also signals from a child that it's time for you to turn to a trusted pediatrician, school counselor, or other professional caregiver to conduct an evaluation and see what is going on.

Depression is rare among preschool children. Thereafter, young boys are three times more likely than young girls to be depressed. After puberty and during adolescence, the rates for depression among both boys and girls increase significantly, with some studies showing that as many as 18 to 20 percent of adolescents experience an episode of depression sometime during this phase of life. By age fourteen, the rates of occurrence are similar to those in adults, with girls twice as likely to meet the full criteria for depression as boys.

Children, even within the same family, differ from one another in the way they can talk about events and in their risks for depression. In general, however, children are far more sensitive than adults to dramatic changes in their environment, such as divorce or bereavement, and childhood depression very often emerges in response to such events. Similarly, the failure to accomplish usual tasks, especially such peer-related tasks as learning to read, is a potent risk factor for depression in younger children.

When unrecognized and untreated, childhood depression is a serious and debilitating disorder that, over the long term, will recur for most sufferers. Yet most children who experience episodes of depression in this country are not diagnosed and do not receive the treatment they need.

Having a depressed parent does increase the risk for depression, although how much depends almost entirely on how severe the parental depression is and what other things are going on in the family. This is discussed more fully in chapter 6. But even at this point, it's important to reiterate that the great majority of childhood depressions do not occur solely because of parental depression, but because of a constellation of reasons.

Childhood depression often goes undiagnosed because the symptoms mimic other common symptoms — being withdrawn or sleepy, having stomachaches, or being irritable. That's why it is key for parents and caregivers to ask directly about being depressed, about feeling sad, and even about having thoughts of suicide. Often parents worry that asking about suicidal thoughts or plans will actually suggest this to the child. This is unlikely to occur. In fact, it is important to ask about these concerns directly if the child is manifesting symptoms of depression, and children are often reassured by being able to talk about it. But if a parent is concerned and does not feel able to ask, or is unsure after asking, then the parent should seek the help of a trained caregiver to evaluate concerns about suicide.

Getting Treatment

Above all, the key to treatment for depression in adults or in children is a long-term relationship with a skilled professional who can outline an approach that includes alternatives. If one treatment doesn't work, then another standard strategy can be tried, or two can be tried together.

Those with depression should be able to choose the kind of treatment they prefer based on knowledge of the risks and benefits of different approaches, as well as the evidence of their effectiveness. Some individuals will prefer medication, others will prefer talking therapies, and others, a combination of the two.

Caregivers will ask about the sufferer's history of depression, focusing on how often someone has been depressed and how severely. They will ask detailed questions about all the symptoms in an orderly way. They will ask about suicidal thoughts. They will also ask about other disorders. This information helps make the correct diagnosis, which then guides treatment. The history also helps you and your family assess what your children have had to deal with. Caregivers will ask about whether others in the family have had a history of depression and how they have responded to treatment. If a particular approach worked for one family member, often it will work for others in the family.

Cognitive Therapy

Cognitive therapy, developed by Aaron Beck in the 1960s, is recognized as one of the most potent approaches for the treatment of depression.[5]

Beck focused on the affected person's thoughts about him- or herself, about the world, and about the future, and attempted to help the individual see that these thoughts, which were gloomy and unpleasant, were distortions of reality. He also showed how these negative thoughts occurred continually and automatically whenever the person was depressed. The depressed individuals either believed that they had no control over what would happen in their lives, or they inappropriately blamed themselves for things that were indeed beyond their control. When they stopped being depressed, their thoughts escaped from these patterns of helplessness and hopelessness.

Based on this rationale, Beck articulated a therapeutic sequence that clinicians can follow. Patient and clinician together address these distortions, taking the most pressing issues first. Once they establish that these negative thoughts are in fact distortions, the clinician can gradually help provide alternative ways of viewing life's experience through a careful series of steps, using the Socratic method. This can be done either in groups or with individuals once or more than once a week, usually for a specified period of between ten and twenty sessions. This approach has evolved over three decades and is widely used.

Cognitive-Behavioral Therapy

A somewhat similar approach, behavioral therapy, focuses not on the patient's thinking process but on what is called the theory of conditioned behaviors.

The original models for behavior therapy focused on observable responses — the patient's actions and reactions. More recently, a number of prominent clinicians have moved from a focus on behaviors to the relationship between the behaviors and the inner world of the person. By giving the patient a stronger sense of his or her own influence or control, behavioral therapy builds confidence.

Both cognitive and behavioral approaches have an explicit set of steps with well-defined goals. Many practitioners have combined the two approaches in what is called cognitive-behavioral therapy.[6]

Interpersonal Therapy

A different approach focuses primarily on interpersonal relationships. It was developed by Gerald Klerman and Myrna Weissman, and follows the work of pioneering psychiatrist Harry Stack Sullivan. Interpersonal therapy addresses the life stressors associated with depression. After an initial assessment, interpersonal therapy focuses on four areas:

1. Unresolved grief
2. Troubles in various kinds of social roles
3. Life transitions that involve relationships
4. Interpersonal deficits or difficulties

There is a strong educational component to interpersonal therapy. The sufferer is taught to deal directly with the impediments to moving on with his or her life, with special attention given to relationships. If there is significant difficulty within a marriage, for example, the clinician will explore how to enhance the marriage or, if the relationship is unworkable, how to leave it.[7]

Medications for Depression

Almost every year, new medications for depression become available, changing the pattern of what is most commonly prescribed. Basically, antidepressants act by increasing neurotransmitter functions. The ones most widely used are called SSRIs, for selective serotonin reuptake inhibitors, for example, sertraline (Zoloft), fluoxetine (Prozac), and paroxetine (Paxil). As we discussed earlier, they increase the presence of the neurotransmitter serotonin by preventing its reabsorption at the junction between neurons.

Combined with other interventions, such as talking therapy or decreasing stress in the person's life, medication allows the body's equilibrium to return. It improves one's mood, helps one sleep better, and restores energy. This in turn helps the sufferer have the resources to address what's wrong in his or her life, to stop being overwhelmed by guilt, and to begin to move back to normal patterns.

In addition to the SSRIs, which act upon serotonin, there are several other main classes of antidepressants, grouped according to which kind of neurotransmitter they primarily affect. For example, some tricyclic antidepressants (desipramine, nortriptyline) affect the neurotransmitter norepinephrine. Imipramine affects both serotonin and norepinephrine. Bupropion hydrochloride affects dopamine. Most pharmacological treatments take at least several weeks to become effective, and they do so by a reequilibration, or rebalancing, of the disrupted patterns that are part of depression. Also, because of the many interconnections in the nervous system, medications which affect one system (like serotonin) also affect other systems.[8]

In rigorous testing, each of the drugs mentioned above has proven its value. Still, there is no evidence to say that one kind of medication is any more effective than another when the medications are compared to one another in large groups of people. The guidelines put forward by the American Psychiatric Association recommend beginning with a drug from the serotonin reuptake inhibitors class because they have fewer and less intensive side effects than the others.[9] The side effects they cause will vary greatly, and different individuals may respond quite differently to the same medication, and even to different doses of the same medication. This means that there is every reason to try a different medication if the first one doesn't work. The critical point is to find the drug that is best suited to you and to recognize that trying several is routine. Because these are powerful medications that affect the body's regulatory system, they can only be given after a complete history, a physical, and a review of other medications you may be taking. They are usually accompanied by the monitoring of blood pressure and sometimes monitoring of the level of medication in the blood.

If the initial antidepressant prescribed doesn't work fully or doesn't work at all, physicians usually try another drug in the same class. Only if a second SSRI, for example, doesn't work will you switch to a different class, such as the tricyclic antidepressants.

Lithium is most often used for the treatment of bipolar disorder and sometimes as a supplement for antidepressant medication. Treatments for substance abuse and anxiety disorders are needed for those individuals who suffer from those conditions in conjunction with depression.

Both the American Psychological Association and the American Psychiatric Association have set standards and guidelines for the treatment of depression that should be used by all, and revised guidelines from the American Psychiatric Association recently appeared. Similar guidelines have appeared for primary-care physicians.[10]

Although the research provides broad evidence of treatment effectiveness, the follow-up of a recent National Institute of Mental Health study that showed the value of both medication and talking therapies emphasized a different point: One year after the cessation of treatment, the positive effects had greatly diminished. This underscores the value of refresher sessions for each of the talking therapies, spaced at four-to-six-month intervals after the initial treatment. This allows you to consolidate the gains made previously and to help prevent the reemergence of the full-blown disorder. Similarly, there is often a need for maintenance medication to help prevent recurrence of depression.[11]

Other Therapies

Although they have not been subject to the same level of large-scale testing in multiple trials as the treatments described above, other approaches to depression have merit, either as additions to the core treatment or in their own right. Couples therapy can offer partners considerable help. For families in which there are systematic difficulties and patterns of miscommunication, family therapy is similarly valuable.

Because depression overlaps so much with loss, approaches that address recovery from bereavement offer great promise. There are also general short-term, well-studied therapies that have proven effective for many conditions, including depression. And while I have emphasized the empirical evidence for specific therapies, many practitioners use combinations of different approaches.

There is great interest in alternative therapies to the standard ones described, including meditation, exercise, and medications like Saint-John's-wort. Undoubtedly, these will eventually offer help to many, but they need careful empirical evaluation before they can be recommended with the same certainty. Most of the treatments for mental illness in general and for depression in particular in this country at this time are rendered not by mental health professionals but by general practitioners. What matters is not the kind of degree the practitioner has, but his or her experience in treating depression.

Treatments for Childhood Depression

It is only in the last ten years that effective, validated treatments for childhood depression have appeared, but now they offer great promise. The same two basic approaches described for adults are used in the treatment of childhood depression; that is, talking therapies and medication. In studies conducted in the last five years, cognitive-behavioral approaches, interpersonal approaches, and medications have all shown evidence of being useful and valid treatments.[12]

There are also effective interventions to help with reading problems, problems with attention, or long-term struggles with parents that often precede the onset of depression. We can also treat such precipitating problems as anxiety.

Key Principles in Getting Treatment

It is important to recognize that the course of recovery from depression in children or adults is not simple and is sometimes profoundly disrupted by sudden changes, such as feeling overwhelmed, feeling completely out of control, or experiencing an episode of feeling high.

Whether it is being unable to make it through the day or being truly suicidal, depression can precipitate crises. This means you need to get to a caregiver and insist on being seen right away. If it's at night or on the weekend, this will mean visiting an emergency room for evaluation. The results of such an evaluation may lead to a brief time in a hospital or an intense treatment as an outpatient, either through talk or through medication or both. But it is never something that families should attempt to handle on their own.

Sad to say, health insurance often dictates treatment based not on rational considerations but on cost control. Navigating the maze of restrictions and regulations that our current health system imposes requires being an advocate for yourself, your spouse, or your child, or finding an advocate outside the family.

Nevertheless, it is possible to find good treatment for depression even within the complicated maze of managed care. Usually, this means finding one person, typically the primary-care doctor or pediatrician, who understands the system and can help. The task often is to be assertive.

All of the information about depression supports getting help immediately, not holding back. Above all, parents concerned about the effects of their own mood disorder on their children should know that getting treatment itself is an important and vital step in helping them.

Five

Resilience in Action

Resilience is the emergence over time of unexpected strengths and competencies in those at risk. The term derives from experience with metals that are changed in shape by stress and then bounce back. Other terms such as "hardiness" also have been used to describe children who, when subjected to serious major adversities, remain strong and do well in the long run. In this chapter, I will provide an overview of resilience — how we learned what we know about it, what processes contribute to its emergence, and how knowing about it can offer help to you and your family.[1]

The strong evidence of resilience in children provides hope for families because it shows that not all children of depressed parents will experience difficulties. The characteristics of resilient children and their families provide a model of what families can try to promote in order to prevent the emergence of depression or other problems.

As we have seen, depression in adults is almost never the product of an immutable genetic sequence or the inevitable result of a difficult life experience. Instead, it occurs when the interactive balance between risks and resources goes awry.

The futures of children are even less predictable, because they are far more flexible and adaptable than adults. Children are constantly growing, developing, and maturing. Children are also more powerfully affected by their immediate surroundings — their homes, their parents, their schools, their neighborhoods, and their communities — than are adults. For these reasons, there are many different kinds of opportunities to shape their lives for the better.

When we began our work in the early 1980s, no one understood how children could do well in the face of parental depression. Very few studies existed. Because we didn't know what enabled youngsters to thrive, we turned to those who had done well. We asked them to describe in their own words how they were able to manage, what they did, and what most helped them.[2]

Each child, of course, was different. We tried to talk to them without preconceptions and didn't try to fit them into any diagnostic framework.

All the youngsters we talked to had parents who had been gravely ill with depression, averaging four years of major episodes with a much longer time of less severe symptoms. In more than two thirds of the families, both parents had been ill, and most parents had suffered from depression and another illness. The rate of divorce and separation was over 60 percent, and the illnesses for the most part were very long-standing. When we asked for their reflections, our survivors were late adolescents and young adults.

One young woman's story epitomized many.

Kate and Mary O'Reilly: Resilience and Commitment Despite Multiple Hardships

Of all the children we studied, Kate O'Reilly faced the most severe and chaotic challenges imposed by parental illness, and yet she emerged resilient, safely on the other side.

Kate's parents had separated when she was young, and at the time of our first interview, when she was fourteen, she'd had no contact with her father. We talked to her again when she was seventeen, and again when she was in her early twenties. When we saw her at seventeen, her brother was in jail, and her mother had been severely depressed and recently hospitalized. Not long after, because of the mother's uncontrolled illness, Kate moved out. I talked to her last when she was in her mid-thirties, and have talked to her mother a number of times in the past ten years.

Thoughtful, attractive, and shy from the first interview on, Kate spoke carefully but with much warmth. She had a strong sense of herself and a deep awareness of what she had to do in order to get on with her life.

As she looked back from the vantage point of her early twenties, she said: "I came to know that eventually I'd get away from it, that I'd make things go for myself. I was on the outside. I didn't have to be affected by my mother's moods." As we would learn, this strong sense of a separate self is a vital part of resilience. She also added, "I could talk to my sister. I wasn't alone." Another common marker of those who did well.

Kate's mother, Mary, was born not long after the end of World War II. A clinician would describe her history by focusing on the severity of her disorder. And yet, through it all, she maintained her focus on her three children and emerged a successful parent.

Mary had serious depressive symptoms starting at sixteen, a time when she felt very down for weeks, but her first episode of full-scale depression occurred in 1966, when she was twenty. She was in the middle of a precarious and difficult marriage, living in a foreign country, and having her first child. Her second major episode occurred in 1968, when she was struggling with some of the same issues, as well as leaving her marriage. This was after Kate, her third child, was born.

Mary had a long period without symptoms, and then her depression returned in 1977. She was treated and the illness remitted, but then it began to recur more and more, starting in the winter of 1979–1980. This led to a hospitalization in 1981. Thereafter, the depressions became frequent, with sixteen episodes of overwhelming major depression between 1981 and 1990.

Her experience with health care providers was indicative of how few people get adequate care early in the course of what is a treatable illness. In 1968 she'd received medical advice only. It was in 1977 that she first received consultation and was treated with medications, well after the illness had begun to wreak havoc on her life.

Mary had many close relatives with depression, including her mother, who had been hospitalized for the condition. In addition, both Mary's parents struggled with alcoholism. Mary O'Reilly had gone through a difficult marriage and moved out with no support. She would have been described as poor for much of her life.

Thus, she had many risk factors, but she was far more than someone who'd simply endured a series of calamities. When I met her, she was a tall, friendly woman with bright blue eyes. She looked at me directly and answered my questions with a piercing honesty. She had a remarkable understanding of her illness, her kids, and herself.

Thinking about what she'd been through, struggling to make sense of it, reflecting about it, and learning how to deal with it over time were essential for her. She was even trying to figure out how to be helpful to her grandchildren. As we shall see, her commitment to parenting endured despite her illness.

Mary's father had been a war veteran, her mother a nurse, and in her early years, she was a deeply involved baby-sitter for her younger siblings. When she was nine years old, her parents' severe and recurrent alcoholism brought out the extraordinary tenacity, the commitment to doing what is right for a child that would become evident later as she raised her own children.

She told her story this way: "It just got to the point, the drinking went on for so long and I never knew how much time went by, but I came to think that I couldn't really take care of my younger brother and sister anymore because I really didn't know what I was supposed to be feeding them. They were eating ice cream and potato chips, and the floor was really sticky. My parents would pass out. I'd have to call up my father's work and tell them what he told me to say. I hated it because I could hear them on the other end of the line saying, 'What's wrong with him?' and I had to lie. I just realized I couldn't take care of my sister and brother anymore, but I knew I could take care of myself. I remember walking up to the police station. It was about a fifteen-minute walk. I kept walking back and forth, back and forth. I didn't want to go in. I didn't want to have to do it. But finally, I stood outside and the policeman saw me standing there and said, 'Can I help you?' So I finally told them. The ambulance came and took my parents away. We were taken before a judge, and the judge put us in a foster home, which I hated, for at least a month."

Perhaps even more important was what happened afterward. The judge was skeptical about the parents' ability to care for their children. But both of them stopped drinking and they got the children back. The family stayed intact in the years that followed. Mary remembers her parents fondly, but she also remembers that their drinking and other family problems were never discussed.

Mary grew to be a tall youngster and somewhat self-conscious, though she was socially active and breezed through school. She had little experience with boys until, at the age of sixteen, she met Anthony, twenty-eight years old, a cheerful and energetic man from Costa Rica who'd recently left his wife and four children. They dated, and he moved in and out of her life. On the spur of the moment, he proposed to her. She accepted, and just after graduating from high school in the early sixties, she moved to his home in Costa Rica. She bore three children, each a year apart. The marital relationship was fraught with difficulty. Although always engaging and cheerful, Anthony was unfaithful and unreliable as a provider. Mary's first depression came when she realized how lonely and cut off she was.

"I got really depressed," she said, "but I was married and living in Costa Rica, and we'd broken up and I went back to him and felt really trapped because I had no money. A lot of times I'll act on things if I have to — I'm better off doing that than just sitting there and saying, 'Oh, we'll see what happens.' Nothing happens unless you make it happen. So I broke off the marriage because it simply wasn't working. You know, we never talked about it. It was just, 'See you later.'"

She moved back home with her parents. They provided support to her and adored the children. She started on Aid to Families with Dependent Children and soon found a part-time minimum-wage job. She quickly advanced to being regularly employed, and gradually things improved. She moved to her own place with her children, but remained near her parents. She liked working. She really enjoyed Kate and the other children, and for the most part, the early years of their lives were positive. The grandparents were loving caregivers, and despite the usual minor scrapes, the children did well.

Mary spoke with great warmth of this period with her kids. She said, "I found it pretty easy to bring them up. They were on a schedule. I was a drill sergeant living in the housing project. I didn't want the home to be chaotic, and there weren't too many fights. It was just me and them."

Even as a child being raised on public assistance, Kate flourished. She was in Head Start, was an exemplary student, and had many friends. Then Mary began a long-term relationship with a man with children of his own, and things became harder, for Mary and for Kate.

"I found the teenage years the hardest," Mary said. "The girls dating, and Richard [her son] getting into drugs." Richard began abusing alcohol and marijuana in 1975, and later used hallucinogens. When he became addicted, he participated in petty vandalism and theft.

Mary's very serious depression started as two powerful challenges coincided. Her youngsters were going through adolescence, and she received a proposal of marriage from the man she had been seeing.

"He had three kids, I had three kids. He liked my kids. I think I was gun-shy because I had been in a bad marriage and I just didn't want to get married. When he said he wanted to get married, I didn't want to, and then he broke it off."

In 1977, Mary developed a depression so severe that for the first time she got help. She recovered slowly, but then toward the end of the decade, the pressures again began to mount. Her son became increasingly troubled, using drugs more and more. He got into constant fights with both his mother and his sisters, and, in Mary's words, "ran with a bad crowd." Increasingly, he got in trouble with the law.

Unable to control her son, Mary began to feel worse and worse. And then there were other pressures. Mary's former husband returned from Costa Rica. Although she chose not to get back together with him, she found his presence in her life overwhelming and disorganizing

Then she was assaulted in a parking lot, badly injured, and confined to home. She couldn't work, couldn't see anyone. She also discovered a lump in her neck that she thought might be cancerous. She became frightened, and then the feelings of hopelessness escalated.

She didn't describe or understand herself as experiencing "risk factors," though in formal terms she was. What she lived through was simply being overwhelmed when a whole series of adversities came together. These circumstances would have been hard for anyone. She had panic attacks, which got out of control and led to a hospitalization on a psychiatric ward. Gradually, though, she recovered. For a time, Kate tried to manage everything for her mother. Ultimately, though, she moved out.

After Mary's hospitalization, Richard continued stealing to support his drug habit, and eventually he was incarcerated. Mary managed tenuously until her father died unexpectedly a year later, and then she descended into a deep depression, unable to function or focus.

In the years that followed, Mary's depressions lasted longer and longer as the many risk factors came together. Her mother developed an illness that drained her vitality and eventually killed her. "After she died in 1986," Mary said, "I just didn't want to live alone anymore. She'd come down on the weekends and I'd cook for her. With my father, the end came out of the blue; with my mother . . . she had cancer."

In time, Mary put her life back together and eventually got the treatment she needed. Through it all, she remained in touch with her children, showing the commitment to parenting despite the ravages of illness that shines through the accounts of depressed parents who nonetheless have resilient children.

Mary had called her parents to task for not being responsible when she was nine. After she'd gotten into a marriage that did not work out, she'd courageously left it. She went out on her own, then reestablished relationships with her parents, who were able to help her a great deal. Despite a devastating depression, she fought through it and established long-term relationships with her kids.

Mary's experience showed me that despite extraordinary adversity, wrestling at times with devastating depression, she and many like her could be effective parents. Part of this is expressing love and warmth. Part of it is being firm and setting limits. Mary was able to do this throughout much of the children's early years, until she became overwhelmed with depression. Later, as she recovered, she was able to reknit the bonds with her kids. And even more, her commitment to her children was vital for her as she faced the storms of the illness, and it kept her going. It was the single most important good part of her life.

All three of the children are now in stable marriages. Nancy, the oldest, is a child-care leader, active in a parenting group, and by all accounts a wonderful, deeply committed mother. Richard, after the episode of drug addiction and incarceration, found religion, has been drug free, and is now faithfully committed to his marriage and his children. Interestingly enough, what led him to give up drugs was not being able to go to his grandfather's funeral because he was in jail.

Kate, who had wrestled with minor depressions off and on, eventually found herself. She is married now, successfully raising two young children and running a family day care.

When we talked to Kate about her situation at seventeen, after she'd just moved out of her mother's house, she spoke of her mother with love. It was also clear that she felt resignation and separation. At that point, it looked as if the relationship between her and her mother was broken. Later, when she was raising her own children and had found her own way, they reunited and became close again.

Kate contemplated giving up at times, disturbed by what she saw as her mother's lack of will. "When she got depressed, I thought, 'What is there for me? Am I ever going to do better than she as far as happiness?' Part of her depression was that she never got anywhere. Her depression made my problems and transitions much worse. Sometimes I was angry that she couldn't be more supportive of me. It seemed like she took a lot. She wouldn't fight back. Why wouldn't she fight back?"

When asked about how she found the strength to survive after moving out, Kate said: "I've always been a loner. I could always overcome it myself, but now I know I can't. I have to lean on other people. And the people I lean on are my family, my friends, and I have a roommate who's very supportive. I know when I'm down, I'm my own worst enemy. The negative thinking and all. If I'm too quiet, [my roommate will] distract me from thinking."

Kate had at times wrestled with mild symptoms of depression, but she never became fully depressed. She had the capacity to think about herself and the actions she could take, and to act on those understandings. As she came of age, she could leave her mother's house and not feel responsible for all the life issues that only her mother could resolve. She was able to separate herself from her mother, which meant that she could get on with her own life. Her success exemplifies three important traits of resilience: relatedness, a sense that her actions made a difference, and above all, self-understanding.

Kate also commented on what would help others growing up in a household with depression. "First, somebody should explain why people get depressed," she said. "You really don't know what it is and if it can happen to you. You don't know why your parent feels that way. You don't know if you're going to feel that way yourself or how to manage it if you do feel depressed. If someone has a disease, you want to know how they got it and how you can prevent it from ever happening to you. Otherwise, you have fear. You can't ever trust something that doesn't have an explanation behind it."

After a twenty-year struggle with a devastating depression, Mary came to a similar conclusion: "It's important for kids to be brought up in a house where they can express themselves," she told us. "In my childhood, we never had that. It was difficult when I grew up. Bad feelings were something I feared, something I suppressed. My kids can be open. If there's a problem, we talk about it and try to figure out what's going on at the time and fix it."

When I asked Mary if it was lonely raising the kids by herself, she said, "I guess so, but I never thought of it. I didn't realize it at the time." And then she described how the kids were so close. "It seemed like at times it was just us. Even to this day, my two girls are my best friends. Even though they don't live near each other. But we went through hard times and they always had jobs in the summer. They never hung on the corners, because they didn't have the time. But they respected me. Richard said, 'You always were there, always there for me.'"

All the resilient youngsters we studied had parents or others who they knew cared for them. So learning from these resilient kids meant learning about their interactions with others who gave support, such as Kate's grandparents, her sister, and much of the time — despite the illness — her mother.

Becoming Separate

We learned other things as well. All of these children wished they were able to cure their parents. All came to realize that they couldn't cure them but that they could do other things. Kate put it this way: "It made me feel a lot better [to understand] that I couldn't do anything to make her feel better or worse. I could only keep in touch with her and listen to her. And she was just a friend, not someone who would affect my whole life." In this sense, by separating from her mother and understanding what depression was, she was able to help her.

Kate also could acknowledge much of what she'd been through. She knew she was angry with her mother for not helping out. She also deeply respected the process of looking at herself and trying to understand. She noted how other people affected her. She said that when others felt helpless, she began to feel trapped. When she began to feel this way, she knew she needed to take action, as she did in moving out.

During her twenties, this issue came up with a roommate who became depressed. Because of her experience with her mother, Kate acted decisively. She said, "You can only help someone so much. When my roommate was depressed, I'd make myself as busy as possible. Work with her for five minutes and then I'd do something else."

She also was able to reflect on her own approach to problem solving: "I mull [problems] over, try to talk them through. Try to think of a way to get through it. Try not to get upset."

Listening to dozens of stories like Kate's emphasized the extraordinarily unpredictable paths that youngsters' lives can take over time. The life histories didn't fit a single pattern, and many youngsters turned out far different than expected.

Putting the Experience into Words

Kate and others like her helped us to recognize that what bothered children the most were the actual disruptions in their lives. The resilient children, however, emphasized that they were aware of what they were facing and were able to put the experience into words.

One young woman whose mother was depressed talked at length about financial problems. She had even lost an apartment because of her mother's inability to manage money. This was only part of the mother's depression, but in the foreground of her daughter's account was the loss of the apartment, the financial irresponsibility, and the young woman's having to manage the resulting disruption. Another young woman's parents went through an angry divorce when she was in sixth grade. Subsequently, her mother lapsed into a depression. She put it this way: "All of a sudden my mother had to go out on her own and raise four children. Whatever went wrong, she had no one to share anything with."

Many children recalled their confusion about what was going on and a sense of helplessness. A young woman who was fourteen when her mother became ill said, "It was bad, feeling like you couldn't help. She was far, far away. You didn't know what to do to make her feel better. She was also drinking a lot. I knew something was wrong. The most painful part of the illness was feeling like I couldn't talk to her. She wasn't my whole mother."

Though they were unhappy at times and even felt some symptoms of depression, these young people all struggled to understand the illness. Many talked directly to their parents. As one said, "She doesn't like to talk a lot about what's going on, but I get it out of her. I keep asking her. I can tell when she's upset, probably by her body language, the way she acts and talks."

Eventually, we recognized in resilient youngsters three main characteristics of self-understanding in the face of parental depression:

1. *They were realistic about what they were dealing with. They were able to see that the illness would recur and that they could recognize when it did.*

In all cases, resilient youngsters noticed that there was something wrong with their parents and concluded that they were not the cause of their parents' depression. They claimed that knowing they were not the cause was crucial to understanding what was happening. This also meant that they saw themselves as separate from their parents. As one young woman put it, "To understand that their problems are not caused by what the kids are doing is essential. Knowing it's the parents' problems — that they need help. I knew it couldn't be my fault. It's nothing to do with anyone else."

2. *They were aware of and could articulate strategies and actions they could take to offset the effects of the illness on them.*

They all wanted to cure their parents of the illness, but they learned they could not, and still found some action that they could take.

We learned that it took children time to understand their parents' illness, often months, sometimes years. However, even in very difficult circumstances such as Mary's, when families face multiple adversities, they can overcome the risks over time. In part, they do it by understanding depression and putting that understanding into words. And in part, they do it by building the resources they need to survive, including nurturing connections to the larger community. In Kate's case, it was her friendships, and her relationship with her sister and eventually her husband. It was also her trying to figure herself out and then acting on her understanding: as in moving out, as in recognizing her roommate's depression.

3. *Psychologically, they believed their actions made a difference, and they took action based on their understanding.*

Entering into the World of the Other

Broadly, resilient youngsters had a well-developed capacity to enter the world of others and to see things from others' points of view. Dr. Robert Selman and colleagues have described how this capacity both to enter into the world of others and to think about the needs of others, the capacity for mutuality, develops through a series of levels. This capacity grows across the span of childhood from impulsive action to reflection to seeing the world both from the other's point of view and from one's own perspective, and then thinking through alternative strategies and choosing actions. Selman's work informed ours.[3]

Two young women in particular showed us how relationships and being able to think about the world of other people can come together in the service of resilience.

Angela, especially, emphasized how her mother helped her. Bright, alert, and constantly on the go with her three siblings, Angela had a father who had been intermittently depressed since an automobile accident had left him with seizures and unable to work. He had been on permanent disability since Angela's childhood. She saw her mother as "the rock of the family": reasonable, strong, loving, and capable of a range of feelings, the organizer of her family and Angela's role model. Angela said, "She doesn't really depend on other people. She's today's woman. If she needs something, she'll ask and I'll do it." She and her mother talked things over.

Only over time, through repeatedly experiencing her father's illness and figuring out her relationship to it, did Angela gain an understanding. "My father would yell at me for something that had nothing to do with me, and then I'd be mad because he yelled at me, and then I'd get it out and apologize and turn around and figure out why I'm angry. Sometimes I don't know, sometimes I know something is left over from something else. Just having friends and family — they know my yelling is harmless. I always say later, 'This is what upsets me, and I don't mean to take it out on you.'" Angela knew she could call her friends night or day, and sometimes she did, even at midnight.

Another young woman, Martha, somewhat older and an only child, emphasized the other side of the process of coming to understanding on one's own. Her mother became depressed when one of her sisters and a close friend died at the same time. Martha said of her mother, "She seemed really unhappy for a long time, withdrawn. It was frustrating for me because I didn't think there was anything I could do. I'd say I missed them too. I couldn't imagine what it would be like to lose so much at once, but I tried to think about it." She said that imagining what it was like for her mother "helped me understand my mother and how major a loss the loss of a sibling must be. I tried to understand it myself."

Martha also dealt with the situation by moving on and establishing her career as a teacher, independent of the family. She emphasized that ultimately she needed to be in control. She said, "My mother holds her feelings in, and I used to be a lot like that. I'm less like that now."

She too came to understand herself only over time. "You have to find a lot of strength in yourself, and then understand your parents. They're human. They have feelings. They can be hurt. They need your comfort once in a while. They've always comforted you. It helps them to know that you're there and that they have someone who loves them." She talked about different ways of fostering understanding. "Talking to someone helps, but it's hard to find someone who can listen. With me, it took the understanding of others."

Along with being able to get outside of the home and on her own, Martha credited learning to express feelings in a relationship with her boyfriend. She says that she and her mother cannot talk about certain things even now, and although they remain close, she has learned to express herself in other ways. "Now I can scream into my pillow. I have a journal. I write things down. It gives me a clearer picture."

She had some trouble upon leaving home but stuck with it. "I'd be sad at night when no one else was awake, but I enjoyed the time alone. It made me feel good that I could do it. I missed my family, but they'll always be here. I haven't lost them."

For a young man named John, the "others" who encouraged his resilience were his teachers. Perhaps more troubled than any other youngster in our study, John exhibited a symptom universally regarded as very disturbed: He was cruel to animals. He had so many risk factors coming together that most psychologists would have predicted he would do badly. He suffered from ADD and dyslexia, and had such difficulty learning that he repeated two grades in school before he was twelve. His three brothers also suffered from dyslexia. His mother had moved to the United States from Italy after World War II. Both parents struggled with drinking and recurrent illnesses, including depression, and through much of John's early life they fought constantly. Those battles receded in intensity when his parents separated, but John lost most contact with his father. Luckily, John's teachers understood his various difficulties, and he did better in the middle years of school.

Still, John's mother's depression worsened as he grew older, complicated by medical illness and a downward economic spiral. John came to see that his activities away from home meant a great deal to him, and he chose to separate from his family even more. Once again with the help of teachers, he was able to gain both admission and a scholarship to a private school and to be away in the summer.

During the last year of high school, he was able to live on campus rather than at home.

Though he remained in touch with his mother, he made many friends at school. He achieved well academically and gradually was able to move away from his mother emotionally as well as physically. At times he wrestled with feelings of depression, and occasionally he experimented with drugs, but neither derailed him from the course he chose. His life was not without considerable struggle, but he continued to show that he was remarkably resourceful in initiating actions. He didn't have enough money to attend college at first, so he worked for a year as a fisherman. He then attended college and did well. After college, he founded his own architectural firm, in a sense building homes for others as his own family had not been able to provide a home for him.

In all these stories, we see that resilience is not the romantic emergence of a superchild, but rather the hard, slow, earned growth of overcoming obstacles and gradually mastering developmental challenges despite the odds.

Six

Enhancing Strengths and Reducing Risks
The Vital Balance Across Time

Every parent wants to know what the likelihood is that his or her children will suffer depression. Every parent wants to know what can be done to strengthen his or her children and prevent depression's onset. In this chapter, I'll share some of the recent findings from studies of families and children's development, findings that help parents promote resilience in their children.

As we emphasized in the discussion of risk factors, in most instances children don't get depressed, or do well for that matter, because of any one occurrence in their lives, but rather as the result of many influences coming together. Although parental depression is one factor that does increase the likelihood that a child will experience depression, parental depression alone, in the absence of other adversities, often conveys far less risk than parents imagine.[1]

Work on the study of resilience and strength in children of depressed parents takes place in the context of a much larger body of research, which emphasizes the remarkable capacities of children to change and adapt. In the medical and psychological literature, this capacity is called "developmental plasticity." What this means, once again, is that there are many different outcomes for children who face difficult life circumstances, and that at many different levels — gene, cell, child, family, and neighborhood — there are actions that can change a child's course for the better.[2]

We now know that genes, once viewed as clear instructions for a fixed outcome, are actually affected by a wide array of factors in any developing child's surroundings. The basic blueprint for the individual may be laid out genetically, but how those genes are expressed varies widely. Genes interact with other genes. They are turned on or off by things that happen to the child over the course of time. Perhaps the best example is the complex interaction between the profound caring, support, and stimulation of the parents, and the intricate, complex evolution of an infant's brain. This process is genetically guided, but only expressed when the child is well cared for. In situations where this caregiving is profoundly interrupted, the child's nervous system may not develop to its full potential.

One of the seminal insights came from studying infants who had damage to their nervous systems at birth but who did well because they developed alternative pathways around the damage. This is developmental plasticity at its most literal.

The Ecological Framework

Youngsters can only be understood by considering the complex, interlocking web of caregivers, family, neighborhood, and community that surrounds them and that changes over time. In psychologist Urie Bronfenbrenner's phrase, this is the "ecological framework." This complex network emphasizes once again that those youngsters who do badly are often subjected to multiple adversities, not just having a parent with an illness. And once again, it reinforces the idea that there are many different ways to help youngsters deal with adversity.[3]

In one hallmark study, psychologists Emmy Werner and Ruth Smith examined resilient youngsters in Hawaii, many of whom were poor. Some had also suffered physical injuries; still others were also the victims of racial discrimination and ethnic prejudice. Early on, Werner and Smith found that the most resilient children shared the same experiences we associate with children who develop and do well without the presence of adversity:

1. Good relationship between the mother and the child in infancy
2. Good relationship between the father and the child in infancy
3. A match between parental expectations and the temperament of the child

Werner and Smith also found that smaller families with a spacing of two years between siblings formed a protective environment, probably because the parents had more time to attend to the needs of each child. Above all, they emphasized that for resilient children compared to nonresilient children, good relationships with both parents and siblings did not exist merely in the first five years of life but were continuous throughout the developmental stages into adulthood. This included not just expressions of love, warmth, and empathy on the part of the parents, but structure, rule setting, and establishing reasonable but high expectations. Resilience emerges in children as a result of underlying processes and interactions that support their development over time.

As the youngsters went through adolescence, the role of the community grew in importance because it provided opportunities for relationships with peers and participation in religious and cultural activities outside of the immediate family. For resilient youngsters, this is when opportunities provided through education, employment, and the availability of mentors demonstrated their power to further promote resilience.[4]

This kind of research on the ecological framework demonstrates the importance of good day care, good schools, and stable, safe neighborhoods. It also explains why prevention efforts such as ours try to provide interventions to strengthen children, not just at the moment of clinical crisis, but through all the ordinary developmental transitions. Most of these preventive interventions take place outside of a clinic. They can take the form of a home visit, or a course in negotiating skills for adolescents, or direct intervention after job loss to help parents become reemployed quickly. The effects of positive experiences accumulate over time, gradually helping children develop deep inner strengths.

A recent review found that 50 to 70 percent of youngsters facing adversity manifest some aspects of resilience. Even among those at the most severe risk, 10 to 20 percent of youngsters were found to be truly resilient in almost all areas of functioning.[5] Even in a group of children seriously impaired in late childhood and adolescence with the most paralyzing and most difficult-to-treat symptoms — including antisocial and criminal behavior — Dr. Lee Robins found that a substantial percentage (about 40 percent) did well in adulthood.[6]

Those children who emerge resilient often have a flexible temperament, making it easier for them to adapt to parental expectation. Good physical health is obviously a plus, as is the absence of any learning disability. But other characteristics associated with resilient youngsters are much more subject to parental influence. These include a sense of purpose, hope and optimism, well-developed reasoning, insight, spirituality, and the capacity for intimacy. These qualities develop over time and are nurtured by protective resources surrounding the child, including caring parents, peers, religious leaders, mentors and teachers, and supported in schools, neighborhoods, churches, and community organizations. How can you, the parent, instill these characteristics in your child? In the chapters that follow, I hope to offer some assistance.[7]

What of the Risk for Depression?

For parents concerned about the effect of their own depression on their children, there is good news. Two classic studies have helped us come to this conclusion. Michael Rutter examined groups of children on the Isle of Wight, and Arnold Sameroff looked at parents with mental illness during the early stages of a child's life.

Rutter examined risk factors, including maternal psychiatric illness, depression, fathers who were criminals, the absence of resources, poverty, and being in foster care. Rutter found that any one of the factors put the child at no greater risk for difficulties. When four of these were present, however, the child was seven times more likely to become ill.[8]

Sameroff focused on mothers during and after pregnancy. These women had mental illness far more severe than most sufferers experience, yet the results were similarly encouraging. Having a mother who was ill did not determine the child's outcome. What did matter was the severity of parental illness and the presence of other risk factors. If the illness occurred alone and was not overwhelming, then there was not much risk to the children. In fact, children from poor, uneducated families with a healthy mother did worse than children with an ill mother but few other risk factors.[9]

In short, what hurts is a cascade of negative influences hitting all at once.

Michael Rutter coined the term "negative chain of causality" to describe the series of different negative events, none of which alone would cause a serious illness, that, as they accumulate over time, can lead to a paralysis of development. That is why children living in difficult inner-city neighborhoods often have a particularly hard time — because so many negative influences come together at once. But Rutter's work also shows how particular openings or opportunities can lead a child on a different course. He studied a group of girls raised under very difficult circumstances in foster homes. Those who, while in foster care, found mentors, friends, and teachers were more likely, in the next phase of life, to get into healthy relationships with men. These healthy relationships in turn enabled them to escape the negative cycle that many of their age-mates did not.[10]

In our own work, we developed a model of how adversities come together for families facing depression. Using families from an HMO, we looked at which children became depressed over a four-year period, from age fourteen to eighteen. Three factors were important:

1. Depression in one or both parents
2. Other problems the parents faced, particularly alcoholism or anxiety
3. The presence of difficulties earlier in the child's life, such as problems in learning to read, problems with attention, or a prior episode of depression

It is well worth noting that fighting and arguing in front of the children and divorce also increased risk. Also, girls were more likely to become ill by late adolescence than boys were.

When none of these factors was present, only 6 percent of the children became ill with depression over the four-year period of adolescence. If only one of these factors was present, including just parental depression in the absence of other factors, only 12 percent became depressed. In short, having a depressed parent increased the risk, but not dramatically. On the other hand, if all three risk factors were present, half of the children became depressed.[11]

Overall, because depression in most studies comes attended by these other problems, there is an increase in risk for the child of a depressed parent.[12] But let me underscore that the risk is directly proportional to the *number of risk factors*. For a parent suffering from a mood disorder, it should be reassuring to see that depression alone, without the associated adversities of divorce or other psychiatric illnesses, leaves ample room for a positive outcome in children. But there is also in this an implicit call to action.

The message is: Get help for yourself before depression can lead to the "negative chain" of other events that, together, can harm your child. Build your child's protective resources and do not let your depression cascade into the multiple risk factors that can undermine your child's health.

How do we best understand the connection between parental depression and childhood depression? Such a connection can exist either with a possible genetic link in some families or without any genetic influence, either because depressed parents may be less available to their children or because the children live through the same risk factors and adversities that the parents do — exposure to violence, divorce, job loss, and so on — and this in turn affects both of them.

As we discussed in chapter 3, many risk factors for depression in children are independent of parental depression. Vulnerable children include those who constantly feel rejection from their peers, those who have experienced repeated failures, those who see themselves as helpless, and those who already have some symptoms of depression or have a prior history of depression. Those who have been victims of abuse or violence, or have witnessed violence, are also at high risk.[13]

Anne Petersen has traced the onset of depression during adolescence in girls to the combined effects of a stressful developmental transition event, such as moving from grammar school to junior high, the onset of puberty, and a family adversity factor, such as an acrimonious divorce. The transition from the familiar surroundings of grammar school to junior high, with larger classes and more demanding intellectual work, as well as the exposure to older kids, provides ample developmental stress. The biology of puberty itself is stressful.[14]

If your depression as a parent doesn't automatically mean your child will become ill, what does it mean for your family? And what can you do to change the effects?

Certainly, your depression attacks your sense of confidence and the desire to positively influence your children. Just as it does with your spouse, depression colors your interaction with your children, and this is where, as Michael Rutter has documented, parental depression is most significant. It changes the interactions between parents and children.[15] The approach I describe in what follows is based, above all, on making these interactions more positive.[16]

Undiagnosed depression contributes to poor communication, misunderstandings, discord, and conflict in the family, and can profoundly disrupt your parenting. Sometimes depression will spark hostility and excessive criticism. Sometimes you will become preoccupied and forget your children's need for affection. Divorce or depression may also make you unavailable at a crucial developmental point, just when your children feel they need you the most.

But there are ways — and this is firmly grounded in research — to be supportive of your children, to reestablish your focus on parenting, communicate well with one another, and decrease discord, despite depression. The first step is to understand both depression and the needs of your children. This understanding helps you make your interactions positive, which helps enhance your children's resiliency. This is true no matter what other risk factors are present, and it will help you overcome whatever has happened in the past, whatever the ages of your children.

This pursuit of understanding, along with getting adequate treatment for yourself, your spouse, and your children (if needed), is the core of our approach to countering the risks of parental depression.

Just as certain individual characteristics emerged in the resilient youngsters we came to know, so did family characteristics. At crucial points early in life and throughout adolescence, our resilient children had strong figures — parents, grandparents, or others — that helped them through. They often had other mentors or guides as well, emphasizing that if one parent is impaired, the other parent, a grandparent, or some other concerned friend or relative can step in and help out. The power of parenting, to combine warmth and support with effective limit setting and discipline, has emerged repeatedly as the critical positive factor in studies of resilience. As parents, we can't be superhuman, but we can strive to do our best.

Once they reach adolescence, children begin to address their parents' depression in depth. This is the point at which the three aspects of self-understanding we articulated in chapter 5 become evident. Also, the central characteristics of resilience become clear. The characteristics are:

- *The capacity for and deep involvement in intimate human relationships*

Almost all of the resilient young people we followed spoke of valuing close, confiding, intimate relationships, especially during difficult transition periods. These relationships, for the most part, were not with just one other person but a wide range of people. Resilient youngsters spoke of friends, older siblings, their parents, teachers, and people in the community. These wider relationships provided a sense of security to offset any unpredictability in the relationship with the depressed parent and allowed the young person to separate from his or her ill parent.

- *The ability to get tasks done outside the home*

Psychiatrist George Vaillant's study of a group of youths growing up in difficult circumstances in Boston concluded that the single best predictor of who would do well over the subsequent forty years of life was the capacity during adolescence to be productive, whether in work or study. In support of Vaillant's conclusions, our young guides to resilience were convinced that their activities were important. They spoke of their work with pleasure and pride. They persisted in it, they had good work histories, and their involvement was intense. They saw that their actions did make a difference in their feelings about themselves.[17]

The activities of our resilient kids took place in a variety of circumstances. Those who were in school were good students, deeply involved in their academic pursuits. A number attended fine colleges after high school, and those in college all had part-time and summer jobs. Those still in high school had jobs as well, the majority holding down two jobs. One young woman was working full time but also spent at least fifteen hours a week dancing with two different companies. Another, in high school, was active in his church youth group, spent time taking care of younger children, was a fine student, and took courses at a local music college. Several others were deeply involved in sports.

- *The capacity for reflection and self-understanding*

In an earlier chapter, I showed how resilient children knew that they were not to blame for their parents' illness. Their self-reflection deepened into a profound sense of psychological separateness and independence from the depressed parent and, with that, an acceptance of what they could and could not do to help their parent. They all wanted to cure their parents, to make them whole, but over time they realized they couldn't. Nonetheless, the sense of separateness, and the absence of self-blaming, allowed them to do many other things that were genuinely helpful. When some who appeared resilient for a while experienced setbacks, the inability to separate appeared to play a role.

As I have said repeatedly, there are many possible futures, not a single path, for a child growing up in a home with depression.

I described the essence of resilience in terms of deep understandings within the child in chapter 5. In this chapter, I have shown how those understandings become manifest in constructive behaviors as the youngster engages the world, including interactions with parents.

Now I want to restate this core message as action points for you, the parent. In the chapters that follow, I'll show how families have made these action points part of their daily lives.

Here are three things you can do to protect your children from susceptibility to depression:

1. Help them develop and maintain relationships, especially those that have been disrupted because of your (or your spouse's) depression.
2. Help them be successful away from home — in school and in the community.
3. Help them reflect on and understand what they've undergone in the family.

In spite of the sense of hopelessness and helplessness that depression often entails, you can help your children maintain and expand their friendships and connections with others outside the family. You can help reweave the social bonds that depression weakens by focusing on making your house a place in which your children can play with others after school. And you can help your children have a sense of individual accomplishment and understanding. If you struggle with depression and worry that your children are being damaged, letting them go is hard. But children need to succeed outside the home, to develop their own independent interests, and to know that their parents' illness won't dominate their lives.

Seven

Breaking the Silence
The Family Meeting and After

In the preceding chapters, I've tried to present a deeper understanding of depression and resilience. All of this becomes groundwork for a family meeting. I hope that this chapter will help you and your partner, if you are sharing child raising, to be able to put the knowledge to use in talking with your children.

You need to spend time planning for a family meeting before having it. You need to spend time alone with your partner, and then alone with each child.

Parents, of course, have many encounters with their children throughout the day, but a family meeting is a different kind of experience. You need to prepare your children for it. Talk with each child separately and tell him or her that a meeting is coming up. Ask if there are questions or concerns that they want addressed. Be ready to hear whatever they have to say. It may take more than one conversation for you, your spouse, and your children to get ready.

Children represent our greatest hopes for the future and also our most intense worries and fears about what we might have done wrong. This can get in the way of seeing them for who they are and what they need from you. Children also have their own unique perceptions and agendas. They may not be as focused on the influence of depression as you are. Talking directly to children can alleviate their unspoken anxieties about what is most important to them. However you choose to communicate, your aim is to give each child an opportunity to speak, to express concerns. This is the only way you have to find out how he or she is really doing.

To speak directly to your children, you yourself have to believe very strongly in what you are saying. You have to have begun your own journey to make sense of depression in your life and in your history. You also have to understand your situation well enough to explain it in language that children can understand. If you have a partner, this means sharing that understanding with him or her. Make sure you have talked through what has happened to you both with depression. Review and make sure you both understand, together, what depression and resilience are before trying to explain them to your children.

Everyone has to feel safe, and this means making sure that if anyone does speak up, he or she will be heard and not criticized. It also means making sure that everyone is ready to talk.

Talk to your children only when you have reframed your family story, when you can accept depression as an unwelcome illness rather than viewing it as a shameful secret.

Like the Petrocellis, discussed in chapter 1, many families take considerable time to plan, to find the right moment for a family meeting. Some take six weeks, some take six months. First comes deciding when to do it, then preparing the children by talking to them beforehand, and then actually doing it. This sequence gives each family member time to prepare. It also gives structure to a conversation about events that have often been experienced as chaos.

Addressing the Needs of Children

Your goal in preparing for a family meeting is to draw your children into the process, all the while making sure that they are not overwhelmed. Here I will share some of the questions we've found helpful. You may choose to ask the same questions, but only after thinking through what you hope to achieve with the exchange.

I generally start by asking youngsters about their strengths, interests, skills, and relationships — things that have been going well in their lives but might have been obscured by depression.

Then I ask what they know of the parents' illness, how they perceive it and how they've responded, sometimes referring to events that the parents have told me about. Each child should have a chance to speak alone, as each child's experience is different.

Many children find it difficult to talk directly to their parents about their concerns. Others find it more difficult to talk to someone they don't know. And of course, children don't follow scripts or guidelines. In one of the first families I worked with, after careful preparation, I was meeting with a thirteen-year-old girl in her home. I asked, as thoughtfully as I could, "What do you think will help you?" She looked me directly in the eye and answered, "I know one thing that won't help — and that's talking to a psychiatrist."

Because painful feelings are hard to own, children sometimes find it easier to describe what they imagine someone else's experience to have been — sibling, father, mother, sometimes a friend or even an imaginary companion. Keep in mind that for most younger children, what they can say generally pertains only to their immediate day-to-day experience. It is as they get older that children begin to think directly about cause and effect, guilt and blame.

Children often minimize or deny what they have been through. Some worry that voicing their fears may actively harm their parents, and others worry that they have caused the illness. Above all, they want to know when a parent might recover, and they crave assurance that a parent will definitely recover over time.

Other stressful family events that may have occurred, such as excessive drinking or divorce, are inseparable from a child's experience of depression. If a child attaches shame to these events, he or she will attach shame to depression.

If a child is depressed, asking about it directly is the most effective way to get an honest answer. You should watch for warning signs — a change in activities, crying, or unexplained irritability. The meeting with the child can then provide a forum in which to ask direct questions about how the child is doing. Always ask children directly if they feel blue, unhappy, or tired a lot of the time if you are concerned about this.

For the rare child who actually seems depressed, a direct question and response makes it possible to acknowledge the depression and then get appropriate support by seeking an evaluation from a professional, such as a pediatrician or mental health worker, as we discussed earlier. For most children, the meeting establishes that it's okay to ask these kinds of questions about feelings. It can also help you learn the distinction between true depression and the more common mild and transient disturbances in mood that many children experience.

Planning the Family Meeting

I've drawn up a list of general guidelines for planning the meeting that families have found useful, but, of course, each family is different. When and how you choose to talk to your children has to work for you.

Decide together with your spouse what to talk about before the family meeting. The process of deciding together is more important than any of the details. If you are a single parent, it is often helpful to talk over what you plan to say with a trusted friend.

Choose also what not to discuss. Events you are deeply worried about, like feeling suicidal or fighting with other family members, that children don't know about do not need to be discussed if you wish them to remain private. Tell your children at the outset that there will be more than one family meeting, and tell them that you and they will be able to talk about their feelings at any time.

Don't attempt a major family conversation about depression and the family's history in the midst of a crisis. Deal with the crisis first and come back later to the larger issues. Families can and need to talk with their children about what they are undergoing as soon as possible, but trying to find a new way to talk to one another while in the midst of an acrimonious divorce, for instance, is not a good idea. The same is true when there is clear-cut abuse of alcohol or other drugs, or when a family member is acutely psychotic, out of control, and is either hospitalized or needs to be. In such circumstances, all of the family's resources need to be directed toward dealing with the crisis itself. Similarly, if a child or parent is acutely depressed, get care first. Reassure everyone in the family that the necessary steps to evaluation and treatment are being taken and then emphasize that other conversations will come later.

Tell your therapist or whoever is taking care of you that you are going to talk to your children. These caregivers can provide help and reassurance.

Try to show your children that you and your spouse are united in caring for them and that clear plans are in place. Take whatever time you need together to reach this point.

For some of our families, it took time for the couples or the single parents to feel safe and ready for the family meeting. Many choose to rehearse several times what they want to say. Each time, it is not only a practical attempt at mastering a specific conversation, but also a way of learning to anticipate how the children may feel.

Children of different ages understand and deal with depression very differently, and many families have more than one child. While a six-year-old will need concrete reassurance that tomorrow will be fine, a twelve-year-old not only will be able to remember and talk about the past, he or she will be able to ask questions about the long-term future. In one family, a six-year-old was afraid that she would catch her father's depression by using his toothbrush. In another, a twelve-year-old worried that she had caused her father's depression because she had been angry with him and because she unfairly blamed herself for her parents' arguing. Thus, in talking with the family as a whole, parents can both address general concerns and tailor certain aspects of the conversation to each child.

We always include every child in the household who is able to sit and talk in the meeting, with some as young as three and some well into their teens and beyond. Children younger than three are very much part of the planning for how to deal with depression and may or may not be included in the meeting, depending on what a parent wishes. Often, children return home from college or elsewhere to participate. Children, after all, live in a family with their siblings, and older children can learn from hearing simpler explanations for younger children. Conversely, younger children can appreciate the feelings and tones of caring expressed through more complicated explanations for adolescents.

Holding the Family Meeting

What children want to know more than anything else is that their parents will be all right. Letting children know ahead of time that a meeting will take place, specifying a time and place, making sure that they know that whatever is said is okay, and leaving the way open for further conversations all contribute to their sense of security.

By talking about depression and what a parent is living through, children receive a different framework of understanding than that of terrible and undiscussable adversities striking at random.

Although each family meeting is unique, the four key objectives of the family meeting are:

1. To reassure your children that you will be okay and that the illness will not overwhelm the family.
2. To emphasize that no one is guilty or to blame.

3. To speak to the positives, the strengths that exist and will be enhanced.
4. To present some knowledge about depression and treatment.

A family meeting is far more than a simple recap of issues that have come up earlier. You need to address specific concerns that your children have raised and to deal directly with at least some of the events you have lived through together. You also need to plan for ways to continue the dialogue. Knowing ahead of time that there will be a follow-up session to review what has happened, to acknowledge the positives, and to plan for the future can help you organize the meeting. It's also important to acknowledge the possibility that another family member may become depressed or that depression in a parent could reoccur, and to explain what you will do if this should happen.

Once you begin:

1. Tell your children what actions you're taking: getting treatment, talking with your spouse and with them about depression, and trying to be there for them. Reassure them that life will go on for all of you.
2. Discuss events your children have witnessed.
3. Talk about those things that are unusual, clearly upsetting, and undeniable, and help your children find ways of understanding these difficult experiences so that they don't blame themselves or feel responsible for the family's pain.
4. Help your children feel comfortable enough to talk about what frightens them, addressing their concerns directly.

The basic information about depression, treatment, and resilience presented in earlier chapters is important, but knowledge has a completely different meaning when parents talk about it in their own words and tie it to their own experiences, then let their children ask questions about it. By doing this, the adults reassert their role as parents and signal that the family is becoming a family again. After a period of pain and hopelessness, the family is free to hope and think about the future once more. With careful planning, almost every family we've worked with has been able to hold a successful meeting.

This is not to say that one successful family meeting resolves everything and all the issues are swept away. Quite the contrary; a successful family meeting merely begins a process of healing that can be revisited over the years that follow.

The journey of Fran and John O'Connor shows how understanding in families develops over time and is tested again and again by unanticipated but important challenges.

The O'Connors: Beginning and Continuing the Family Dialogue

Fran and John O'Connor each worked as teachers and were deeply committed to public service. They lived outside the city, but had many friends of like mind in the surrounding community.

Fran was an attractive and personable woman in her thirties who was alternately upbeat and withdrawn. Her life had been racked by a series of major depressions brought on by many losses, increasing in frequency over the ten years before we saw her. She was receiving both medication and intermittent counseling. John, tall and thin, was soft-spoken and often followed his wife's lead.

They wanted to talk to their twelve-year-old boy about his mother's depression. What was striking in this couple, as well as in most couples we worked with, was the fact that although they were thoughtful, intelligent, and reflective people, they had never talked in depth about her depression with each other and had only spoken of it in the most general terms to their son.

Fran voiced her concerns immediately in the first session with one of our clinicians. "When I'm depressed, I can't see why John loves me and I don't see how he can want to continue." On several occasions in the throes of depression, she had left the house and stayed at a hotel for a few days, unable to bear her fears of being with those who loved her.

John had struggled to make sense of this. "I try to cater to her mood when she's depressed. I try to get her involved with something else if I can. Sometimes, I just get discouraged or upset. Over the years, I've learned to believe that it will pass, although it took me a long time to learn. It's sad for me when she's unhappy and can't enjoy life as much as she should."

Fran and John were worried about how their son, Frank, their only child, would understand what was happening and, over the long term, that he too would become depressed.

The family had established a nice routine, with Frank having a set time to do homework, then spend some time relaxing, and then go to bed. This all went out the window, however, when Fran was depressed. As she said, "I can't follow through with anything, and I just tell him to plop down in front of the TV or go to bed, and then I call John and tell him to come home early."

Frank was somewhat disorganized, and when Fran was depressed, she couldn't monitor him and provide the organization and direction that he needed. "Anything that has to do with discipline or with making mistakes or being noisy is impossible. I have a hard time with it when I'm depressed."

The difference between how they talked about the depression and how they talked about Frank was striking. Fran's voice changed when discussing her son. There was a lilt and energy to it. She saw him as bright, fun, and articulate, and with "incredible negotiating skills." She described him as a good student with many friends, although there was some concern that he was insecure at times and had trouble dealing with change. He had been asked numerous times to participate in advanced programs in school, but he had refused because he didn't want to change his routine. John had more worries about their son, indicating that he, in contrast to Fran, thought Frank had some difficulties in getting along with others. In John's view, Frank seemed somewhat isolated.

Following the sequence I've described so far, Fran and John were presented with the basic information about depression: that depression is a biological illness, that no one is guilty or to blame, and that help is available. The risks to children were discussed: that there are somewhat higher rates of depression in the children of depressed parents, but that this is largely due to the accumulation of many risk factors. The clinician working directly with them also presented the characteristics of resilient youngsters in terms of their ability to engage in relationships, to take action in the world, and to understand what was happening to them, to understand depression.

As is customary in our work with families, the clinician asked to have one session alone with Frank, and Fran and John readily consented. When the time came for Frank's session, though, the O'Connors called and canceled.

Families need to take time, proceed at their own pace, and feel safe in opening up. Information comes alive only when families deal with their underlying fears, and talking about depression is not simple. For many, it involves rethinking the depressions they have experienced, the families that they grew up with, the events that led to depression — and the veil of silence that has surrounded these events. Fran and John took more time to talk things over, and it became clear that the tradition in both their families had been to deal with adversities by not talking about them. In Fran's family, there was a deep-seated fear that talking about negative things might make them worse.

For Fran, this style of not talking extended back to the age of twelve, when her mother was severely ill with cancer. She remembered seeing her mother crying many times. At the same time, she and her brother were told that her mother was getting better. They were not told of their mother's impending death from cancer until the night before it happened. Fran's loss was compounded after her mother died. As her father couldn't manage both her and her brother, Fran was sent to live with an aunt. While she thrived in her new environment, she missed her family terribly. Her brother, on the other hand, developed a severe recurrent depression with many suicide attempts and failed relationships. The pattern of depression and suicide attempts extended to her brother's own children. As a result, Fran was desperately worried about childhood depression, not as an abstraction but as a very clear image of her brother's decline.

Frank was now about the same age that Fran had been when her mother died. Likewise, Fran was now reaching the age at which her mother had died. When she eventually began to talk with her son and her husband about her depression, Fran expressed her fear that her life would be the mirror of her mother's and that she too would die at an early age.

Fran's father was a vital part of her life, upbeat and optimistic, but his style of dealing with many tragedies was to deny them and simply emphasize the positive. A devout Catholic, he attended mass every day. He had become depressed during a hospitalization for pneumonia and then cured himself, he reported, by simply "snapping out of it."

"He thinks you should be able to just stop feeling depressed," Fran told us. "When I'm feeling guilty, I feel like I should be able to look at what a good life I have and be happy. I feel it's my fault that I can't be happy."

The idea of talking about depression with Frank, or letting him talk to one of us, raised all these powerful specters for Fran and John. These fears translated directly into day-to-day, minute-to-minute encounters between them and their son. These were the fears that made them hesitate about letting their son talk to one of us.

Both parents were worried that they would somehow irrevocably alter their relationship with Frank if they labeled Fran's illness as depression. As she said, "I don't want him to think I'm crazy." John had a different issue. "I've always felt he was too young to hear about it," he said. "I don't want him to think that Fran is impaired." Fran summed it up this way: "I'm afraid Frank will hear something that will change his world." Inevitably, though, that change was coming. The only question was whether the change would be for better or worse.

Gradually, with John's help, Fran's efforts, and our support, the O'Connors decided to go ahead and let the clinician talk with Frank alone, and then hold a family meeting. During the session alone with the clinician, Frank played with a handheld video game and mostly gave one-word answers, typical for a twelve-year-old boy, but he did talk about specific events related to his mother's depression. For Fran, talking with her son meant developing a new way of understanding her depression and the losses she'd experienced. To have a new view of depression, one more accepting of herself, she would have to break with the view held by her father, the single person who'd been there for her most throughout her early life — her loving father, who was alive, sane, and helpful. But this break also meant moving more into the present, the present she shared with her husband and her son.

The O'Connor Family Meeting

With our help, Fran and John planned their family meeting very carefully. They role-played and rehearsed it repeatedly before talking with Frank. As they began, they talked specifically about what they'd been through together, and because they had taken time to plan, it went well. They emphasized that Frank was not to blame. They outlined the actions they would take to protect him. They explained that Fran's behavior came from a biological illness. They described the depression, her irritability and her upset, in terms that he could understand. Frank was mostly quiet but listened intently. At the most poignant moment of the meeting, Frank said, "I don't think you like me when you're depressed." Fran answered, "It's not that I don't like you. I love you. I will always love you."

Fran had her own fears that she wasn't loved. She feared John's utter confusion about what was going on, and they both feared for Frank. But all the anxiety was compounded by the deep-seated patterns of not talking.

After the Family Meeting — Frank

In the weeks and months following the meeting, Frank asked far more questions about Fran's depression. He asked in detail what caused it and voiced the fear that he might get it, fears he'd had long before the family meeting but had never voiced. He, like most children, was quite concerned about the arguing at home. He wondered if the arguments his parents had were caused by depression.

Clearly, he knew that his mother experienced some changes in her behavior. When Fran descended into episodes of depression, manifested both by withdrawal and irritability, he would either steer clear of her or be nice to her and try to make her feel better. As Frank put it, "Lots of times she gets into a bad mood. I don't get her aggravated when she's grumpy, because I'll get into trouble." He had also seen how a good mood could suddenly turn into a bad mood. Once he confronted her and asked, "Why are you picking on me just because you've had a bad day?"

Concrete actions — talking directly about the behaviors Frank had witnessed, his mother's reassuring him periodically that she loved him, and a more general emphasis on talking — made Frank a more active participant. As Fran said, "I learned to tell Frank that I loved him every so often, regardless of my being depressed, and how happy he made me. It doesn't come naturally to me. It's easier to complain about his dirty laundry."

Change comes both from broad understanding and from continuing to take small specific steps. Both parents reported talking to Frank about what to do when Fran wasn't feeling well. Both parents remained open to talking. After a while, Frank admitted for the first time that he was worried that he had caused his mother's illness. Both parents were able to reassure him, above all, by reasserting their love for him.

After the Family Meeting — Fran and John

Over the next year, Fran noticed that her many stresses caused her to get distracted and not take her fluoxetine and then to get more and more upset. Once she noticed the symptoms of depression and felt as if she was going to lose it, she would make a conscious effort to start taking her medication again. She and her husband said that her depressions were less severe and caught earlier because of their talking together.

Gradually, Fran began to have more confidence. Periodic low moods became "just a phase." She saw the illness in the context of her family's history. She ceased seeing herself as some pitiful person who was at fault for her own suffering. Perhaps most important, as she put it, "I retained my awareness that others can help, especially my husband and my son."

Likewise, talking openly helped to validate Frank's sense that the depression wasn't his fault. A year or so after the first meeting, Fran said, "I'm hoping that it will help to be able to separate my being depressed from my rejecting him."

Talking about depression together also enabled Fran and John to sort out other issues in their marriage that needed attention. Removing the veil of silence about depression relative to their greatest fear, their child, helped Fran open up about other topics. As John said, "It gave us a framework to try to understand things together." He felt it profoundly changed the way they related to each other as husband and wife.

At various points, Fran and John asked Frank how he was doing. Progress took time, but their conversations had already gained a new and different dimension. John said, "We talked about it in the same room and established that we could do it as a family, that is, all together." Talking helped John understand his role as a buffer between his wife and son, so he was able to be much more helpful when she became depressed.

Instead of withdrawing and despairing, Fran spoke up, enabling John to be more helpful. They both became stronger and more equal in being able to disagree and yet work things out. "Before, I wanted to be alone," Fran said. "Now I realize I want my husband to be there with me, and it helps me that he's there. It helps to talk. Before, it didn't seem worth it; I had no energy. Now I push and he pushes to talk." Years later, looking back, she said, "We have a kind of intimacy that not every family has." John too confided that he thought the approach had helped save their marriage.

The change in the family was especially clear when Fran became ill again. When she began to feel depressed, she asked for help from both Frank and John, and they listened and responded. This led to other major changes. When Fran became more depressed and felt like leaving, she didn't. She stayed and talked about what she was feeling, and at various points they got help together. Sometimes when she felt the impulse to leave, she and John went away together for the weekend while Frank stayed with friends.

Developmental Challenge

Even so, Frank O'Connor took a long time to make sense of his mother's illness, and only came to a full understanding after he'd left home. Along the way, he challenged and upset the equilibrium of the family, particularly in his late teens, when he began to refuse to talk to his parents.

Perhaps this is not unusual for rambunctious, somewhat ornery athletic boys, but it was particularly difficult for this family on a journey to try to talk through an illness that paralyzes the capacity to talk. Our meetings with Frank during this period reflected the same black hole of noncommunication — mostly one-word answers.

During this time, Fran experienced a catastrophic series of major depressions that, according to her husband, were the worst she had ever experienced. She struggled with sleeping, with terrible doubts about herself, and with wild periods of irritability. Frank, although mute about his mother's difficulties, began to struggle more and more himself. His reticence continued. He seemed uncomfortable with questions regarding depression, although he and his father did talk about how to manage when his mother was having a very difficult time.

After his mother's most serious episode, his grades dropped below the honor roll for the first time, and he tried marijuana. There were furious arguments with his parents. During these arguments, Frank even threatened to hurt himself. He also began to fall in with a bad crowd at school and, very uncharacteristically, he got into fights. His father's efforts to talk him through all this did not succeed. Yet, when another child from the neighborhood who had struggled moved in for a few months, interestingly enough, Frank became this boy's defender against his own mother's bouts of depression.

When Frank was fifteen, his maternal grandfather became acutely ill with diabetes, and the family decided that he would move into their home. This was a joint family decision. Over the year that followed, Frank and his grandfather became very close, and Frank actually helped his grandfather monitor his insulin levels and his diet. During the same period, Frank had more fights with his parents and further troubles at school. In short, he became a mildly rebellious adolescent, one who particularly aggravated the disruption in family rhythms brought about by his mother's depression.

Given all the turmoil in the family, the grandfather's presence represented a kind of restoration or reassertion of the family's bonds. His grandfather's presence, along with his father's, represented islands of safety in the midst of the tumult of Frank's adolescence. Unfortunately, bonding with his grandfather may have reinforced Frank's refusal to open up. His grandfather had suffered many losses, yet believed that people should simply cope as best they could — in silence.

Suddenly and unexpectedly, Frank's grandfather died, and both Fran and Frank were bereft. This would be a terribly hard event for any family, but it threw Frank into a tailspin. He lost interest in work and school, and one night he got drunk with friends. His parents worried that he would start to drink regularly. He told them that he was convinced he'd caused his grandfather's death because he hadn't paid enough attention to monitoring the insulin the day before he died.

This was a crucial juncture for the family. Fran faced an extraordinary array of tasks. She herself, battling long-term depression, needed to grieve the loss of her father, and it was quite possible that this death would precipitate an even more profound depression in her. And, of course, grieving that loss meant also reliving and rethinking her life with her father, all that he'd given her. It also prompted her to remember the other losses she'd endured — her mother's death and the many tragedies in her brother's life. At the same time, she had to keep on with the tasks of daily living, working, being in a marriage, and raising her son, all the while facing the specter that her son was developing the same illness that afflicted her.

Helping her son gave Fran a focus that allowed her to get through this time. But it also challenged her deeply. She realized something was very wrong with the way things were going with Frank. She talked it over with John and called the clinician from our team who had worked with them over the years to review the situation. Fran and the clinician met with Frank and succeeded in continuing the dialogue.

Fran conveyed her feelings to Frank. She reassured him that her sadness was not another depression and that it was normal for her and for anyone suffering the loss of a parent to cry a great deal, that it was in some ways an affirmation of how much she loved her father. She also offered the opinion that Frank's attempt to deny his own sadness came from an identification with his grandfather's repressed emotional style. This created an opening. Frank was able to admit his fears for his mother and express many positive memories of his grandfather.

Parenting is constantly going back and forth between understanding and taking action. And the actions often require firmness, discipline, and even battling with children. Fran and John took a series of actions together, directly and authoritatively, to help Frank, and also to try to understand with him what they were all undergoing together. They kept talking to him and refused to let him retreat. They removed him from social situations in the neighborhood and on the school bus with the gang he'd fallen in with by switching him to a more rigorous, time-consuming, and demanding academic curriculum. They continued to set limits. They also decided that Frank would benefit from having someone outside the family to talk to. Suspecting that he was wrestling with symptoms of depression, they arranged for him to have his own therapist. These changes did not yield a compliant child who suddenly shaped up and said "Thank you," but the combined weight of the changes led Frank not to drink, to get into less trouble at school, and to seem less depressed. Frank liked having someone with whom he could discuss his own views separate from his parents. He went to see this person on his own for over a year.

The O'Connors were still not out of the woods. In the next year, Frank simply didn't talk about what was important to him with his parents. But his attitude and demeanor continued to improve. He was in better spirits, he reported that he was generally satisfied with his life, and he did very well meeting social and academic challenges. He even started dating and took up a new sport.

It took longer for the O'Connors to come to peace with one another. For at least several years in his late teens, Frank could not give up his anger at Fran. John continued to step in and act as a buffer between them when Fran was depressed. After an argument, John agreed that Fran might have appeared unreasonable because she was depressed, and this was comforting to the boy. When John was away, though, tensions escalated between Frank and Fran. In an effort to avoid the conflicts, Frank stayed out of her way and didn't talk much to either parent. But like all our resilient youngsters, he had other resources. He talked at great length to a family friend and, gradually, to his peers. He also talked to his girlfriend about family issues.

All the family took pleasure in Frank's academic accomplishments and in his friendships. He was admitted to a top college out of state. In a senior essay, he emphasized the importance of family members talking to one another. He reported to us that the family's conversations had helped him understand that his mother was suffering from a biological illness. Ultimately, he could acknowledge what had happened. Once, when riding in the car with his mother, he told her, "I couldn't imagine having a more wonderful family."

Perhaps it is not accidental that the O'Connors came to us when Frank was the age Fran had been when she lost her mother. Her adolescence had been very difficult because of that loss, but the difficulty had been compounded by not being able to talk about it with anyone. Years later, her family was tested by the loss of her father. In their journey to understanding, many of the themes talked about in the first family meeting recurred for years. The

O'Connors together had many strengths — a strong marriage, a strong commitment to helping others in their work. Also, when they needed it, they found help for their difficulties: treatment for Fran's depression and assistance for Frank, as well as some help from us. But above all, they were able to move on because they worked out a way to talk and solve problems together.

Their views of what happened, once very divergent, came to be very similar. They all reiterated that they stayed together in the family struggle and then eventually persevered. In the struggle, there was a great deal of anger, and many situations that were not resolved when first discussed or even months thereafter. In time, however, things did improve. Fran and Frank became close, in part because they could survive each other's anger without letting it overwhelm everything else. Also, their story emphasizes that each of them, but in particular Fran, had to journey forward to a new way of being within the family, to rethink and reunderstand their history.[1]

In the chapters that follow, we'll see other families wrestle with the same issues in different ways.

Six Principles for a Successful Family Meeting

In general, there are six principles that we offer for any family getting started:

1. Pay attention to the timing of the meeting.

Wait until everyone feels ready to devote the energy to start. Anyone currently wrestling with an acute depression — for example, the crisis of hospitalization, the recurrence of a depression, or a job loss — is often unable to manage the work of prevention and learning a new way of talking. Katherine Petrocelli waited a few months before having the family meeting, and it made a great difference. Fran and John O'Connor timed their talking to Frank for a moment of relative calm, but it took place at a time when the issues were very intense for them, as Frank started adolescence.

2. Gain commitment to the process from the entire family.

A family conversation involves everyone — reluctant spouses, nonresponsive children, and those who clearly want to do it. Very often, the parent who suffers may want to participate, but the other will be reluctant. Often, parents may wish to have a process go forward, but adolescent youngsters resist. Learning a new way to talk only works when everyone agrees to be part of the process, and the whole family's agreeing to be part of the process is an important ingredient of success in and of itself. The dialogue just doesn't work if it's only among selected family members. Often, gaining agreement means talking about why people may not want to talk and being patient until everyone is willing to participate. In our work with families, we have found that one family member or another would often refuse to participate, but a month or two later would want to be part of the process, and then the conversations took place.

3. Begin by identifying specific major concerns and addressing them.

The more a family knows what it is worried about, the more those concerns can be addressed. Sometimes, families are caught up in the chaos that erupts when family routines are shattered by depression: bills unpaid, cars not repaired, cavities not filled. Such disruption must be addressed to provide a secure base from which children can begin to understand.

4. Bring together and reknit the family history.

Recognize from the beginning the need to build a new family story that incorporates new ideas about the meaning of depression and its effects on the family. Many families have had experience with depression that completely disrupted normal life, and for the most part, families don't see depression as something that can be part of their history. It is reconstructing a family story and putting depression in that context that's most important.

5. Plan to talk more than once.

Children will rarely grasp what's been said fully and, even more important, they will not be ready to ask their own deep-seated questions the first time you talk to them. Any serious change takes time.

6. Draw on all the available resources to get through depression.

Those struggling with depression need high-quality care and an ongoing, trusting relationship with a caregiver. When different caregivers are involved, they need to communicate with one another effectively and consistently. Over time, children need to reknit the bonds that have been broken, find friends and mentors, be with their grandparents, their cousins, their aunts and uncles, participate in sports, go to church, and resume other normal activities. Help from others is crucial in raising children, yet such help is often shunned in the midst of a depression. Inevitably, then, families need to develop alliances with those who can help them. Understanding how depression isolates them helps families overcome that isolation and access the resources they need.

Opening a dialogue is an enormous accomplishment for any family. But for many, the illness doesn't magically go away as a result of the journey to openness and sharing. Depression recurs, sometimes very painfully. What has changed for many families and can change for yours is the ability to manage the illness. Many families, including your own, can come to recognize their strengths, to find help from outside and within.

Eight

Finding the Healer Within

The rain drums down like red ants,
each bouncing off my window.
These ants are in great pain
and they cry out as they hit,
as if their little legs were only
stitched on and their heads pasted.
And oh they bring to mind the grave,
so humble, so willing to be beat upon
with its awful lettering and
the body lying underneath
without an umbrella.

Depression is boring, I think,
and I would do better to make
some soup and light up the cave.

Anne Sexton,
"The Fury of Rain Storms"

Breaking the silence about depression shines a light on other aspects of many families' lives. The aim is to return to the tasks of daily living, to, as in Anne Sexton's phrase, "make some soup and light up the cave." But this only happens gradually.

Promoting resilience in your family, above all, means returning to the subject of depression periodically, continuing to build young children's friendships outside the home, and continuing to deepen your understanding of depression.

Raising a child through any major transition is difficult. Being aware of the dual set of challenges that most families with depression face helps master them.

As children grow older, they spend less time with their parents and siblings and more with their friends and in their own pursuits. As they reach adolescence, they often engage in risky behaviors — driving too fast, experimenting with alcohol and drugs, becoming sexually active.

And they do all this not in a simple, predictable, intentional way but with many fits and starts. Most of these things happen without their parents' knowledge. The demands this places on parents are immense: to be at once loving yet limit-setting, to adjust to change, to provide comfort to children as they become bitterly disappointed in themselves, and above all, to communicate clearly, both with the children and with each other so that children see parents working together. The difficulties parents face have only become worse in the last three decades with the breakdown of the extended family and the lack of stable, long-term communities.

Against these evolving challenges, depression casts a long shadow and presents a second set of obstacles. The last thing a person acutely suffering from depression wants to do is be flexible, try new things, think of new possibilities. In much the same way that someone recovering from grief needs quiet, a safe space, and time to heal, depression causes a retreat, a withdrawal to protect oneself from pain and loss. The most reassuring thing for a person with depression is continuity, predictability, but raising children inevitably involves discontinuity, challenges you can't anticipate, and sudden plunges into uncertainty.[1]

It's particularly unnerving for someone who has courageously taken action, who has begun to talk openly about it, to have depression reoccur. Mary O'Reilly, whom we met in chapter 5, conveyed just how devastating this can be: "Everything is gray, nothing is good. But I think with me it's the overwhelming sadness. By sadness, I mean the losses from the past. The man I was involved with in a ten-year relationship that ended when I was thirty-eight. I think it's the man-and-woman relationships that are harder than anything, even harder than the deaths.

"The physical is very hard, extreme loss of weight, either sleeping too much or not at all. The emotional side is suicidal thoughts, just let it be over. How much longer can I go on feeling this terrible, and will it ever lessen? I know the depression has eased in the past, but when it's a long haul, if it continues too long, I have suicidal thoughts. No matter what I'm doing, thoughts keep coming back. I'm watching a program on TV, everything is extremely sad to me. It could be a comedy, and I'll find something devastating about it.

"You know, it comes on with a couple of symptoms and suddenly it hits you full force. You run to the doctor. They always put me on medication. You try to figure out what's going on, what triggered it. Stress will trigger it. I notice that when I get tired of a job, rather than go looking for something else, I feel trapped, and the trapped feeling is a trigger for me. Then, when I come out of it, it's a huge weight off me. Then, when I recover, I feel I know where I am and I know it's the last time I'll go through it, so when it comes again, I feel devastated."

But families can and do learn to cope over time. Just as there is a series of stages that families pass through after they first break the silence, so there are further stages that emerge over time. As they understand depression anew, gradually family members move from being alone to being with others. Thus, depression becomes a shared adversity to be overcome together, not a withdrawal into pain and silence. And this often begins in the common ground of parenting.

The Rothsteins: Finding Common Ground in a Sea of Adversity

For the family of Clair and Len Rothstein, a series of troubles came all at once. When one of our team began to work with them, Len had just lost his job, Clair's mother had recently died, and to make matters worse, the family was feeling quite isolated, having just moved from the Midwest to Boston.

Len looked the part of a well-educated and successful man. But the fact was that although he had an advanced degree, he'd been unable to sustain a career and find satisfying work. Clair was a tall and attractive woman who dressed nicely and who had a part-time job. Both parents struggled with depression. Making matters worse, they had been almost unable to talk about it. Even with us, Len spoke hesitantly, taking a long time to choose his words.

As she began talking about herself, Clair quickly moved to a discussion of her mother, a woman she described as frequently depressed and fearful of crowded places. She had to "treat her carefully," Clair said. As a child, Clair had not understood what was wrong with her mother. Her family had never talked about feelings, and so opening up now was still a struggle.

Clair's first battle with depression had occurred in college. When they moved from the Midwest to Boston, she had been depressed for nearly a year and a half and had been placed on medication. She found her religious community a great help and had received counseling through her Episcopal priest.

Len first became depressed during his senior year in high school, after his brother attempted suicide. He described feeling very guilty about having failed to anticipate his brother's needs or to help him. After his brother's attempt, Len began to feel suicidal himself. He now had a hard time remembering what life was like without depression.

Len's father had appeared kind in public but was very domineering at home. He criticized Len for making wrong choices, and Len coped by trying to become "invisible." His mother was ineffective in protecting him from his overbearing father. Growing up somewhat isolated in the rural South because of his intellectual interests and abilities, Len had found some relief in college but continued to struggle, experiencing six episodes of major depression that profoundly sapped his energy. The most severe of these had occurred seven years before he came to us. Then, he had lost his job and been hospitalized. At the time of our first intervention, Len was being treated with sertraline, doxepin, and psychotherapy.

Len saw himself as having two lives: a supportive home life that enabled him to confront his daily struggles at work over many years, and an unsupportive and demanding work life. But the sanctity of that home was threatened as he had gradually built a wall around himself.

Brought together out of concern for their two daughters, the couple reviewed their history with our clinician. For the first time, they addressed a central event in the early years of their marriage — Len's hospitalization. Clair spoke movingly of how alone she had been, how frightened and helpless she had felt when she was pregnant and Len had stayed several weeks in a locked ward. Len was able to tell Clair how comforting her presence had been during his depression and hospitalization, but he was amazed to hear of her fears. As she spoke, he began to cry. Learning how much she had feared losing him helped him understand how much she loved him. He also very gradually began to see that he could be there for her in a way his parents had not been for him.

Acknowledging their mutual tendency to retreat also helped them to understand each other. Len, for example, wanted his home to be more of a refuge, an inviolate sanctuary from the pressures of the work world. Clair also wanted the home to be the central part of their lives, but she wanted it to be more than a resting place. She wanted help with the day-to-day tasks. She wanted Len to be more involved with the children, something he needed help learning how to do.

The couple worried about their two girls, ages six and nine. Both were quite shy, and the older one, Emily, was deeply aware of her father's depression.

"There's a change in him, and I don't really know how to describe it," she said. "Dad doesn't have a job. He can be unhappy. He cries sometimes and loses his temper. Dad is more grouchy since he lost his job. Mom's the same. Dad doesn't make as many jokes. He's not himself. I try not to complain like I usually do. I don't let it affect my moods. I just stay out of the way."

Emily mentioned in passing that she didn't think any good would come of talking. Both parents feared she would become depressed, because she had some trouble sleeping and some fearfulness and difficulty making friends. Amanda, at six, also was somewhat fearful.

Len's severance pay was running out, but his depression sapped his will to search for another job. Despite all his worries, though, Len's primary concern was how his depression affected his daughters. He saw much of himself in them, and he was worried that they too might feel inadequate, because he felt inadequate and because he saw himself as becoming more and more detached from them. He knew, as he put it, that "I need to look beyond myself when I'm depressed." He wanted to change how he was with his children, but his statement could easily have applied to his work and his marriage.

The challenge of bringing their children into the room and speaking to them revealed just how deeply ingrained the patterns of not talking were for the Rothsteins. Clair voiced the realization that her inability to speak about Len's illness echoed the pattern of her own mother, who could not stand to have anything out in the open.

When they met with their children for the first time, the Rothsteins talked blandly and with little focus about the facts of depression and its biology. Len and Clair mentioned the kids' crankiness and the yelling that went on around bedtime, and tried to think about a more appropriate routine. Len said he wanted the girls to be more responsible. He became irritated with them. But then, for the first time in their memory, he stopped himself and simply said, "I'm being too critical. I'm being too hard on them and I don't want to be this way." His daughters saw him trying to think about how to avoid being negative and withdrawing. This led both parents to describe on a deeper level the experience of being depressed. The girls responded by asking for more information — what was it really like? What did it feel like?

Equally important, when the topic of Len's job search came up, each of them discovered how uncertain and worried the others were. The girls wondered if they were going to have to move again and what would happen. Would they lose the house? Each member of the family was operating alone and had never talked about it. What would a change in job mean? Where would they live? The parents filled the girls in on what was happening on the job front and promised to keep them informed. They all affirmed that they would stick together during difficult times.

As the meeting ended, the entire family made an agreement to talk at dinner once a week. Interestingly enough, they followed through with great regularity and came to count on these sessions. Len kept a record of the conversations so that the family would know what they had talked about. It was also a way they measured how they were doing. But, perhaps more important, they realized that they actually enjoyed talking and looked forward to it.

The process of talking was a welcome counterpoint to the relentless self-criticism that Len had endured. It reinforced his sense that his home life was a refuge. While he'd been unable to get moving in many other areas, he was able to mobilize here — in talking to his children and helping his wife out around the house. He learned to speak to them differently, and in the records he kept he emphasized the accomplishments as well as things to be overcome.

Clair and Len both had been worried that the girls were becoming depressed because of the family strain. This proved not to be the case, and the discovery gave them all great reassurance and confidence. Based on hearing the girls' concerns, Clair made other concrete changes. She made sure that the kids had friends over no matter what, and that she was there for them. Even when depressed, she made certain that she did not push the kids away when they wanted to talk. She also found herself more aware of what her daughters were going through. She realized that Emily was expressing her anxieties by being clingy. Spending more time with her and being more reassuring began to alleviate this problem.

In the months following the family meeting, Clair went back to work full-time. Eventually, this led to an episode of depression because she was trying to manage too many things at once. But now she knew to go immediately for treatment. She had come to believe, as they had talked about in family sessions, how important it was to intervene early in the course of the illness.

Gradually, Len and Clair came to understand themselves differently. This understanding was shared, but it also drew on their separate journeys. "As children," Len said, "we did not have the right to our own feelings, both of us, Clair with her mother and me with my father. We were faulted for our feelings." He now recognized the difference between the sense of doom he felt about his life and the reality of the kids' lives. His daughters were different. They were going to be okay.

It took time for Len to break the pattern of self-criticism so deeply established by his father. He struggled in a variety of jobs, not able to stay in any one for very long, but two years later he was able to refocus his career search when a major opportunity came to him. It was different from what he was used to, a position working in another city. The Rothsteins were able to carefully weigh what it would mean to leave Boston, both the negatives and the advantages. They used the strategies gained initially in talking about depression and about unemployment to sit down with the girls, talk about the possibility of moving, and listen to their concerns. They planned the move carefully as a family.

The move turned out to be quite successful. They came to like the other city. In getting away from Boston's high real-estate prices, they were able to afford a house rather than an apartment, and because it had two bathrooms, this made a huge difference to two girls going into adolescence.

When we saw Emily after the move, she had grown three inches in height and looked like a young woman. She talked knowledgeably about depression and now emphasized the value of openness in the family. In particular, she appreciated how her father had reassured her. She also insisted that neither she nor her sister felt guilty.

Emily emerged as the stronger child. There were worries because Amanda, the younger girl, did not make friends easily in the new school. She also had a teacher who was extremely strict and critical. Clair realized that she herself had recoiled from criticism as a child. With the guidance of one of our team, Clair sought the assistance of the school counseling department, which gave Amanda some help with the transition and probably staved off a serious illness. They talked with Amanda and with the teacher and worked things out. The Rothsteins helped us realize how much talking to kids is a shared endeavor, and how important it is to keep track of conversations, to know what's been said, to go back and see where you've been and how you've moved on.

In time, in addition to receiving treatment for depression, Len was diagnosed with attention deficit disorder and received additional medication. But large events continued to challenge the family. Clair's sister died in a car accident, and it took months for her to get over her grief. Len's brother made another suicide attempt. Len relived his guilt about not having done more for him. Clair herself developed serious medical symptoms that gradually cleared. But these events did not derail them from talking to one another or from helping one another on their shared journey to understanding.

For Len, the lesson was about isolation. "It's important to get the kids involved outside of the family," he said. "The kids don't have to be like I was — a lonely teenager in a rural community." Len also came to see his illness differently. "I feel less that there's something wrong with me. It's now part of my life that I just have to take care of. [Talking together as a family] removed a lot of guilt."

Clair's assessment provided the name for the key process in talking together: *"It's been helpful in breaking the silence,"* she said. This meant not just the immediate cycle of silence around her and Len's depression, but the generational cycles they had been going through for decades, cycles they had come to believe were perpetual because they were so deeply ingrained. The family met regularly and talked often. Over time, they became healers for one another. The way that these conversations and strategies continued, despite the onslaught of further losses and a move to another city, emphasized how change can take place and can be sustained.

There are many factors that contributed to the Rothsteins' being able to move forward. They actively sought treatment for depression, and both had psychotherapy before starting to talk together — an important element in breaking the pattern of self-criticism. They also got help from us. Moreover, Clair and Len had strengths within themselves that they could draw on. They both had the benefit of a good education and were deeply committed to each other. They also had a strong religious faith and a deep commitment to being involved in the community.

Making sense of depression for kids means making sense of it for yourself first. For the Rothsteins, change began with a focus on the kids, which opened the way for much broader changes. Len's wrestling with his critical father, his resulting sensitivity to criticism and devaluing of himself, had been going on for years. He had worried that his children would be like his brother. But his daughters were not his brother and were not doomed to relive his experiences. Len acquired confidence, in part by realizing how much Clair cared for him. This came out not only when they talked about their relationship, but also as they planned how to describe depression to their children.

As is true in developing resilience, a central quality in being able to deal effectively with depression is optimism, or confidence that one's actions do make a difference. Both Len and Clair had always been pessimistic, perhaps the most pessimistic of all those we treated in our study. They gradually acquired a sense of hope about the future, first by correcting the misunderstandings brought on by depression, and second with the immediate actions they took. This began a process of counteracting in concrete ways the legacies of pessimism and failure from their past. A central part of developing optimism is being able to see positives in oneself and one's children despite the pall that depression casts over one's life. But optimism only occurs over time, as parents and children become convinced through repeated actions that circumstances can be changed.

Maura Temple: Uncovering the History and Seeing the Strengths

Maura Temple faced perhaps one of the most daunting combinations of adversities of any of our families. But her story illustrates a central theme for all families. It is essential to not become embittered and overwhelmed with anger; instead, one must be able to see and recognize strengths in oneself, in one's child, and in one's family. Like many others too, Maura had to make sense of her own upbringing to raise her child.

A single parent by choice, she had made a series of tough decisions to maintain her independence throughout her life. Deciding whether to accept any help from us or from other caregivers itself was a struggle precisely because she had survived so long by maintaining her independence.

A tall, slender woman in her mid-thirties, with striking red hair, she had, for the most part, educated herself, and although she had worked as a waitress, her real interest was in painting. Her already difficult life had been complicated the year before when a man in the neighborhood attempted to rape her. When she took legal action, she had to testify against him in court.

A middle child in a family of eight, Maura suffered abuse from both her father and her brother. Her mother had abandoned the family and left Maura at age eleven with her abusive and alcoholic father (although Maura did reconnect with her years later).

Maura described herself as having felt lonely and isolated from then on. She had struggled with depression for years as a teenager, retreating into drug use throughout her teens to try to alleviate the pain.

In her mid-twenties, she entered a stable relationship, and she lived with a man from Panama for over ten years. Gradually, though, she came to see herself as his caretaker. She felt that she could not communicate emotionally with him. He begged her to marry him, but she refused because she did not truly love him. Not too long after her son was born, she broke off the relationship.

Her struggle with depression continued with deepening and longer periods when she simply felt down all the time. When her son was four, she became profoundly depressed. She felt she wanted to die, but she stopped herself because of love for her son.

"I hit rock bottom," she said. The bottoming out led her to turn her life around. She got into Narcotics Anonymous and found this support group very positive. She said that these people enabled her "to feel her own sorrow." She began then to deal directly with her depression and to figure out her family.

She thought of her mother, Nell, as a tough-minded survivor, and she often attempted to model her own life after that of the woman who had abandoned her. She called her mother her best friend and deeply admired her success in putting herself through nursing school and separating from Maura's father. When Maura was in her twenties, her mother died and Maura was devastated.

In addition to the positive, there was also a negative legacy from her mother who, in her view, had "dumped her shame on her kids." Her mother, born illegitimate, had been raised by nuns in a convent. Maura's mother gave Maura's son, Ted, a special set of rosary beads from the convent. In Maura's view, this was an attempt to perpetuate Nell's deeply held shame.

Maura disliked questions about her history of depression and the sadness she had to deal with all her life. She also disliked the bland explanation that depression was a biological illness. She wanted to control her moods herself, and because of her history of drug difficulties, she felt that antidepressive medication was a "crutch" that she should avoid. Taking control of her own life was essential to her survival, in managing her depression and in raising her son alone. In her view, accepting the biological explanation was "giving up." Although she talked to a therapist from time to time, it took her several years before she decided that medication was a legitimate form of treatment for depression, and that only when she could see the medication as possibly helping her to be independent.

Maura struggled with how to tell her son about depression, and it took several scheduled meetings with one of our clinicians before a conversation actually took place. Maura began by telling Ted how nervous she was. She told him about what she was going through and how she was trying to get help, and how shortly before we all met she'd begun to take medication. (Lacking health insurance, she had used a friend's coverage to get the prescription filled for herself.) She told her son that her sadness was not his fault nor his responsibility to cure. She said, "I want you to have a better understanding of my illness so you're able to get along with your life without worrying about it. You've brought a great deal of joy to my life. I want you to know I love you very much. There's a lot of guilt about my illness. Everyone wants to live in a perfect world, and I'd like to make things perfect for you."

After they talked, there was some relief for Maura and her son. Like so many of our parents, she remained very committed to helping him. She struggled at times over a period of years, but she really was able to help him succeed, first in junior high and later in high school. Along with this, becoming a very different kind of parent from her own forced her to rethink her history, yet this realization of difference did not mean rejecting her past entirely.

"I feel driven to find out about my mother's family because she never talked about it. That's one of the things I regret never having done with her. And part of the reason for not talking about it was her own shame. We could never talk about it. I can understand how she couldn't talk about it given what I've been through."

After a family reunion, Maura consulted records in a neighboring town. She found out that not only her mother but also her mother's mother had been an orphan and had been raised in the same Catholic orphanage. This did not lead her to be angry with her mother, but rather made her more sympathetic to her mother's struggles.

She also reached out to her father's family, and by talking to his sister, learned something about the hardships of his life. This softened her feelings for him. There were so many children in his family that he'd been forced to go to a work camp during the 1930s, and he had never learned to read.

While she fought against the idea that there could be a genetic vulnerability, she came to see that her father, in her view, had been depressed. "My father's father always suffered from depression, but they weren't even allowed to be children, so of course they never dealt with it. My father shows no emotion; he doesn't talk much." She came to understand the silence in her family and she also realized that her father's alcoholism was an attempt to deal with depression.

As she gradually worked away at these issues, she struggled to set limits for her son, who was in his early teens and had begun to slack off in school. At the same time, she had a series of reverses, including a brother who died of cancer, which touched off a depression in her. Then she broke off with her boyfriend and noticed that she was more irritable with Ted. Despite both great loss and terrible episodes of depression, she did not become angry at her son or embittered toward her parents.

Gradually, she moved on to a new job, her depression began to clear, and her son began to do better. She came to believe in the biological aspect of depression and that it was helped by medication, but this was only because she saw that she did not have to lose control. She had to see herself as not abandoning her profound core commitments — understanding herself and helping her son.

She had many worries about her son, but as he emerged into adolescence, she continued to set limits and in time noted that he actually responded well. In fact, he liked the limits. She had a good relationship with her son's father, which made it easy for the boy to go back and forth between the two homes. At a certain point when his father's new wife was giving Ted a hard time, Maura intervened and worked it out. She was very careful not only to keep Ted from being caught in the middle, but to help him draw on the resources and strengths she saw in the other family. Finding the positives in her parents despite their limitations, and seeing the positives in her son's life and in her own real ability to care for him were essential elements for her in finding the healer within — and for many others we worked with as well. In this sense, a part of resilience in parents is to see the positives and to avoid the pit of recurrent anger and recrimination.

The Polaskys: Surviving Mania

At the opposite end of the behavioral spectrum from the Rothsteins' silent suffering and from Maura's recurrent battles with depression is the manic behavior associated with bipolar illness. The Polaskys came to us when Glenda and Jerry were in their mid-forties and their two boys were ages twelve and nine. Glenda had had a diagnosis of both depression and mania for several years.

"The biggest thing is the nonstop talking," she said. "I'm doing something all the time. It's a feeling you can do anything, a false sense of security. You do too much; you are constantly on the go. I don't get much sleep because something just kicks in like a motor."

Glenda's mania was all the more devastating because she couldn't always identify it herself. "Sometimes it's hard to tell. For example,

I was busy with back-to-school shopping. I had to ask myself if I was doing these things because I'm manic or am I just busy. Sometimes I feel I have to rationalize everything I do, that I'm doing it because it needs to be done, not because I'm manic. I have to watch myself. Sometimes I think too much about everything I say."

Although she was not formally diagnosed until she was in her twenties, Glenda recalled extreme mood swings during most of her life. She remembered a time in junior high when she was so depressed she missed several days of school. Her parents downplayed the situation, though, and no one in her family or at school helped her to get any treatment. When she was married, neither she nor her husband had any idea that she would be afflicted with such profound mood swings, and for a while she was ebullient, upbeat, fun, and energetic. After her first son was born, she was hospitalized for what was in retrospect an episode of depression. Two other episodes of mania required further hospitalization. During manic episodes, road signs had special meanings for her. She heard voices, which caused great embarrassment.

"When hospitalized, I told the nurses off, threw things, and refused to take meds. I seemed to pick certain people at the hospital to fight with. This isn't like me. I feel guilty about this. I said things that were out in left field. I felt like one part of me was looking at the other. I was so embarrassed later on!"

As she sat before us, carefully groomed, slim, attractive, focused, very sad and very reflective, Glenda seemed anything but out of control. In contrast to her warm, friendly smile, her dark eyes darted nervously, her voice was deflated. Introspective by nature, Glenda pondered the illness, wondered why she was rendered crazy at times, wondered what precipitated the episodes, and wondered which "self" was the real one. She had an understanding of the genetic and chemical factors contributing to her illness — her father had suffered from a serious depression — but she also acknowledged stress. Other times she felt, "Maybe I did something to deserve it."

Mania complicated her marriage. When Glenda behaved abruptly and in unpredictable ways, she particularly needed her husband, Jerry, to be there for her. For his part, though, he felt confused, drawn into something he hadn't bargained for. When she wasn't manic, Glenda often felt lonely and abandoned. Once Jerry had gone out and spent the night away from her. Compounding the problem was the fact that he was an accountant and watched money very carefully. When manic, Glenda spent money very freely.

"He is quiet," she said of her husband. "He doesn't talk too much about things that are bothering him. Maybe he doesn't realize things *are* bothering him! In his family, psychotherapy is taboo. I think he thinks he's very supportive. Unfortunately, he sees things only his way. He has very set opinions and won't listen. I only wish he would open up a little more about himself."

From Jerry's point of view, he did not see the illness as biological, but simply as a complete rearrangement of their agreement. "Things come to a screeching halt, like our remodeling the house. There was no maintenance being done. There's a reversal of roles, and I pick up the slack. I become more the mother. I'm cooking more, shopping more, dealing with the children on a daily basis. I'm not away from the house as much. I won't travel on any business trips when she is sick."

Jerry described the family as "walking on eggshells" in an effort not to stir things up. He felt the best approach was to avoid any confrontation or situations with emotional content, as these were likely to aggravate Glenda's condition. But this avoidance of emotionally laden topics seemed to preclude meaningful communication and problem solving. It also led Glenda to feel more and more abandoned.

They both acknowledged that because of their inability to talk about the real tension, conversation in general had come to a standstill. Other issues in the marriage were neglected. They fought frequently, and their two children knew it.

Glenda had acute memories of how out of control she had been at the hospital and was very worried about its effect on the children. "When they came to visit me in the hospital, they all smiled. I'm sure they were upset, but they were afraid to show it. They wanted me to feel better. You can tell they're afraid. They get quiet more than anything."

"They're as affected as I am," Jerry said. "They're worried about their mother and also about fights between us. I couldn't begin to say what could be going through their minds. They're scared. They'll sit back quietly in a corner and watch from afar when she's displaying really manic activity. The kids don't see the buildup as much. I don't think they know what to do."

Their son Bobby spoke of being "confused" about his mother's illness. When asked if he ever talked to his mother about the problem, he said, "No, I never really tried. Nothing came up that I asked her. I don't think I had questions."

But he did recall feeling awkward visiting his mother in the hospital. "I didn't know how to act around her," he said. "I had to be more responsible, help Dad with the laundry and stuff more than usual. I wished I was the youngest, not the oldest."

After careful preparation, the Polaskys were able to talk with both children, together, without exploding at each other. They chose to talk quite frankly about the genetic risk in mania and emphasized to the boys that they should get help if needed. But Glenda's main agenda was to bring the mania out into the open and to emphasize that she was a person independent of the disease.

As Glenda and Jerry made the journey toward breaking the silence, there were many fits and starts. Frank descriptions of her mania led Glenda to feel betrayed. Arguments followed. But through the discussion of the biology of illness, she was able to get to a core difficulty that almost all the families wrestled with. Glenda spoke of the painfulness of having her credibility questioned all the time, even when she was not ill. She felt condescended to. The mania cast a shadow over her entire life and invalidated what was most important for her — her role in the marriage, her role caring for her kids

In the months that followed the first family meeting, there were many difficulties, but the pattern of talking continued. Jerry too had changed. "Now we're talking to her when she is not ill," he said. "Talking together gave her a sense of legitimacy." Perhaps more important, when she began to become manic, they both saw it as an illness. Jerry had feared that his wife enjoyed the manic symptoms and had not known how frightened she was of them.

In the year that followed, Glenda had several periods when she became hypomanic, a less severe illness that often precedes mania, but their newfound openness relieved stress around the house. It allowed Glenda to ask her parents to help with the kids, and for everyone to pitch in more with the housework. Glenda, each time, went directly to her psychiatrist to review her medications. These actions together prevented manic episodes.

Characteristic of many children of parents with severe illness, Bobby, the older boy, had put great pressure on himself to be a good student. When he had a period of low mood, the family, aware of the genetic risks, became concerned. Ironically, what led to the low mood was not failure but achievement — election to student council — which carried with it a heavy burden of responsibility. Not unlike his mother, Bobby noted that things were always running through his mind. Drawing on what he had learned about depression, Bobby was able to go to his father for help. With his parents' support, he saw a guidance counselor at school, and over time the problem was resolved.

A year later, Glenda broke down, overcome by the combined weight of Thanksgiving, Christmas, and financial worries. On the eve of the new year, she was hospitalized with mania. The hospitalization lasted a week, but it took her two months to return to normal. This severely tested the family's understanding, and many of the issues that had been there before — fighting, worries about money, resentment about illness — resurfaced. But both children spoke to Jerry of their concerns about their mother, family meetings continued, and they stayed with it despite unpleasantness. In fact, it was a family meeting that led to Glenda's voluntary hospitalization. She was able to reassure the boys that they were not to blame. Bobby again had several days of low mood, but this also cleared up.

Glenda feels that one clear legacy of learning to talk together about depression was learning to communicate in general much more with her children. She says she tries to listen more than she talks. Although mania does not afflict most sufferers of depression, the issues of guardedness, not wanting to talk, and of each family member retreating out of fear characterized almost all the families in our study. Fortunately, for Glenda and Jerry, their new strategy changed all that.

As in Clair and Len Rothstein's sharing their experience of the pain each had endured during his hospitalization, Fran and John O'Connor's finding a way to talk that opened up many more conversations, and Maura Temple's making sense of her own history and focusing on her son, in Glenda Polasky's coming to be strong in the face of mania there was a blending of small continued actions, parenting in the face of depression, and finding the good in the present and the future.

Focus on Communication

Certain issues came up again and again in talking with families with depression. Knowing about these can help you to anticipate what may happen and help you plan for it.

Many spouses of depressed parents talked about how they had not planned on marrying a depressed person. In most couples, although spouses might have been depressed before the marriage, the illness didn't fully emerge until later. As one husband said, "I really didn't know what 'for better or worse' meant."

Naturally, no one dreams of marrying a depressed person. But, as with other crises, dealing with adversity can bring out the strengths in marriages and in our love for our children. One father mentioned, for example, braiding his daughter's hair when his wife was ill. Many mentioned similar instances of reconnecting with their children in a way they had not previously, and how knowing that the children needed them was a positive experience.

It can be very lonely during a spouse's bout with depression. Some compared the illness to the loss of a best friend. Compounding one's concern for a wife or husband is the need to acknowledge the loss of friendship and of a sexual relationship. The pain of watching someone suffering from depression is serious, and often lived through alone.

Many couples don't go out with other couples or make it to their usual engagements when depression enters their lives, so their networks are disrupted just when they need them the most. If the depressed spouse is the one who made the social arrangements, isolation can be complete.

Some parents emphasized that they were consoled by the knowledge that depression is episodic and there was an end to it.

Precisely because one spouse isn't functioning, the challenges of keeping the household and the kids going are crucially important and require prioritizing, but this is easier said than done. Doing the laundry may not be difficult, because it is done at home and can be done on its own timetable, but driving a daughter to Girl Scouts may be harder, because it requires being there at a specific time in the afternoon. In short, when people in families change roles, and in particular when people working outside of the home suddenly have to do more domestic tasks as well, it requires a profound shift.

Parents emphasize that it's important to know that it's okay to say no. Not everything will get done. It's okay to get help: house cleaners, baby-sitters, take-out food. One husband emphasized that it was very important simply to get out and have time alone, that he'd had time for himself before the illness and missed that. Just as with any other serious illness, there is a financial impact — the cost of eating out, the loss of work, the time a person has to take off work. Thus, families must plan for some loss of income and rebudgeting, just as they would have to with rheumatoid arthritis or a heart attack.

Having a depression can also change relationships around money. If the person who is in charge of paying the bills is the one with the illness, then the bills may not get paid. Also, if a couple has either been used to making decisions together or even arguing and then compromising, these dynamics get completely changed when the person with the illness can't speak up.

In a religious family, depression can often be equated with sin, and therefore the victim is blamed even more. All the more important, then, to try to understand one's spouse and not get into the framework of judging and blaming.

Time and time again, we have noted that children are often at their most resilient during a time of crisis. Many times they pitch in, making sure the household keeps going, and indeed are happy for the opportunity to feel useful rather than helpless. They are proud of their contribution, but afterward they need special care and support.

One woman summed it up this way: "It's important to know that the illness will end. The person who is ill is not responsible. We'll be okay. The irritability is the illness. The signs and symptoms are there. The treatment is being obtained, and it's okay to talk about it. Talking together. Kids won't know unless it's made very explicit, and it's important to indicate what the treatments are and how they're working."

Sustaining Change

It was enormously rewarding to follow these families over time, to have them share with us what happened. Families showed again and again that they could change and did, and that the changes were sustained. Inevitably, some families made more dramatic changes than others.

We learned that it took months for a family to put together and begin to use what they had experienced in breaking the silence. The changes were often far more evident a year after the family began to talk, as the information came alive in their own experience. We were pleased to find that while families initially believed they'd made the changes because of our help, five years later they claimed this was simply their way of working together as a family. They had made these strategies their own, and healers had emerged within families.

To recap, here are some of the strategies that you can use to sustain change:

1. Continue to put into words what it is you are trying to deal with, and continue to explain it to others.
2. Be clear about what concerns for your children's and family's welfare you are trying to address.
3. Decide what needs to be addressed immediately and what can be addressed later.
4. Take action quickly in a crisis, especially getting help for you or your child if depression recurs.
5. Be willing to explore your history in a new way.
6. Go over the conversations and actions that work and use those strategies again.

Nine

The Children
Understanding Depression Anew Over Time

> "If a man does not keep pace with his companions, per-
> haps it is because he hears a different drummer. Let him
> step to the music which he hears, however measured or
> far away."
>
> — Henry David Thoreau, *Walden*

C hildren definitely march to different drummers, and they
also make sense of depression in their own way. No matter
what age children are when they begin to talk about
depression, their understanding goes at a slower pace than that of
their parents.

In this chapter, I will present the three key themes in our work
with children over the years: (1) how changes in the parents' illness
affect young people's understanding; (2) how the kids' own needs
for different and more complex explanations develop as they grow
older; and (3) how their parents are able to provide an ongoing
forum to talk about depression, assisting their youngsters in making sense of it in new ways over time.

I will focus on the stories of four children, each of which shows
how the parents' journeys are inextricably bound up with their
children. Ultimately, for all of these youths, making sense of
depression is dealing not just with the experience in the present but
with what is remembered. The same event can be experienced differently over time and, perhaps more important, made sense of
differently at different points in time.

Conversations about these matters are not easy for children.
Often, children and adolescents appear to hear only a part of what's

been said to them. They often will not acknowledge what they do hear. And, of course, it's difficult to sort out what's a response to talk about depression as opposed to a response to all the other conversations that go on between parents and kids.

The same explanation will be heard differently by different children in the family. Boys differ greatly from girls in how much they will talk about depression. It is also true that children talk not just to their parents, but also to their brothers and sisters, so they influence one another's journeys.

Most important, children change dramatically over the course of childhood. Their capacity to understand their world in depth, to understand cause and effect, to plan, to be masters of their own destiny, all develop over time. The ability to ask questions, to probe deeply, to try to fit things into a moral framework, to take action, and to define themselves in terms of how they stand within the culture from which they come, the religion in which they grow up, and their family traditions change profoundly during the course of adolescence. The explanation that works for a child at age ten will not be enough for the same child at age fifteen, when he or she can understand a much more intricate, multifaceted view of depression. But the way children marshal all this to make sense of their family's unique circumstances, including depression, reflects not just a general growth in reasoning but the application of this general capacity to the specific day-to-day circumstances of their own families.

As youngsters mature, their awareness of relationships and of themselves deepens. Their growth drives the need for families to continue to talk about depression and to fit depression into their broader awareness of the context, continuity, and traditions in their lives. Older children will ask deeper and more penetrating questions and require, and sometimes even demand, more complex explanations as they define their identities and fit parental depression into that process. They will also encounter depression outside their parents — in the media, in their peers, and perhaps in their grandparents or other family members. Also, of course, the parents' depressions may change, be more prominent or less prominent. For all these reasons, as they mature, their questions drive the need for young people and their parents to understand depression anew.

Despite the many differences, children, like their depressed parents, face a common set of challenges in learning to speak up. No matter how old they are, children in families with depression do not want their parents to be ill or impaired. When parents are ill, their children want them to get well. And if their lives have been disrupted, children want them to be made whole. They also do not want their parents to drink or get into terrible fights, or get divorced. Above all, they do not want to witness violence or be abused.

Once frightened that any or all of these things are happening, they want some reassurance that calm will return and that some part of their lives will become predictable and stable. If no stability is present, no immediate safety available, then children, for the most part, will simply remain quiet and wary.

For children to become partners in a dialogue, first they have to believe that their parents will be all right. Thus, reestablishing the structure of their lives is an essential precondition for their being able to talk.

The idea that parents are injured or hurt or suffering from a mental illness that impairs the very way they relate is foreign and scary for children. Children look to parents to be the authorities and providers. They need their parents to be strong so they can argue with them, confront them, feel that they are invincible. They don't want to have to worry about them. They want to ignore them so they themselves can move on with challenges outside of the home. The idea that a parent is injured pulls children back into the sphere of the family, and they may feel they have no choice but to stay at home.

Children naturally try to anticipate their parents' responses. And when they sense pain in a parent, they try to get inside that parent's world, to see things as the parent does, so they can communicate with the parent and try to change what is wrong. Children are a great source of comfort and pride to parents, and their growth and development can in fact cheer them up. Unfortunately, this natural empathy leads many children to take on a downcast mien, imitating their depressed parents.

Children of almost any age believe that their actions have an impact on their parents. When they're angry or have a bad day, or don't meet parental expectations, it's natural for them to attribute some of their parents' emotional responses to their own behavior, to blame themselves and feel guilty. This is even more true when parents don't fight back, or when illness is inexplicable and unspoken.

As youngsters move into adolescence, they demand more complex explanations than they did when they were younger. But they also have a much exaggerated sense of personal responsibility and can feel even more guilty. For all these reasons, it takes time for children to find themselves and be able to speak their minds.

The entire course of raising a child is ultimately directed toward helping him or her become independent. Early in childhood, the task is learning to live without mother or father (or both) present on an hourly basis. The next task is to leave home and go to school, followed by increasing involvement in school and with peers. Much of this in high school and beyond involves not talking to parents about inner feelings, but in fact learning to live outside the parental realm. For most youngsters, this culminates in their leaving home in their late teens for higher education, jobs, relationships, military service, or other pursuits.

Letting go of children, particularly for a depressed parent, is very hard. And it is equally hard for children to let go and move on if they feel that separating will harm their parents.

Peter: Overcoming Denial to Make Sense of Depression

When Peter's family first chose to talk about depression together, he was fourteen. He was the oldest of four children whose parents were deeply committed to artistic endeavors. His mother, Julia, had wrestled with depression for several years and that depression had its origin in a complicated family pattern of denial. Despite her illness, Julia had a strong relationship with each of her four children. Indeed, the children saw her, when she wasn't depressed, as the more focused and well-organized of the two parents. Peter's father started out less involved, but during the times of Julia's greatest need, he stepped in and carried the load of parenting largely by himself.

Peter got along well within the family. He was a gifted student, a talented visual artist, active in a wide array of school and outside activities. Aside from drawing and working with a group in designing theater sets, he liked playing Dungeons and Dragons, basketball, football, and the saxophone, and had a group of close friends.

Peter's mother described him as a very self-aware person. But because he was so concerned about others and could see others' points of view so well, she was, as she put it, "afraid he'll not speak up for himself."

Unless asked directly about it, he would not mention depression at all. Despite having lived with his mother's illness for many years, Peter was very anxious when the subject came up. He seemed compelled to be loyal to his parents, rattling off long lists of their accomplishments and showing confusing and contradictory layers of awareness. For instance, he knew about depression in an abstract way, but he steadfastly insisted that his mother had never shown any signs of it. He didn't know the symptoms of depression. He was unaware of treatment options, and his ideas about why people became depressed were vague. "I guess I don't understand depression," he summed up, emphasizing that it was not easily discussed, even inside the family.

Yet Peter offered these reflections in the wake of his mother's most recent illness, during which she'd been unable to come to meals and often spent time alone in her room crying.

When one of our clinicians began meeting with them, the family had gradually found a way back to its regular routines, and Julia was feeling quite upbeat. She was on an antidepressant that she believed was helping and was also in an individual therapy that she found quite valuable.

For Julia, the episodes of diagnosable depression were inextricably woven into the fabric of the family life from which she came. By Julia's account, her mother had hidden everything, and indeed was depressed for many years but never talked about it. Julia herself had been sexually molested repeatedly by her brother but had never been able to speak about it in the family. During her episode of depression before our work began in the fall, she'd experienced flashbacks. She had scared the children by sobbing and telling them something had happened to her as a child that caused her to be depressed. While this particular episode of crying in front of the children was riveted in Julia's consciousness, Peter never mentioned it.

Peter's father, Sam, drew a contrast between Julia's openness in many areas and a tendency to hide her feelings. "Julia's surface is not the same as what's underneath," he said. None of Peter's siblings was able to talk about Julia's depression.

For Julia, preparing to talk to the children meant reliving the worst of the depressions, in particular, her profound battle with thoughts of suicide and the many family secrets. Her journey to understanding meant dealing with all these things openly, both in work with her therapist and with her husband and children to prepare for the family meeting.

Julia's mother had presented an idealized version of the family in the local community. Julia saw herself as having learned as a child to conceal her true self and not let anyone know she often felt hopeless, lonely, and very angry. Far worse, she somehow felt she was responsible for all her negative feelings. Because she felt horrible, she thought she *deserved* to feel horrible. As with many who survived terrible experiences in childhood, Julia blamed herself for following the family code. When her brother came into her room at night, she pretended to be asleep and that she didn't know what was happening. Then she felt worse because she had not spoken up.

Prior to the family meeting, Sam and Julia forged a new understanding as they struggled to figure out what they might say to their children during the meeting and what effect it would have on them. Both worried that Julia would lose control. Both were quite anxious and constantly went over what to say ahead of time. They decided to talk about the abuse only if asked. They didn't want to attack Julia's mother, and they didn't want to scare the children by talking too much about the abuse.

One comfort they found was in reviewing their children's strengths and resiliencies. Likewise, knowing there were things that could be done to help the children if they became depressed was also an important motivation for them as they planned the family meeting.

This family, which had so many different strengths, had never before held a meeting to talk over anything. When they began, the children, for the most part, were quiet and serious, listening attentively but saying very little.

First, Sam and Julia presented general information about depression. Then Sam, very directly, talked about his own reaction to his wife's depression. "I know intellectually it's not my fault, but I feel it's my fault. That's why we have to talk about it so you can see it's not your fault."

Sam and Julia then defined depression in terms of what had changed in their family — Julia's missing dinner, her withdrawing. The children began to remember more and more. For the first time, Peter began to see these as manifestations of depression. "I never made that connection," he said. "Now that we've put it in a new light, I do remember."

The youngest of them all, Peter's sister, looked directly at her mother and said, "What happened to make you depressed? I remember you telling us something that happened to you when you were a little kid." This time, Julia responded without shame or embarrassment and said that someone had molested her when she was young, but she did not elaborate. She felt this was a much better explanation than the previous confused and anxious one.

In the weeks that followed, Julia, with much help from everyone around her, began to feel better. In high spirits, she told her family that her depression was a thing of the past. She said she began to see how separate her children were from her. As she put it, "I had an opportunity to speak to them and hear about what are my issues. They're not their issues; they're my issues."

Peter's reflections on the meeting, just like his youngest brother's, were tempered by restlessness and anxiety. He had many questions about his mother's illness, but he still didn't want to talk about it or ask the questions. But, as is characteristic of many children, when asked, he and his siblings remembered things that had gone on before the meeting but which they had been afraid to speak about. On reflection, Peter and his siblings admitted they tended to stay in the house more and didn't feel like going out when their mother was depressed, almost as if they were protecting her, making sure she was safe. Peter made one particularly startling statement as he realized his mother's effect on him: "My mother's depression put a limit on how happy I could get."

In the months that followed, Peter's father noted that both boys almost never initiated any discussion. "It's hard for them," he said, "because she's a bright, funny person and they enjoy interacting with her, but her depression makes them feel closed off from her."

A year later, when asked if any stressful events had occurred within the family over the prior year, Peter talked with great intensity about the loss of the three family cats, which had to be given to an animal shelter. Offhandedly, he acknowledged that his mother had been hospitalized, but he hastened to add that this was trivial because it didn't really change things. Peter's bland description belied the seriousness of the crisis the family had faced.

In fact, the winter before, Julia had experienced increasing difficulty making it through the day. She became profoundly preoccupied with suicide and for the first time had to be hospitalized. Her hospitalization, sadly, was born of her recovery from the previous episode of depression. She had felt so much better that she had gradually tapered off her antidepressant medication, convinced that she no longer needed it. She had also considered joining a group for incest survivors but kept postponing it, getting ready to go and then not being able to. Moreover, her mother made a particularly definitive and rejecting gesture toward her, giving something of great value to someone else, completely ignoring everyone in her own family. Julia could not rid herself of recurrent, intense thoughts of dying. She even wrote a suicide note. In her view, she did not carry out her plan to kill herself because one of the children came home unexpectedly. At that point, Julia and her husband realized that something was very wrong. Despite their hesitancy about getting care, they went immediately to the caregiver who was treating Julia. She realized that Julia was not safe and arranged for her to be hospitalized that day.

The first few days in the hospital were extremely difficult, but Julia, like many others, found that the hospitalization helped a great deal. She felt she was in the right place and getting what she needed. She also was amazed that she could talk with people who knew exactly what she was going through.

After hospitalization, she was in day treatment for months. Through this experience, she found a group of women all struggling with life-threatening depression, and they formed a bond, a bond that countered Julia's lifelong isolation and tendency to hide. Julia was not an easy sell for group therapy. As she said, "We don't do the touchy-feely thing very well in the family." But as Sam described it, "Julia's experience in the group made her want to try again."

Sam was able to keep the routines going for the children — getting to school, having meals, even seeing their friends. Sam described his experience of the hospitalization this way: "It scared the hell out of me. I had to take over with the kids and deal with them, so my own needs were subordinated immediately to their needs and to her needs. Sometimes I was angry. I'd love an excuse to fall apart and have someone else pick up the pieces." But he realized that he needed to go on with his own life and routines as much as possible. "I'm much clearer now. I can say gently that I need friends and activities too. Thinking of depression as a disease helps me to figure it out, to know what to do and what I have to do, like leaving her at the hospital and recognizing my limits and dealing with it."

Seeing Julia's illness starkly through the hospitalization helped Sam depersonalize the symptoms. "I used to think she didn't like me or that I was failing her in some way. Now I try to be more supportive."

He also said he and Julia were kinder to each other and blamed each other less. He felt that the children had not been traumatized by the hospitalization because they had received information ahead of time. Sam and Julia had not repeated the family pattern of making up a story, but instead were honest with the children.

In her journey to understanding, Julia came to see her depression primarily in terms of the devastating isolation it caused. She said her depression was left over from having grown up in a household full of people isolated from one another. As she observed, "You accept those things that are really enough to cause my depression. You get over saying simply, 'I should try to be a better person.'"

Both Sam and Julia credited talking to the children together with helping her overcome her isolation within her own family. She came to believe that the children's experiences could be different from hers and that she wouldn't trigger depression in them. She gradually came to realize this by understanding the factors that led to her own depression, factors that had exercised more power by remaining unspoken and mysterious.

While these parents functioned well against a devastating illness, their children didn't come and reassure them that they were on the right course. The children were much more like their parents before the first family meeting — they simply didn't talk much. The younger two were somewhat open and curious, particularly the spark plug of a younger daughter, but the two older boys almost never initiated any discussion.

For example, the peacemaker brother, a year after being in a family meeting and a few months after the hospitalization, denied that anyone in the family had ever been depressed. He said specifically that his mother had not been ill, that he hadn't worried about her for a long time, and that "things don't change if she is ill." But later, within the very same conversation, when asked to review what had gone on in the previous year, he said his mother's hospitalization had been very hard for her and that the month of the hospitalization was the most difficult month for him. In a sense, in that brief half hour interview, he recapitulated his entire struggle to understand, as well as the struggle of many children: first deny, then insist that things don't change, and only then gradually talk about what had been so scary. This pattern was true for Peter as well.

Over the next two years, Peter grew inches taller, his voice deepened, and he experienced considerable success in his art, his friendships, and his schoolwork. Julia's recovery continued. Although she did descend into repeated periods when she simply couldn't manage, she remained on medication and in therapy, got a new job, and was able to function outside the home.

Three years after the hospitalization, after a particularly severe recurrence of his mother's depression, Peter was at last able to open up to his parents, his friends, and to others. He reported for the first time that when she'd been depressed he "felt sad and worried, and like I wanted to get her in a good mood but I couldn't." Like many children, he had mirrored his mother's sadness, but he also remembered the effect of Julia's depression on everyone else. It had affected the whole mood of the household when she'd been irritable and hadn't come to dinner or hung out or joked around. He said, "I felt like I didn't see her much, and it was weird and uncomfortable."

At eighteen, some four years after first beginning to talk about depression, Peter was poised to move forward with his life by leaving home to pursue a liberal arts education. His reflections were very different from those when he was fourteen. He emphasized that it had taken him many years to understand what had happened. As he said, "I think it's only recently that I've begun to address the whole thing. I do think it's such a long process. I never dealt with it while I was experiencing it." And he said rather sadly, "This left me without any details." He echoed his father, who talked about having an intellectual grasp of the mother's depression but only a very recent inkling of the impact. He could finally say, in retrospect, how much he had missed his mother during those depressions. "She just wasn't there."

But Peter also acknowledged that he and his mother had a kind of intimacy not every family has. "The bond between us became even stronger because it was broken and then reaffirmed," he said. Although no one would wish a family to wrestle with mood disorders, the mastery of experience can be a source of strength.

Peter's father had taken each of the children aside and tried to get them to talk about their mother's hospitalization. Peter, although he had been largely silent during those attempts, later described the discussions as very revealing. "It wasn't like I didn't know my mom was in a bad mood, but it was like, 'Oh, *that's* why!' and it helped."

Sam directly pursued conversations even though he wasn't getting much back from the kids. He did so because he was aware of the family style of keeping things secret, and aware that repeated conversations offered a much better chance of understanding than a single interaction. His kind but firm persistence characterized the actions of many of the parents we worked with who dealt successfully with depression.

Peter also felt that his relationship with his father had changed because of these conversations. Before, he'd been much more comfortable speaking with his mother about issues in his life. It was strange having his father be the one he'd talk to when his mother was ill, but all in all, it proved very positive.

Peter said he'd found the periodic, regular, and predictable inquiries from us and from his father annoying. He was put off by questions like, "How did it feel for you?" because, as he said, "I didn't know how it felt." But he did think they'd been important for him, and he was grateful that he had been encouraged to keep talking about his mother's depression.

This underscores a point that is important for all families. It is necessary to periodically revisit what's been talked about, review understandings, and go over the same information again and again: "You're not guilty, you're not to blame, and there are ways to talk about depression."

As Peter said, "Being asked about it forces you to look back on it. Depression doesn't happen to everyone you know. I realize now it's had an effect on me."

Woven into Peter's story are many lessons for parents, suggesting what they can do even in the midst of the challenges brought on by recurrent illness. Providing for daily routines, talking things through, and gradually helping the depressed person reemerge into the family are all important strategies to employ, not just initially but over time. When Julia was hospitalized, Sam made extra efforts to step in and be, as he said, both mother and father. Also, there were many strengths in this family: a strong marriage, strong religious bonds, a rich shared experience, and many talents, not the least of which were humor, art, and much closeness not colored by depression.

But for Peter, as for almost all the children we've worked with, it was only as the threat posed by a serious depression receded that he could begin to talk about his feelings. This, combined with an acknowledgment of what had gone on, occurred only over time, and in a somewhat uncertain and unpredictable fashion.

Peter had actively struggled to wall off the pain his mother's cold and uninterested expression caused him. First he said his mother's illness was not a problem, then he said it was. He wanted to stay home with his mother, wanted to get her into a good mood. Both parents recognized the distress Peter was in, even though he couldn't tell them about it. Gradually, they were able to help him, both indirectly, by showing that he could go on with his own life, and directly, by leaving the way open to talk about it. They each kept encouraging Peter to speak about his emotional reactions, no matter how painful. They also showed him he could safely separate yet maintain and even deepen the close relationships he had. As his father said, "He will not need to use up his energy to avoid thinking about these problems or hide them anymore." Then he added, "Hiding is exhausting."

Lisa: Caught in the Middle of Divorce, Alcoholism, and Depression

Among the most difficult issues that children must deal with are feeling caught in the crossfire between fighting parents, particularly when one or both struggle with depression again and again.

When we first came to know her, Lisa was a shy girl of ten and an average student with few, if any, close friends. She loved drama and competitive skiing, and both her parents, who adored her, helped her to pursue these interests. However, they could not protect her from her mother's increasingly intense episodes of depression and mania. Nora, her mother, had experienced her first episode of mania when she was twenty. She'd heard voices, felt she could read other people's minds, been unable to sleep, and had even been hospitalized on a medical ward. As is so tragically common in so many of the families we worked with, her illness wasn't recognized. She was discharged with no diagnosis, no treatment, and no explanation. She went in and out of episodes of depression, some of mania, for years thereafter. It had been treated gradually but only partially. And these episodes continued from the early years of Lisa's life, with the bouts of mania becoming more and more frequent. Lisa saw many episodes when her mother couldn't control herself, leaving home at unexpected times and behaving in odd ways.

Dan, Lisa's father, had a drinking problem, as well as his own bouts of depression. Lisa was constantly in the middle of arguments between her parents and was forced to choose sides, in effect expected to be an adult long before her time.

Despite all this, Lisa was quite reluctant to talk about her mother's behavior. She could sometimes say her mother was "in a different world, or couldn't listen to me that much." She told us how she remembered her mother crying and trying to comfort her. "I just wanted her to stop crying," she said. "I didn't associate manic depression with her crying. I didn't know why she was crying."

Driven by mania, Nora had left Lisa alone more than even her husband realized. While Dan worked, Nora would go out drinking. She would dress provocatively, dance with different men, and then drive home late at night. This in turn led to huge tensions in the family.

As they began to talk together, with our help, Lisa was relieved because she felt she'd "covered for" Nora during this time. She had not told Dan the full extent of her mother's behavior for fear of "betraying her."

Nora and Dan talked about what they'd been through together, assuring Lisa she was not to blame. Yet, as Lisa said, "I told my dad about what you did and my dad got mad at you, and then you got sick. I thought it was kind of my fault."

As they worked together as a family, they recognized Nora's illness as biological. Both Lisa and her father agreed that it was not being helpful to Nora to ignore the symptoms and let them get worse. Nora agreed to a plan to try to recognize the symptoms earlier in the cycle, but said with insight, "Right now I think, 'Oh, that's great!' but then, I might get furious." Lisa still said she felt as if she would be betraying her mother if she mentioned the symptoms to her father, but she agreed she would have to if they became serious enough.

Up until age ten, Lisa had been exceedingly isolated. She'd spent most evenings alone, lying to her father about her mother's bizarre behavior and unable to talk with her mother for fear that her feelings were a threat to Nora. Ultimately, she said, "I'm glad we're talking like this, because at this moment I have a whole new way of dealing with it."

Although she found the talking helpful, it was only as the family revisited the explanations again and again that Lisa's thinking changed. A year after the meeting, Lisa still minimized its importance; two years later, she did the same.

Her father acknowledged that the family style was "to ignore the problem," but he changed over those two years. He realized the extent to which he denied many things and tried to cover them up by lying. He also came to see the role of drinking in his denial and he joined Alcoholics Anonymous. As he stopped drinking, he began to understand that he had been depressed himself for many years, and so he began both counseling and antidepressant medication. Nora's manic episodes continued unabated, with frequent forays out at night and much rage at Dan. When Lisa was thirteen, they separated for the first of several times.

But Dan and Nora remained undivided in their caring for Lisa. They even asked for a second family meeting, which they used to talk about the separation and to go over once again both of their illnesses. They had found someone for Lisa to talk to, and they talked to that person to develop strategies that would "keep her out of the middle." Then they implemented those strategies. They told Lisa that they wanted to be sure she knew she had their permission to "go her own way."

After this meeting, Lisa still denied that she was much affected by either parent's illness, perhaps because she had to wait and see whether they could hold to their agreement.

Gradually, over the next year and a half, she blossomed. She had some success in school. She said she genuinely appreciated her parents' effort to help her understand what was happening. Above all, she liked the family's openness.

Lisa also came to a new level of understanding about both of her parents' difficulties. She could describe much more fully what it was like for her. She said that when her mother was depressed or manic, it was "like having a totally different parent around." And she defined mania in startlingly clear terms. She summed it up as, "You are not thinking about what you're doing and you act out."

A year later, Lisa said she spent a lot of time thinking about her mother's illness. She admitted that she'd done the same for years, but for the first time, at age fifteen, she directly acknowledged it. Although her parents were no longer secretive, she said mania and depression were "not a daily topic of conversation." She had been able to tell her parents that she felt somehow responsible for their illnesses. She felt it was very helpful when they both told her she was mistaken. This allowed her to place herself in the story in a different way.

At this point, she had a kind of "I get it now" experience. She said, "I've always known it, but I wasn't too clear in my mind about it. Somehow, it hadn't been as traumatizing for me then. I understand it more now, and so it's more of a shock for me."

Lisa echoed the stories of many children as they mirror and try to get inside the world of their parents. "I think I go through it with them, actually," she said. "I tend to almost get depressed myself. I'm not as serious as my mom, probably. I kind of go up and down with her because the whole house feels more subdued."

Dan became the stable parent, remained sober, and attended AA faithfully. Nora took on a nomadic lifestyle, changing residences and relationships freely, although she kept in daily contact with her daughter.

Speaking of her mother's departure, Lisa said, "I'm a really different person since that event. I think the episode with my mom really changed me. Now I'm more withdrawn. I don't really like to be with people. I've been kind of moody and high and low. I've known a lot of anger lately, and I don't know why." She went on to describe several things that made her furious, including an argument with a peer. But perhaps because she was able to put these things into words, they didn't overwhelm her. She continued to do well in school, developed a relationship with a boy, and became involved in Al-Anon and deeply involved in church.

Despite their profound conflicts, Nora and Dan found trying to help Lisa do well to be the one thing on which they could agree. In this sense, they reaffirmed the centrality of caring for children despite the ravages of depression, mania, and divorce. And they did not try to do it alone. They were open to getting help. They used a wide array of services — psychotherapy for both, repeated attempts to find the right treatment for Nora, Alcoholics Anonymous, the church, and getting Lisa her own therapist to talk to, as well as working with us. They permanently changed the context in which Lisa experienced the chaos brought on by repeated separations and recurrent mania. They helped Lisa understand and accept that Nora's depression and mania, as well as Dan's alcoholism and depression, were not her fault. They also consistently encouraged Lisa to pursue her own life and interests, helping her separate herself from them. Nora's decision to leave actually may have represented an attempt to protect Lisa from being drawn in.

Because she couldn't always talk to others about this illness, Lisa saw her regular talks with us as important signposts in measuring how she was doing. Lisa's strategy changed from "going with the flow," as she put it, to "going my own way." Above all, this took time as she endeavored to make sense of very large difficulties and painful questions when they arose and come to terms with them years after beginning to break the silence.

Andrew: Taking Care of One's Parent

Andrew's story gives some insight into another issue that runs throughout children's accounts of depression: the desire to take care of the depressed parent.

The youngest of three children, Andrew lived on a rolling estate south of Boston. Even though his mother's depression had gone on for at least ten years, he began to be clearly aware of it only around the age of fourteen. Fortunately, he came to understand his mother's depression at a time when other things in his life were relatively stable.

Andrew, a stocky, athletic youngster, was a good observer of the facts of her illness but minimized its seriousness. "She was really kind of depressed all fall and kind of freaking out. It wasn't much fun being around her, but we supported her and now she's out of it." Although he knew he wasn't responsible for his mother's illness, he saw it as the sum total of "little events, like my sister's getting in trouble or maybe my grades going down." He tended to deny that it affected him in any significant way but did admit, "I get a little depressed when she's down."

His mother had actually talked to him about depression a number of times. But his awareness of his mother's disorder became more acute when his older brother and sister were away at school. He noticed that he missed her attentions when she was depressed. "It sucks. It's not fun at all," he told us. "I come home at five-thirty or six, and she's home at six-fifteen. My dad comes home at seven. If she's depressed, she just goes to bed or goes out or something."

The parents worked effectively with one of our clinicians to begin a family conversation, and all five members attended. Afterward, Andrew reported, "It gave us a whole new vocabulary." He learned for the first time that his father and siblings were concerned about his mother's illness and that it was all right to talk about it. He had firmly believed that his siblings didn't know anything about it, and thought his father was in the dark as well.

A year later, Andrew was quite concrete about the symptoms of depression. He said repeated conversations with his brother and sister were very helpful. He poignantly recalled a conversation in which one of them cited a well-known statistic — that one out of every three children of depressed parents will become depressed. "I wondered which one of us would be the one to get depressed. We were sitting at the table talking about it, and it made an odd moment. It was weird."

Of course he wondered whether he would be the one. He anticipated "the day when I won't be able to go to sleep because I have thoughts, things racing in my head. I'll be tense and suspicious." These were the very symptoms his mother had described when she was going into depression. Clearly he had been listening.

That summer, his mother became depressed while Andrew was away at summer camp, but she recovered by the time he got home. His parents discussed it briefly, and he did not seem particularly worried after the episode had passed.

As time went on, despite the depression, his relationship with his parents deepened. During a year at boarding school to prepare for college, he was acutely aware that his mother was experiencing "the empty-nest syndrome." His father was a great support. They began to talk much more openly, and Andrew came to see his dad as a friend and peer as well as a father. Their openness about the depression allowed them to share many other things as well.

Youngsters learn about depression not just by observing it in their parents but by seeing it in others they are close to. Depression and, sadly, suicide too are very much in the news. Andrew's girlfriend also suffered from depression. He described her as becoming "aloof," meaning, as he put it, that "she doesn't want to be put in a good mood." He saw her depression as "periods when nothing seems good. You get frustrated by things that are normally okay. Little things bug you." When depressed, she only wanted to talk about depression and, as Andrew put it, "didn't want to hang out with me."

As he grew older, Andrew became much clearer about the characteristics of his mother's depression and how separate he was from them. He now saw depression as much more complex — "an extended period of void, which makes people feel insignificant, like nothing really good is going on."

At eighteen, just before going off to college, Andrew described his relationship to his mother as positive and warm even though it had been interrupted by depression. "She looks out for me and I look out for her." He also remembered the family meeting well. The meeting had opened up unanticipated connections between family members. Interestingly, Andrew's understanding of the meeting changed as his degree of comfort with depression changed. Andrew said that he no longer viewed depression as "an alien taking over my mother's body," but something that affected many people and was very much in the mainstream of American life.

At twenty, Andrew had a fright when his roommate in college on the West Coast became depressed. Then, while he was home for a visit for spring break, his mother was hospitalized and Andrew spent a lot of time helping out at home. "She was very open about it," he said. "It was sad as hell. It was all so weird. It was just such a feeling of helplessness. You wanted to shake her back into place, but there was nothing we could do. I don't think she was suicidal, but she was really out of it. She was really forgetful, leaving the door open to the car and house. She'd say, 'Come and talk to me,' and I'd visit her in the hospital. She'd say, 'You know I'm fine. I'm just going through a tough time. I just need you to realize I'm not crazy,' which was cool. It was definitely helpful. The first few times it freaked me out. Actually, maybe it was the other way around — the first few times it was okay and then it freaked me out. But it was helpful in figuring out how she was doing. It really helped me gauge how she was feeling."

His father, he said, tried to be "Super Dad," wanting to protect him from the illness. While he understood his father's intentions, Andrew was actually upset with his dad for trying to isolate him. He wanted to do more for his mother, to care for her, so he felt somewhat betrayed. As he put it, "Why should it be a burden for me to help?"

When asked what impact having a parent with depression had had on him, he said, "You know, it's made me more receptive to other people, what's going on in their lives. I used to be more callous. It makes you aware of how other people are feeling, what's going on with them. It makes you aware of other people's emotional well-being." Then he continued, reflecting more generally, "You know, having something bottled up is not a good thing. Being able to vent it and explore it is definitely helpful."

Over time, owing to his growth, his experiences with depression outside of the family, continued conversations within it, and his helping his girlfriend through her own bout of depression, Andrew's understanding became more complex. As with Peter and Lisa, the process involved continually working away at it and trying to make sense of it.

Starting with the first resilient youngster, Kate, these young people universally expressed the desire to take care of their parents just as if they were suffering from a physical illness. The difference with depression is that it first has to be understood as an illness. Once that is established, children, adolescents, and even young adults then have to be free to choose; that is, they cannot be coerced into taking care of someone against their will. As with Andrew, when they have that choice, they often contribute a great deal.

Stefan: Changing Perceptions Over Time

When we first spoke to Stefan, he was eleven, and despite having lived with a depressed father for many years, he said he had no idea what depression was and described it as simply being very angry. His father, George, suffered from posttraumatic stress disorder and had wrestled with drug and alcohol abuse complicated by lingering neurological difficulties. Nonetheless, he was a caring and thoughtful man who held down a regular job.

Throughout the years of kindergarten and grammar school, George worked in the evening and took care of Stefan during the day while his wife worked. One afternoon, Stefan noticed his father lying in bed and called his mother, Agnes, at work. She immediately sensed that something was wrong and called an ambulance. George was taken to the hospital, where he was treated for an overdose that was an attempt to take his own life. Agnes, a clear, articulate woman, and very much the strongest one in the family, made a decision she'd stick to from that time until we first talked to her five years later.

"I think it was probably very scary for Stefan, but I don't think he realized it was a suicide attempt. He thought it was a heart attack. When I asked him why he thought his father went to the hospital, he said he knew people went to the hospital for heart attacks, so I just left it that way. He doesn't bring it up. When he's old enough and wants to talk about it, I'll certainly correct it. At this stage in the game, I didn't verify one way or the other what it was or it wasn't. We were all just sad that he was sick." Throughout the years of grammar school, Stefan remembered the event as a heart attack.

At thirteen, Stefan told a very different story. By then, in his account, his father's hospitalization was not due to a heart attack but to an illness resulting from having taken too many pills. He remembered vividly his father lying in bed and not being able to get up. Still, he said he had no idea what his father had been in the hospital for and attributed his getting better to "the doctors and different drugs that he took and stuff." He did say that his mother had talked a little bit to him after it had happened. He remembered she told him that his father took something he was allergic to. In short, he still did not attribute the event to depression. He summed it up by saying, "It felt pretty good, because I helped him so he wouldn't die." He indicated that no one had talked to him about it since and that no one in his family suffered from depression.

Stefan's definition of depression was abstract, not tied to his family experience, but it was, in fact, a description of his father. "When you're sad for a long time and you can't get things out of your head that are bothering you; you're really sad about somebody dying."

Two years later, at fifteen, Stefan's descriptions of depression were far more detailed. His father's depression had intensified in the meantime and had become an undeniable part of the boy's experience. For the first time, he identified his father as being depressed. His growing awareness not only coincided with going to high school, but with the fact that his father had stopped working and was "hanging around the house." He also had seen his father taking medications to help himself. Stefan used the phrase "manic depression" to describe what his father was experiencing, although he had little idea what it meant. His explanation was, "It's when you're really, really depressed." When asked if either of his parents had been grouchy, upset, or sad, he said his father had been, "maybe once or twice," but he said he couldn't remember for how long.

He also, for the first time, said he had felt that it was his fault when his father got depressed. But he no longer felt that way because, as he said, "I've learned there's nothing I can do when he's in this mood." He said talking with his mother helped.

A year later, Stefan talked even more about his father's situation. George, claiming to be sick, was still not working, and Stefan's mother was managing her job, the household, and the money. Stefan had learned something of work himself through a part-time job.

As children begin to face the tasks of adulthood, they naturally look at how their parents face such tasks and often look to parents as models. For Stefan, the contrast between his own efforts to work and his father's lack of effort was intense. He was very upset that his father kept saying he was going to work and then wouldn't go. "He kept saying he was sick, but I didn't think he was," Stefan said.

George continued on a downhill course, stopping all of his care. Stefan's mother insisted that something be done. George refused, so Agnes, after consultation with George's doctor, called an ambulance. Shortly before the ambulance arrived, George took all of his remaining medications in another suicide attempt, which left him hospitalized for seven days.

This time, Stefan's mother told the boy in detail about what was going on and what had gone on in the past. She explained that the prior hospitalization had been for depression and told him why she had used the explanation of medical illness before. Stefan asked many questions. Agnes offered him the chance to talk to someone outside the family, a counselor, and he refused. A few months later, one of us routinely asked about the depression, and he denied that anything had happened — this despite the fact that there had been a meeting in the hospital with his father, his mother, the caregivers, and Stefan, at which Stefan had become angry with his father. His grades went down, he had difficulties in school, but he told no one about his father.

A year later, he was able to say that his father had not been going to work and had been around the house, and that his strategy was to avoid him. "I spent time outside or went to my room. I talked to my mom but not him." He said of his father, "He was up and then he went down and stayed down for a while."

Stefan's understanding of the illness was very literal and based on his father's experience. He felt that what his father needed to do to get better was to schedule more doctor's appointments and stay on medications.

At eighteen, Stefan was doing well. Although it was still difficult for him to talk with us about his father's depression, he'd gradually come to see that being silent and guarded made no sense. He had a number of friends and interests, and was meeting the challenges of adulthood. His mother, in fact, spoke with great pride about his easygoing disposition.

By this time, at his mother's insistence, his parents had separated. George remained depressed, was suicidal at times, and was not getting the care he needed. Stefan's mother discussed with Stefan the reasons for and the risks involved in George's leaving home. George moved to a protected living situation but had regular contact with his son, coming over for dinner at least once a week.

Developmentally, at five and even at ten, Stefan couldn't understand what depression was. On the other hand, he didn't feel the need to, so his mother chose not to discuss it. While some parents we have worked with would have chosen to discuss it sooner, his mother's course worked for her and for Stefan. As Stefan became more aware of his father's condition, he required an explanation. When he was challenged by the undeniable fact of his father's suicide attempt, he learned about depression and connected it across time to his father's earlier behavior. And as he faced one of the normal challenges of young adulthood — finding work — the contrast to George's not working stood out in bold relief.

The four youngsters profiled here demonstrate four different reactions to the same illness. Peter's reaction was one of quietly struggling to make sense of things while, for the most part, moving through the changes of adolescence without profound upset. Lisa's was to be aware of the illness but not talk about her feelings. Andrew's was to want to help. Stefan's was to keep quiet until the undeniable pressure of events forced him to make sense of it.

The most powerful common thread among all these families is that in order to be able to move beyond depression, it's necessary to move beyond denial. Families must acknowledge the pain and hurt, the loss that's been borne together, with the awareness that it did not overwhelm them. Acknowledgment works because it puts these experiences into words and because it allows other actions in the family to continue. The loss, the hurt, and the anger are placed in the context of the family as a whole but are also directly recognized for what they are.

Lisa could only tell her parents how guilty her mother made her feel three to four years after they began to talk. Peter could acknowledge not having his mother there only as she began to recover. But having spoken about their losses, and as they mature, children gradually become vital partners in the dialogue with parents. Depression becomes not just a terrible adversity but something they and their parents have mastered together. As Fran O'Connor said earlier, it can give families a kind of intimacy that others don't have.

Jesse

Becoming the Author of One's Own Story

In her room at the prow of the house
Where light breaks, and the windows are tossed with linden,
My daughter is writing a story. . . .

The whole house seems to be thinking,
And then she is at it again with a bunched clamor
Of strokes, and again is silent.

I remember the dazed starling
Which was trapped in that very room, two years ago;
How we stole in, lifted a sash

And retreated, not to affright it;
And how for a helpless hour, through the crack of the door,
We watched the sleek, wild, dark

And iridescent creature
Batter against the brilliance, drop like a glove
To the hard floor, or the desk-top,

And wait then, humped and bloody,
For the wits to try it again; and how our spirits
Rose when, suddenly sure,

It lifted off from a chair-back,
Beating a smooth course for the right window
And clearing the sill of the world.

It is always a matter, my darling,
Of life or death, as I had forgotten. I wish
What I wished you before, but harder.

Richard Wilbur, "The Writer" (selected stanzas)

The incredible courage and resilience of children can teach us much. This chapter tells the story of one boy who, dealing with an extraordinary burden, showed me how children gradually develop the active capacity to understand.

When I first met Jesse, he was a wiry and slender eight-year-old, with quick movements and an athlete's grace. From the beginning he looked me directly in the eye and demanded that I be completely attentive to him.

Jesse showed me how the same challenge — dealing with the suicide of his mother — was revisited again and again at crucial points as he grew older. As he developed, he had to make sense of it differently, just as Peter and Frank and Lisa did of their parents' depression. But above all, Jesse moved at his own pace, and he made the process of understanding his own.

I began to see Jesse a year after his mother's death. He and his father, Arthur, had managed together for a while, grief-stricken, but then Jesse began to present an increasing puzzle to those around him. In many ways he was doing incredibly well with friends and in school, but every four to six weeks he became very angry very quickly about something that didn't warrant such an outburst. Those around him didn't know what this meant and were worried that Jesse was becoming depressed, or even worse, becoming manic, the illness his mother had struggled with, or that maybe he simply found the loss of his mother too much to take.

In a play at school with the other second graders, he was given the role of death. In contrast to the bubbly and upbeat characters of the other children, he gave a haunting and startling portrayal. His teachers and his father observed that he was an extraordinarily determined young man, implacably persistent in getting things done. He drove himself relentlessly and was severe in his self-criticism. His teachers also saw in him a great adherence to rules, so much so that he was often frustrated. He got into struggles with other kids when he believed they weren't obeying the rules.

Jesse's mother was described by others as having been warm, loving, intense, artistic, and unpredictable. Although she'd wrestled with depression, her descent into the mania that preceded her suicide was unexpected. Jesse's father was bereft, wrestling with many tasks at once, raising this boy day-to-day, dealing with loneliness, helping another child from a previous marriage, keeping on with his job, and figuring out how to rebuild his life. But while Jesse represented many worries and much responsibility, he also represented the center of his father's life. In the midst of all these other demands, raising this boy and meeting his needs was sustaining and nurturing for Arthur. In this, he was like many parents wrestling with depression, and his wish to help his son was where he and I found our strongest alliance.

I had a particular window on Jesse's experience because I was asked to see him as his doctor and therapist when he was only eight, and did so for several years. Jesse didn't have a major mental illness, but what he had lived through — a parent's suicide — is the worst fear of patients, families, and caregivers who must deal with depression.

Jesse had a set of characteristics that remained the same over the time I knew him: his intensity, his need to decide the pace at which he worked, and above all, his refusal to be forced to do things without explanation. His discussion of his mother's death followed the same pattern. He showed me again and again that he could not be forced to talk about his mother. From very early on, he could acknowledge how much he missed her and that he knew she was never coming back, but he was steadfast in not wanting to know how she died.

Characteristic of many younger children, Jesse could not put feelings into words but would show loss, pain, and anger through his gestures.

From the beginning, Jesse was quite wary. What got us started was finding things we could enjoy and share together. This was easy because he was fun to be with, loved games, and was extraordinary at drawing. We avidly played chess and cards, and as there was a gym near my office, we often played basketball for part of the session. As we engaged in these pleasant activities, I frequently asked Jesse whether he had any worries or concerns. He would deny it. When I asked about his mother, for the most part he would not answer, except occasionally to recall positive memories. Certainly, he never admitted to being sad or angry.

Jesse loved rituals and always wanted things to be the same. In the building where I saw him, there was a kitchen. We had the custom of going down and getting some juice at the end of each session. Each time, after he drank his juice, he folded the juice carton in the same particular way. For years, we followed that ritual. I knew he liked the juice, that it was a standard and familiar ceremony, and that it represented something tangible that I was able to give him. It's also true that, like any child after school, he was simply hungry and thirsty.

Once, though, the kitchen was closed because of a holiday. His face clouded over and he was inconsolable. As he gradually calmed down, he was able to tell me what was really going on. Having juice was the last thing he and his mother had shared on his final visit with her in the hospital. Our sharing the juice represented an unspoken way for him to keep the memories of his mother alive. Moreover, his mother had been very skilled at folding paper, and on that visit, after they'd shared their juice, she'd folded the carton into the shape of a bird.

The disturbance of our ritual showed the emblematic connection, and once we articulated that connection, he was able to talk about how much he missed his mother and how much he thought about her. For many eight-year-old boys, talking about feelings is difficult, but for this boy, not talking about the loss and all the attendant feelings about his mother's death created a burden impossible for him to sustain. In the weeks that followed, as we drank juice together, I would bring up his mother again, and he would acknowledge that he missed her, but he still wouldn't talk at length. I learned just how much he needed space to figure it out his own way.

Over time, our sessions came to have a rhythm of their own — some talk, some games, and some basketball. I came to understand that his insistence on rules was a result of what had happened with his mother. What could be more unfair and unpredictable in life, more out of his control, than for a boy to lose his mother this way? He simply couldn't figure it out.

I was very direct in telling him he was not to blame, that many people loved him, that his life could go on, and that he could talk about the sadness. His school environment, caring and focused, as well as his father, reinforced that same message. Jesse would acknowledge that he had heard, but still he would not talk about it.

Losing control, being unaware of why, and gradually connecting the disturbance to the unfairness of his mother's loss: these were themes that ran through his life over many years. But the manifestations changed as he developed.

For example, a year and a half after we began, he became very upset on learning that he needed glasses. Apart from any athletic nine-year-old's reluctance to wear glasses, it turned out his mother had worn glasses. Jesse felt he was being unjustly singled out. Fortunately, he was able to talk about this sense of injustice, and he was able to link it to how he felt about his mother's dying.

Jesse watched people very closely. Once, I received an emergency page when I was meeting with him and had to answer the phone. He was very upset with me for taking time away. We talked about how vigilant he was in staying connected to those around him. He acknowledged that he was afraid he would lose them the way he had lost his mother.

Jesse's self-criticism also meant that at school or at home, his face would cloud over or he would struggle with an assignment, and those around him would worry. Although he could not put his feelings into words, Jesse's expressive face showed when he was angry, sad, or troubled. His quick, hawklike gestures reflected his decisive way of dealing with things. He did not want to brood. At the same time, it was just as clear that he did not want to talk.

Jesse's mother was someone who had taken particular delight in holidays and celebrated every way possible, so holidays and anniversaries, particularly the anniversary of his mother's death, were very difficult for the boy. Holidays also meant visits to his grandmother, and her home, with its many portraits of his mother, stirred his awareness of how much he'd lost. Mother's Day was also extremely difficult.

Raising any child is complicated, and for Jesse's father, raising him alone, all the strategies that thoughtful parents use were necessary. But even after several years, when Arthur found a wonderful partner, Sarah, and remarried, there was still a special challenge. Everyone around this child feared that some of the behaviors he engaged in — refusing to talk, becoming so angry with himself that his face darkened and he simply froze — were either symptoms of an overwhelming grief or worse, symptoms of the emergence of his mother's illness. This fear grew more intense during Jesse's adolescence. He had difficult times because he was older, more on his own, and more intense in his reactions to any transition or failure.

One essential role I played was sorting out Jesse's behavior and helping his father and stepmother recognize that he was not developing his mother's illness. Had Jesse been developing mania, immediate treatment could have been lifesaving. But as he was not, misidentifying his behavior as illness would have been a dangerous mistake. Another part of my role was giving him a safe place to explore his anger and hurt, as well as permission not to explore them if he was not ready.

His father's remarriage, which took place when Jesse was eleven, represented a positive step, because Sarah was deeply committed to him. At the same time, it sealed the fact that his mother would never come back, and it required considerable renegotiation of many delicate balances. The house had been left as his mother — creative but chaotic — had arranged it, and Jesse and his father had kept it as a shrine to her special personality. With the remarriage, Sarah rightly believed it should be reorganized. She threw out things and bought new things, redecorating to her own taste. These changes were immensely difficult for Jesse because for him they were a threat that the memories themselves would be lost. Jesse also had a mind of his own, and he didn't take easily to change under any circumstances — certainly not change initiated by his step-mother. The reorganization of the house did go on, however, and he learned that positive change did not threaten his memories of his mother.

Shortly after Arthur's remarriage, Jesse had a good start in school, but then he ran into difficulty. He was assigned a long paper to write that involved expressing his feelings, and he simply couldn't do it. This caused great consternation in his parents, literate and committed intellectuals who saw writing as a way of life. I gently inquired whether his criticism of himself and indeed some of his trouble writing were due to resurfaced feelings about his mother, both the feelings of missing her and the feeling that it wasn't fair. He cried and insisted that nothing was wrong. By the next week, though, he'd completed the assignment, and he acknowledged that his initial inability to write had been a result of his remembering his mother with overwhelming feelings. It was only through better understanding his emotional reactions that he was able to express himself. He had to make the connection between his frustration, anger, and criticism of himself and his sadness, pain, and anger because his mother had died.

This boy lived for sports and practiced basketball many hours a day. He was driven to win, and yet when he was at the point of beating me badly, he often became frustrated with himself and couldn't follow through. He also got very angry if he didn't win. One of the most complex dilemmas, of course, for any child and family is sorting out what's a response to a loss and what's just normal development. I tried to get him to see that it was possible to play hard and not win, and that part of his anger might be because he'd had no control when his mother was taken away from him. Gradually, he was able to put that awareness into words. On the basketball court, he was able to tolerate losing. But it was only after he was eleven that we could truly talk about it together, as opposed to my simply voicing it and his silently enduring it.

When Jesse was eight, nine, and ten, his father and I made repeated offers to talk with him about how his mother had died, but he was steadfast in not wanting to know. At thirteen, he wanted to know more about his mother's mental illness. We talked about these issues in general terms, but he remained steadfast in not wanting to know how she died. It was not until years later that he wanted to know exactly how she had died, or even hear an explanation of what mania was.

As he entered junior high, Jesse gradually saw me less and less, but at each step of his development, the process of negotiating what his mother's death meant continued. At thirteen, he celebrated his bar mitzvah. At this point, he had enough peace with his mother's death to be very positive about her, and she was remembered throughout the service. This was a wonderful affirmation for him and for many of his family's friends. Her presence was very much felt at the ceremony, as was the presence of other figures in his life — his father, emerging stronger, his stepmother, the friends he'd made and developed since his mother died.

That summer, he worked in a camp and was particularly effective as a counselor. He shared with me a little detail I found very telling. When he was playing basketball in the summer and the game would come down to the final shot, he told me he'd first say to himself, "I hope and pray the person makes the shot." But then he'd say, rather, "No, I hope my mother's happy." He was developing a better sense of his relationship to his mother's memory, and also bringing those memories inside himself.

How Jesse managed is not just the story of an individual but also of his family, his school, and his community, all of which gave him a great deal. But Jesse, in turn, gave a great deal back. He had an older sister with whom he was very close. He remained in the same school and with the same friends he'd had since early childhood. These were people who knew his mother and could help him remember her. The teachers and principal of the school were aware of Jesse's loss and occasionally acknowledged it with him. So not only his family, but also his school and his community rallied to support him.

In trying to help Jesse deal with his emotions, his class visited his mother's grave and he talked about her. I was regularly in touch with the school and with his parents, and we agreed that the core message be consistent among all of us. Being in touch with them, I saw how the same behavior, the withdrawal, anger, and implacable intensity, occurred in many different places as he struggled, behind the wall he had put up around himself, to make sense of these things.

I met regularly, although not every week, with Arthur and Sarah. Day-to-day, they had to deal with Jesse's anger, his cantankerousness, his refusal to do certain things. They had to sort out what were normal developmental issues or predictable tensions between parent and child, father and son, or stepmother and son, and what were Jesse's unique issues because of the death of his mother. They had to be able to set limits and be firm. They also had to know when to try to get him to work and when to back off. And they had to do all of this within the context of developing their own relationship. My presence as a therapist helped them reframe or get around logjams more than anything else, Sarah told me.

While Jesse was in eighth grade, the year after the bar mitzvah, I saw him again briefly because there was now a great emphasis on grades in school, and he was very worried about how he would do. As we explored the tensions around grades, he gradually relaxed. He was able to recognize that pushing himself to do well was different from pushing himself in order to punish himself, or to make up for his mother's death.

That year, around the Jewish holiday of Rosh Hashanah, he experienced many memories of his mother, and in November he was asked to read a story about a child who felt he'd caused the death of someone else. When Jesse presented this to the class, he became tearful and admitted that he felt he had caused his mother's death. He'd had a cold at the time of her death, and not knowing how she'd died, he worried that she might have caught something from him.

He had heard many times that his mother had had an illness and that it wasn't his fault. He had never before said it was his fault, but obviously he still wondered about it, and here the question blindsided him.

From a developmental point of view, Jesse at fourteen could consider different explanations for why his mother had died and what his role might have been. But he could also begin to understand realistically that he was not to blame. He could connect his feelings to the loss of his mother, reinforced by conversations with his stepmother about this.

Jesse had kept his mother's memory alive in part by keeping things the same. When he finally changed schools and went to high school in a new community, everyone in the family was anxious, and in fact he was quite lonely for the first three months. This transition from a very familiar environment associated with his mother to a new and challenging one raised a specter of his being alone and isolated because of his loss. He met the challenge with silence and intensity, but in time the things he did well — studies, sports, and making friends — carried him through.

I stayed in touch with his parents, and I saw him again when his father felt that he needed me. The crisis Jesse faced was not unlike that of many other youths — he had lost the first love of his life. But for Jesse, that loss was intertwined inextricably with his mother's death. By this time, Jesse had been involved for years with a young woman whose mother had also died when she was quite young. They had become friends, and early in high school he'd fallen in love with her. But the young woman he had shared so much with, and in many ways had helped through mutual loss, suddenly broke up with him. He described feeling devastated, saying he didn't care about anything anymore. He was overwhelmed by emptiness, hurt, and anger. He talked to his father about how upset he was, and naturally his father worried about a descent into depression.

Here again, Jesse faced what many adolescents face, but with a difference. He and this young woman had found a special bond because they'd both lost their mothers, and she had been the center of his life for a number of years. He said he'd had an image in his mind of both of their mothers watching them from above, caring about them, glad they were together. This image was shattered when she went out with another boy.

He made it through the crisis by using all of what he'd gained in learning how to deal with his mother's loss in understanding what was going on with this young woman now. Although he was upset, I ascertained that he did not have the symptoms of a full depression, nor was he overwhelmed, despondent, or suicidal. He did not need therapy with me but dealt with the loss through conversations with friends, and above all by talking to his sister. She told him his image of the two mothers in heaven was wrong, because the relationship simply was not meant to be and the girl was not for him.

In time, Jesse came to see that what he needed was long-term, reliable relationships and that this young woman, although lovely, really didn't share this need.

Because he had found friendships and relationships in which he could talk intimately about these losses, Jesse did not need therapy at this point in his life. He was making sense of his mother's death and the end of the relationship on his own.

I saw Jesse again, not because of any crisis but because I asked him to help me understand how he'd gotten through the challenge and what had helped. At eighteen, he was a tall, dark, handsome, athletic young man who spoke quickly and decisively. He picked up a basketball and bounced it between his legs, and we joked about the many hours we'd played basketball together. He was an honor student and a peer leader, coaching, teaching Sunday school, and baby-sitting regularly. He said he wanted to be a physical education teacher, but in the upper-middle-class town in which he lived, coaching wasn't a profession held in very high regard. We explored how he could resolve that conflict.

He'd made his peace with his mother's death by remembering the positives about her, what she'd given him and what she would want him to have. He said he thought about her every day and that he had fond memories of her — visits to the children's museum, toys she had given him, images of her in the house and the way it was set up. Echoing many of the young people we've talked to, he said that the experience had actually toughened him. "I think I'm the way I am because of her," he said, "because I've learned to think about things as she would want me to."

Despite the pain, he reflected a lot about his mother's death. As Jesse explained it, because of her death, he had adopted an "I can do better" attitude. "In a lot of ways, my mother's death has really helped me. I really see her — wherever I go, there she is, looking and seeing everything I do. So in a lot of ways it made me want to do the right thing. Because my mother is not there, I sit there and I respect what she would want me to do. It has kept me out of drugs and other things.

"At first it was hard, but having her really watching me and wanting to make her proud of me in a lot of ways has helped me find morality on a larger scale before I would have otherwise. It made me want to do better than I possibly at the time would have. I probably wouldn't have cared for myself so much."

Just as important, he talked often with his older sister and, as he said, he had learned from her that his mother wasn't simply an ideal, that she hadn't always been supportive, and that there had been a lot of fighting at home. "I came to see her as a real person and that different people saw her in different ways," he said. "But I still miss her."

He reflected at length on what the whole experience had meant. "I always think about what it's done to change me and how I am because of her. It's strange, because it's kind of a contradiction in a lot of ways. I think about her committing suicide and I think about how it was a disease — a contradiction in my head, but I'm not sure. I guess in some ways I feel like she is a lot more there for me not being alive than any parent could be alive. Everything happens for a reason. I feel that really strongly. I'm a lot more spiritual than religious. Much of the good parts about me are because my mother's not around and I needed to deal with it. I had to grow up really quickly and become stronger. A lot of things. What doesn't kill you makes you stronger. I really believe in that pretty strongly in terms of dealing with things, overcoming them. Everybody's been telling me it's not suicide in a normal sense, but it's the disease more than anything else that killed her, and I guess I believe that. I've justified that in my mind. It's taken it away from being a suicide. She died of a disease. It makes it a lot easier to deal with. It helps to name it."

I asked him about the long period of not wanting to know how she died, and he said, "You know, physically I still don't want to know. I feel like she's always in my heart."

Jesse had a well-developed sense of who he was in relationships and what he needed. He said even with his close friends, it was very hard to talk on a deep level, but he had managed. "In terms of sharing what's really inside of me, it's a lot easier with women. Now I feel comfortable doing it with everyone."

In my last conversation with him, Jesse insisted fiercely that people had to make sense of things on their own; no one could do it for them. "Your explanations have to come from yourself and not from the outside," he said.

Just as physical development is discontinuous — that is, people make sudden shifts in height and weight and don't grow continuously from year one to year eighteen — so is the making sense of things. Experiences build up for a time and then they come together. Jesse helped me see that an essential part of making sense of things is not just within but is being able to write it, speak it, and declare it to others.

For Jesse, the experience with his mother came up unexpectedly in his applications to college. Jesse struggled for a long time with a scholarship essay that asked, "What's the most important event of your life?" Although he was well aware in his own mind what that event truly was, he wrote about other topics for several applications and didn't write about her death until the last essay.

He went back and forth about it. "You know, my mother dying is really the biggest event in terms of my life. It's changed me in many ways. I've been thinking about those questions from junior year on, got help from the counselor editing it." Interestingly enough, he wrote the last sentence first. *"I apologize for the rawness exhibited in this essay."* But, as he later said, "I had to edit that sentence out. It was important for me to express it in writing because writing has always been so difficult. I always figure stuff out in math, but expressing myself in writing was never my strength. And I shared it with my close friends, my sister, and a couple of teachers. Writing that essay helped. I really pulled myself in that essay in a way I never had before in writing. I didn't get the scholarship I wrote it for, but it was worth it. You know, in making sense of that, it's important to write it down. It's an important step to take when you are ready."

Although Jesse missed his mother very much, he also had been able to move on with the tasks of being a young man. In this sense, he showed the characteristics of resilient youngsters. He was deeply involved in relationships, had two friends from early childhood with whom he remained quite close, he worked well with adults, had a growing sense of what he wanted to do, and had found a deep spiritual and moral side. He was committed to helping the poor. He negotiated with others, especially his parents. He could reflect about himself over time, how he'd been in the past and what had changed. This was evident when he talked about the girlfriend he'd lost.

"Every time I talk to her, I care for her deeply. At the same time, I know how much she's hurt me. But it's interesting, everything we've shared and how I've matured since then, because then I thought I was so mature and was acting like an adult when I was really kind of idealizing her and idealizing the world. I think what I love the most [about her] is also what got us into trouble. She's able to get just enthralled with what she is doing and to leave anything that's bad out of it. She just ignores her pain. There are times when I feel bad about it. I gave her everything she could ask for, and it didn't work. I sort of resisted getting into another serious relationship, but I am going to college and hope to find something."

Jesse had developed a capacity to enter into the world of others and to see the world through their eyes while still maintaining his independence. The path his former girlfriend chose was very different from his, and he could see this. He was able to recognize what he needed and to get it for himself actively.

At times, when he suffered reverses in relationships or in sports or school, Jesse still got very down. But he said he managed through these times by reaching out to friends. "I'm really part of conversations," he said. "If I don't understand something, I'll ask questions. A lot of people just sit there and don't get it and don't say anything." He also recognized that when he was alone and uncertain, it brought back feelings similar to those he experienced when his mother died. By recognizing that link, he was able to get beyond it.

Jesse told me that he remembered a book from my office called the *Diagnostic and Statistical Manual of Mental Disorders,* a guidebook to mental illnesses. He and his guidance counselor had gone over it in detail, in particular the diagnosis of manic-depressive illness. She had explained that it was a biological illness, and this then became part of how Jesse understood, fundamentally, what had happened to his mother. But he had not been ready for that kind of explanation when he had been seeing me, no matter how readily available it had been during that time. This too showed how understanding could only come at his pace, when he was ready for it and when his capacity for reflection had developed enough to understand complex constructs like mental illness. As we've noted many times, this is true for almost all children struggling to make sense of mental illness.

I reminded Jesse of our basketball sessions, and how I tried to get him to accept the fact that if he didn't do well in a particular game, that's all it was. It was not something about the loss of his mother or his value as a human being. He nodded but then said, "Yes, we talked about that. But then I would go home and practice a crossover dribble for four hours after our sessions to get it right." Again, Jesse put his own stamp on things. His intense will to win did not go away because he understood that he was not responsible for his mother's death. That understanding just changed what winning meant. He knew he had too much riding on winning. Winning meant being able to deal with his mother's death, and losing meant descending into an abyss.

I don't think people ever stop grieving over immense losses or questioning themselves at times, and this was true for Jesse. He acknowledged that even at eighteen, he still had lingering doubts about his mother's death. "It was tough. There is still part of me that won't completely accept the explanation. Manic depression in terms of huge mood swings. I still think if I'd gone that day and made her smile, would that have made this incredible happiness instead of depression? Could I have prevented it? Yes, possibly for that day. Then could things have gotten better? Yes, possibly. To an extent, I still feel that, despite the fact that everyone has told me with logic that it's not like that."

Jesse could observe himself objectively. He commented with some humor, but also with insight, on certain things he did that drove his father crazy. At the same time, he expressed a deep affection for Arthur and for Sarah.

No one is fully formed at eighteen, and the issue of being intimate with someone else and risking another overwhelming loss will challenge Jesse again. He may, at some point, seek counseling again; then again, he may not. But in terms of prevention and resilience, he has made it through the crucial developmental stages. This leaves him in a much stronger position to deal with whatever comes. His accomplishments in the outside world, and in mastering the loss of his mother, give him a much firmer foundation to face whatever he encounters. All along the way, his father and stepmother shared in those accomplishments.

Jesse had to make sense of his mother's death because she was no longer there. How he did that changed dramatically over time. Though the information that he was not to blame and not guilty had been there almost from the weeks after she died, he could only come to believe it himself gradually, after he tested it out again and again.

As the years went on, Jesse became more and more the author of the questions. He asked people about his mother. He asked his sister. He asked his friends and many of his friends' parents who knew his mother and had tried to figure her out. He was very intense in the way he manifested his grief and in the way he challenged those around him. In this sense, his developmental task was facing loneliness, the fear of reliving the bereavement, even perhaps being angry at his mother and worrying that he had killed her. What got Jesse through was the evolution of his understanding. This occurred not within himself alone, but through a set of conversations in which he checked out, tried out, and thought through these issues at each developmental stage, involving me, his parents, his friends, and sometimes even his friends' parents.

Jesse's understanding taught me how often understanding is a vital, interactive process. This is above all what needs to be fostered, what the long-term aim of breaking the silence is. Each time Jesse talked about his experience, it helped him through a particular stage, and some of what he learned stayed with him. This eventually led us both to an understanding that he could go ahead with his own life. The act of asking questions and then making sense of things for himself — being the author of his own story — gave him control over what had happened. But it did not give him control because there was a final answer. Making sense for himself became a process that he could use as he needed, not just in dealing with his mother's death, but in dealing with whatever else life might hand him.

Eleven

When Children Succumb to Depression

Despite the best intentions of parents, open communication, community engagement, and the other steps we recommend for promoting resilience are not magic amulets that can guarantee protection for all children.

Children can become depressed. But although the occurrence of a serious depression in a child is a profoundly wrenching and disruptive event, the same principles apply: Start at the beginning and get treatment, use the knowledge base to guide recovery, and gradually make sense of it together.

When a loved one becomes depressed, parents, like their children, are extremely prone to feeling guilty, blaming themselves, and believing that they should have done something differently. But we know now that to blame family patterns as the cause of childhood depression is unscientific and nonsensical; in fact, it contributes to the difficulties families experience. This has come home to me again and again as I have simultaneously had my own children go through the period of highest risk for childhood depression, ages fourteen to twenty-three, and seen many of my friends' and my acquaintances' children struggle with depression, some of them even being hospitalized on the service I run at Children's Hospital. In many of these families, depression has truly struck completely without warning.

"Having a child hospitalized with a depression takes all of your time, all of your energy, and all of your focus," one mother commented to me after her daughter had been hospitalized out of the blue for a suicide attempt. "You know, the first day our daughter was in the hospital, we were shell-shocked, could barely move." Only gradually does one put one's life back in order. When a child is in the hospital, the need to ask questions, to advocate, to constantly force the issue of how plans will be made, is all-important. Only gradually, after the immediate concerns were taken care of, could this mother begin to deal with her hurt, rage, sense of loss, and complete confusion about her daughter's unexpected suicide attempt. The steps along the way to recovery were first adjusting to the ward, then readjusting to her daughter's being home and her gradual reentry into school, and then coping with a continuous back-and-forth, heart-in-the-throat agony about whether she would attempt suicide again.

Just like the journey of many children to understand their parents' illness (or of many spouses or of many sufferers themselves), the journey for parents of a depressed child takes place over time. First, families need to take care of the child's immediate needs. This may mean an emergency evaluation. It may mean a hospitalization or the initiation of an active outpatient evaluation and treatment. And just as in dealing with depression in a spouse or in a parent, feelings will be stored up that need eventually to be acknowledged but cannot be talked about immediately: loss, hurt, pain, anger, sometimes a sense of betrayal, and often great confusion about what will happen. But like adult depression, childhood depression is a treatable illness. With good treatment, the vast majority of children recover.

Being prepared for depression also helps. As we talked with families over time, many said that knowing what depression was, and that their youngsters had had a good and positive interview with one of us, was very important in demystifying treatment for those who later became depressed. Prior discussion made the process of getting help seem a normal and natural response, like getting help for any other medical condition.

Afterward, families come out on the other side, able to see that the experience of depression in their children can become a part of a family's experience that won't overwhelm the other parts of their story. But children who recover from depression must make sense of it for themselves, place it in the larger context of their friends, their communities, and their faiths. They can make their understanding a part of who they are, and they can use what they have learned as they face the future.

Charlie: From Multiple Problems to Multiple Strengths

I had known Charlie off and on from fourth grade, when his mother had brought him to me after her acrimonious divorce from his father. He lived with his mother primarily and had regular scheduled visits with his father, but they were quite circumscribed. His older sister and brother also lived with the mother, though one was often away at school.

Charlie, by his mother's report, had some trouble in his peer relationships. Being the youngest and being from a separated family, he didn't have the same neighborhood circle of friends that many other kids had. At times, Charlie could appear standoffish, even arrogant, partly because of his unusual verbal ability.

From the beginning of our time together, Charlie showed both extraordinary strengths and vulnerabilities. He was smart, and had a wonderful sense of humor, a capacity to reflect, and a determination to get things done. He had a great interest in abstractions and loved to play computer games, which he found soothing. He also was an avid collector of baseball cards and had an extraordinarily detailed cataloguing system for them.

He watched me very closely and, in fact, seemed to enjoy the probing questions I asked from time to time about his feelings or his reactions to me.

Gradually, as he became more confident and as he had success in school, his problems resolved themselves and I saw him much less frequently. In his early teens, however, Charlie's difficulties increasingly returned. He went through puberty somewhat later than other boys and was acutely worried about his thinness. Despite numerous attempts, he wasn't able to gain weight. He missed his brother, who was living abroad. His mother was remaking her life and was involved in a new relationship. She sold the house they had lived in and he became a nomad, staying in a variety of condominiums and apartments until the family resettled. He started high school in an environment very different from his grammar school, and while in the first year he did well, he was somewhat overwhelmed. As time went on, though still living with his mother, he reconciled with his father and spent considerable time at his house. During his first year in high school, Charlie was active in sports and found physical exercise rewarding, but as high school went on and he felt less competitive, he gave it up. Charlie began to experience more and more periods of loneliness and sadness, and he began playing computer games without end, sometimes staying up until two or three in the morning. As a result, he wasn't able to get much done during the day. He also had difficulty sleeping.

His parents continued to have major battles around finances. As their animosity increased, so did Charlie's withdrawal. He later realized that computer games had become an addiction. His mother tried to set limits, but his compulsion kept recurring and he began to become more and more depressed.

In the bland language of clinicians, Charlie had many of the risk factors for childhood depression I described in chapter 6. His difficulties were exacerbated by the onset of adolescence, by going to a new school, which disrupted his friendships, and by his parents' increased acrimony.

By his junior year, Charlie began to experience many of the symptoms of depression all at once, and I began to see him more regularly. Gradually, he met the full criteria for a major depression. He began to ask questions about whether life was worth living. He had marked difficulty sleeping. He withdrew from friends.

What was it like for him? Charlie kept a journal and shared some of it with me: "I have to constantly prove to other people that I'm smart, because being smart is the only tool I have to defend and achieve. I am otherwise repulsive. Too thin, big nose, ugly haircut, skinny, bad posture, weird. People think I'm queer. Sometimes I wish I were, because no girl has interest in me. Or the one that does have an interest in me I find repulsive. I am a physical reject; therefore, all people I can date must be equally repulsive or worse. My friends don't invite me anywhere. I'm not actively denied admission to get together or anything; I'm not invited.

"Maybe, just maybe, after this Friday, everything will be better. No, really. Everything will have a nice golden sheen on it. I'll suddenly gain weight. Girls will find me attractive. I'll have sex. I'll dance. I'll play guitar. I'll start reading. I'll be the big man on campus. No, wait. I'll still be a loser. Everyone will still push me around. My friends will still ignore me. Girls will still ignore me or just be repulsed. My humor won't change. I'll still be condescending. I'll still be sarcastic. I won't think before I speak."

Charlie was thoughtful and capable when he wasn't depressed. And while there certainly were some rough incidents with friends, his intense, vicious self-criticism was mainly a part of his depression. Charlie went on to describe being angry and hopeless, and then wrote *unhappy* over a hundred times. Over the months that followed, his mood went up and down depending on his grades, and he raged against the unfairness of the school's grading system. Some of the school's policies were in fact not entirely fair, but he couldn't see his way beyond it.

At the worst time, he wrote, "My eyes grazed across the room, blurred with tears, frustration, and suppressed panic. My eyes are blurred, the material world is blurred, and the only sight with any integrity is the inward sight. My ruminations, creations, speeches, fantasies, rages, and sorrows are more real than the daily humming of routine, interspersed with moments of epiphany, regret, and pain. But I cry from my thoughts and cringe more often from my inward sight than physical torment. My fingers are slow and heavy now. I am wheezing in my pathetic attempt at crying. I feel robbed of my ability to really have my tears. I can only hyperventilate and cough and squeeze tears from my eyes, and suffocate because my nose feels like it's full of cotton."

In short, while Charlie looked not very different than he always had to his classmates, he suffered a silent agony. His parents, both thoughtful teachers, strongly supported therapy and medication. He and I began to work even more actively together. We met weekly and focused on how he could change things in his life. I tried him on one SSRI and then another. As is often the case, it took many months, as well as a consultation with a senior child pharmacologist, before we found a combination of sleeping medications and antidepressants that worked for him.

I met with his parents and, despite their differences, they were both very committed to his recovery. Once they realized that he was depressed, they found common ground in trying to help him and resolved to not put him in the middle of their disputes, so that particular stress was relieved for him.

Over a period of several months, he reengaged with friends and, although he didn't take up sports again, he took up a new form of Brazilian dancing that was very active. He also came to understand his need to avoid computer games.

Charlie had a long-standing interest in meditation and used this to help himself. He found a guide in meditation, which complemented and supported both his recovery and my work with him. All these things together enabled him to emerge gradually from his depression.

Despite continued acrimony between them, his parents came together around the issue of paying for Charlie's college. When the four of us met together, Charlie told me that it was the first time in ten years that they'd been in a room together and had been able to discuss financial issues. Charlie chose a university far from home and far from the culture in which he'd grown up, and he thrived there, pursuing interests in science, the environment, and alternative healing.

Charlie continued to keep a journal as he struggled to make sense of what the depression meant. Another part of his journey was to try to understand why his parents got divorced and what his role in this was. In fact, he talked with each of them at length about these issues, sometimes with me present and sometimes with them alone. In the process, he acknowledged what he had lost, but he also came to see that he was not to blame.

As time went on, Charlie's journal included far more than self-recrimination. It was another way he kept track of *all* of his history, both the good and the bad. There was great concern in his family about his going to another city for college and the possibility of suicide if he became depressed, but I was able to allay the parents' fears by working directly with him and by helping to plan for different eventualities.

We remained in touch years afterward, and I was always available to him on an emergency basis. He maintained his interest in meditation and eventually became an expert, using the technique both to relax and get a deeper sense of himself. In short, his recovery from depression involved many different parts of himself and the integration of many different strategies.

He continued on antidepressants, both for sleep and for depression, for a number of years and then, after careful consideration of the risks and benefits, chose a period of time off medication.

Charlie also reconnected with the usual pursuits of those his age: doing well in college, having fun, and thinking about what he wanted to do with his life. Profoundly affected by his own struggles, he was drawn to helping others and he became a coach for younger people. He changed his diet substantially and took up a much more rigorous exercise regime. He located himself within the religious and ethical traditions of his family, but chose a different though related course, self-consciously proud of that.

Charlie's strengths were substantial, and it was clear that both parents loved him dearly and that he was at the center of their lives. His depression was not the result of any one occurrence, but the way different things built up. His recovery required every bit of his energy — all of who he was — but it came through building on his strengths and resiliencies. His long-term relationships with his sister and brother, with family friends, and, despite the difficulties, with his parents were also very important. Certainly, at various points he and I worked well together and the various different treatments helped. His parents found common ground, both in being very sympathetic and supportive when they realized he was depressed and in helping him move on. As a result of his asking questions and reflecting, he was able to understand his depression, put it behind him, and move on.

Rebecca: Coping with a Family History of Severe Depression

At fourteen, Rebecca was tall, thin, and dramatic, with orange hair. When we first talked to her, she was sobbing and scared because of what was going on at home. On the positive side, she was very connected to others and willing to talk about anything and everything with her close friends, and even with adults outside the family. From the beginning, Rebecca could put her worry about her mother and herself into words, rather than keeping feelings inside.

Rebecca's parents, Linda and Alexander, both wrestled with depression. In addition, Rebecca's father had been having an affair with a younger woman, and her mother had recently discovered it.

For Rebecca's mother, this betrayal had reawakened memories from her own abusive and neglectful home and contributed not only to depression, but also to a severe posttraumatic stress disorder. At the time of our meeting, Linda had only recently been discharged from a psychiatric hospital after episodes of self-mutilation. She was in day treatment and was finding it hard to manage on a day-to-day basis.

Rebecca had heard her mother crying out at night and had seen her bruises. She wondered whether her father had caused them, when in fact they were due to her mother's banging herself against a wall. Linda, an artist, was frequently unable to stop sobbing when we talked to her. Linda and Alexander both had parents who were severely depressed. Both dreaded that they would repeat their parents' errors in their own marriage.

Despite this very difficult beginning, the parents found some stability as they prepared to talk to Rebecca. The clinician who worked with her focused on explaining how people relive trauma, as well as depression. Both her mother and father were receiving treatment, and for these parents to help their daughter, they had to understand something of what they were trying to get away from — the abuse, neglect, and depression in their own histories — in order to have any chance of not blindly repeating it with Rebecca and not playing it out with each other. After many preparatory sessions, mother and father were able to talk to Rebecca and to her older brother, who had come home from college.

During the basic discussion about depression, both youngsters directed a lot of anger at their father. He had a history of being very short-tempered and domineering in conversations, so for his kids, even beginning to speak was difficult. The parents were able to recognize that they had neglected Rebecca because of their own difficulties. They also recognized that she needed to talk to someone outside of the family and found her a guidance counselor at school.

This started a gradual process in which both parents, in the midst of their own troubles and struggling with their own pasts, were able to unite in helping their daughter.

Rebecca was positive about the first conversation because it allowed the family in general and her in particular to recognize that people can't simply snap out of depression. Despite the undeniable ravages of both parents' illness, it had never been talked about at all. But with the meeting, as Rebecca said, "At least it all came out in the open."

In the year thereafter, Linda and Alexander experienced ups and downs but were less angry and abusive toward each other. Alexander's depression gradually stabilized. Like so many others, Linda tried a variety of different SSRIs and other medications, and it was not until some two years later that they found a medication that helped. Her mood stabilized, and gradually the family began to devote more attention to protecting Rebecca.

Rebecca kept a journal describing how her understanding of her parents' illness was not just her experience with them, but also very much related to her own experience. Her journey reflected a gradual maturing of who she was in relation to them and her growing independence from them.

Rebecca's school advisers understood the depression in both parents and helped her cope, both by providing a counselor and by emphasizing that what was going on with her parents was not her fault. She and her brother also found a new common bond and talked regularly. In the year following the initial conversation, she began to see herself as less dominated by the mood changes and upheavals in her family. As she put it, "I feel like I'm beginning to get away."

At fifteen, she could see herself learning to "cool it," meaning that she had ways of calming herself down no matter what her parents were doing. Unfortunately, her recovery was thrown off by a severe shoulder injury that kept her from competing in sports. She had been a superb athlete and had been about to enter the Junior Olympics.

By the time she was sixteen, she herself was wrestling with depression, brought on largely by medical treatments and not being able to compete athletically. She received a series of active interventions, including medication and therapy for her depression, and she talked with many people about what she was going through. As she gradually recovered from her depression, she struggled to make sense of it. And her understanding of herself and her own depression further helped her understand her parents' experience.

A year later, at seventeen, she could begin to reflect about who she was in relation to her parents. She said that her father was very insecure and, "It's not up to me to fix it. That's a dangerous place to be. It sets me up for failure. I do the little things I can."

At eighteen, she observed, "I'm not so judgmental about my parents. I know what it's like to be depressed. I've learned something about the self-hatred that goes along with it."

As she prepared to go to college, she reflected that she needed to put depression behind her. She said, "It's no one's fault. I don't know what's going on. I don't want to know. It's partly chemical and it's partly who they are."

After a year of some success at college, a gradual recovery from her illness, and an awareness that she had undergone a depression, she was more empathic. She had recently broken up with her boyfriend, and that enabled her to say, "I know what it's like to be really sad. I've had such feelings myself and I can talk more easily about it."

For Rebecca, understanding herself, particularly in relation to her own depression and the risks she faced, left her reflective, mature, and able to move on.

Twelve

Facing the Threat of Suicide

C ertainly, the most acute mental health crisis any family will face is the threat of a loved one committing suicide.

Lisa Petrocelli: Facing a Parent's Threats of Suicide

The Petrocellis were the first family I worked with in depth, the first family introduced in this book. The mother, Katherine, was plagued for years by recurring episodes of sadness and irritability, continued to be obsessed with ending her life, and even at times sliced her arms with a knife.

When I first saw Lisa, the middle child of three, she was thirteen, bubbly, friendly, and very much a teenager, moving from subject to subject quickly. Her mother had had the onset of a debilitating depression two years earlier. Lisa was completely confused by her mother's illness. A doctor's attempt to explain it to her when her mother was in the hospital had failed.

Lisa was the most reflective of the three children and wanted very much to know what was going on with her mother. She had voiced in our first interview the fear that her mother would commit suicide, as well as the fear that talking with her mother would put ideas in her mother's head. She alone in the family remembered what had led to her mother's decline — Katherine's giving an anniversary party at Christmas for her parents. Her reflections about how she dealt with her mother's recurrent suicidal urges show how young people gradually deal with such worries over time.

After the long struggle to have the family meeting I described in the first chapter, and the powerful conversation that occurred, her children were able to move on despite Katherine's depression.

I saw Lisa again much later, when she was a mature young woman preparing for a career in counseling. She had spent a lot of time reflecting on who she was and what had happened. She had also talked frequently with her father about how to care for her mother and was very close to everyone in her family. Her religious faith was vital to her, and the family had continued to celebrate holidays and other events together. She asked to see the interview of herself at thirteen, which I had kept, and she read it carefully. She said she was amazed at how different she was. In recalling the family session, she was still surprised at the behavior of her brother — his anger and denial — but it also brought back images of her mother.

The long day-to-day struggles were organized around a few vivid memories. The first was her mother's initial hospitalization, made necessary by the threat of suicide when Lisa was twelve. As Lisa said, "It was put to us: 'Your mother is going to the hospital because she needs a rest.' Rest from what? What is she resting from? Can't she rest here? I'll never forget helping her pack up things, and saying, 'Why can't you rest here?' How maddening it must have been for my parents. There was no such thing as a question I wasn't going to ask, ever."

On the day her mother agreed to be hospitalized, she took Lisa to the basement and showed her how to do the wash — how to keep the whites separate from the colors, and how to run the machine. Katherine was a meticulous housekeeper, and Katherine's mother was also a meticulous housekeeper. Katherine attached a list of instructions to the wall that is there to this day. Lisa has gone over that memory again and again, one that symbolizes her mother's struggle to hold on to the one routine that might endure in the midst of the breakdown, a concrete physical act that represented her caring for the family, that gave order to the chaos she was experiencing, that perhaps also represented the hope that her daughter could carry on. But for Lisa it was completely confusing. What she remembered was how disorganized her mother had been, and thinking that what her mother was doing made little sense, that doing the wash was not the issue.

Lisa could not stand being lied to and knew that there was more to the story of her mother's illness than they had been told. She also struggled with the fact that her mother could say things and mean them, and yet they could turn out not to be true.

Part of the reason the Petrocellis were so committed to talking together was simply to make sense of what was going on. Both the children and the parents were very confused and troubled. Lisa remembered the meeting very clearly. She said that she and her siblings found the family meeting very helpful in providing a structure for the chaos, and believed that talking enabled the family to come together again. "I think it is pretty amazing that any family could sit down and have the conversation we did and have that process continue." Like many families, they talked again and again about the illness as it recurred.

Lisa helped me understand how intense the need to make sense of things is for youngsters and how the need continues. Like those of many other young people I've described, her questions drove the family to keep talking. "The opportunity [to talk] was there. I know I seized it for myself. The door opened, and it has continued to be open between my parents and me about what's going on. It's going to be disruptive either way for a family, whether you are talking or not talking, but at least when you are talking, there's a kind of understanding about why it is disruptive and that it's not your fault. Christmas might not feel like Christmas, but by talking, I was still connected to my family during that time. I feel connected rather than that 'there's something going on and I'm disconnected.' Every family is different. We were a family and very much operated as one. We are still a close family that has its ups and downs. We see each other and we go to church together. My siblings and I were comforted to know that it could be talked about and then we could support each other."

Lisa remained very close to her brother and sister as she grew older, and, as she put it, "being on the same page helped."

Finding the suicide note in her mother's car began a long period for Lisa of being concerned about Katherine's safety. Katherine remembered writing the note on one of her drives along the coast and sent her husband to try to retrieve it, but it turned up when the car was being repaired.

Over the months that followed the family meeting, Katherine would have inexplicable, unpredictable episodes of depression. "She would leave in the middle of the night and not come back," Lisa said. "There were these long car rides when we simply didn't know where she was. And, of course, there was constant worry about suicide.

"Sometimes she'd come up and kiss us and leave, and then call from a pay phone somewhere. She'd just say, 'I'm okay.' There were some nights when there was no call, and she was just away."

Once, when Katherine had left, Lisa and her sister were sent to a neighbor's camp in New Hampshire. They didn't want to go, but they were made to. She worried constantly that her mother would die while she was away.

She also remembered more dramatic moments that happened right in front of her. Once, she heard screaming and ran downstairs to find her mother and father struggling and her mother trying to leave with a purse full of pills.

During the years after Katherine's first hospitalization, Lisa observed that trying to take care of her mother made her more serious and much more focused than other kids. "After that summer, I changed," she said. "It was so much a fight to keep her alive, in retrospect, that I thank my mother for those things because it kept me from superficial things. I would say to myself, 'This is just not important, all that matters is my mother's life.'"

With that serious focus came isolation, not from being with other kids, but from talking with them about what was going on in the family. "Except for one friend, I withdrew that summer, and then the next fall I started in a new school. I had friends, but there was a lapse in what I told them. In college, I had very good friends, but I remember thinking that I had been lying and hadn't had close friends in those early years of high school because of what had happened. I just didn't go out with friends."

Lisa emphasized that being told she was not guilty or to blame was an important component in being able to move on. However, it took a long time to believe it. As she said, "You asked all those questions about whether I felt responsible or guilty, and of course I said no, but I kind of lied. I said, 'I don't think it is me,' but I really did think, at the time, that it was me, and I think my siblings did too. The less certain things are, the more kids attribute it to something within them. If it is not attributable to anything else, if it is not explained, they are going to attribute it to themselves."

Lisa went on to say, "You know, I think it's like divorce for kids — 'It must be something I'm doing' — so I think it is really important to talk about, as hard as that may be. Maybe you don't have an explanation for what is happening. But things happen for a reason. Kids want to know what the reason is. If you don't provide one, they are going to come up with one of their own, which is probably going to be even more devastating than the real reason."

Again and again, Lisa faced the stark conflict between her mother's wish to die and her own wish to save her. "I'd tell her how much I loved her. I'll never forget this going through my head: 'If she knows how much I love her, she won't kill herself, because obviously she means the world to me.' I know that I was kind of naive. I was going to try to save the world. I was going to try to save

her. All through high school, I wrote down how much she meant
to me."

As she reflected on her constant interchange with her mother,
she said, "It gave me some kind of control, to know how she was.
I'd ask her, and if she felt safe enough to tell me she was feeling suicidal, I'd tell my dad, and he would say, 'If Mom says this, we've got
to make a phone call.'

"Being educated makes you feel comfortable enough to ask the
horrible questions. Not only to have the information but to feel
you have a system of support, so you know what to do with it."

Lisa spoke for many children when she talked about an important component of being able to separate. "The only way I can
really come to peace is to know that everything was done for her, so
I really feel that when she had been suffering or whatever, I never
have to look back and say, 'There is something more I could have
done.'" An essential part of moving on for almost all families was
the belief that good, even excellent care was being provided. This
was especially true during those many times when the path to
recovery was unclear and children or others in the family had to
simply make their peace with what was, whether there was a recovery or an episode of depression continued unabated, and, above all,
when there was a continuing threat of suicide.

Sometimes Lisa was there when life and death hung in the balance. Once, she had come home from college, and the family was
called to her mother's doctor's office on a Sunday. "We went to her
psychologist with her for an emergency meeting. She tried, actually, to jump out of the window. She wouldn't make a contract for
safety, and so they called the police, and she had to go into the hospital. They had to hold her back from jumping out the window. It
was so real. I just couldn't control her. I just couldn't deny it, like
reality hit me, that it was going to happen. Here I was in her face
saying, 'But I love you,' and she was saying, 'I don't care, it doesn't

matter.' Sometime later, as she recovered, she said, 'I couldn't hear you, I really couldn't. I was so irrational.'

"She said, 'I'm going to kill myself, you know. It's just for me.' I realized it didn't have anything to do with me. In a perverted but true sense, I could see her point. It was selfish of me. I realized that before, I was asking her to live for me rather than to live for herself. I'd say, 'But Mom, when you do this, you're happy,' or whatever. But the point is, she was not rational, and gradually I realized that I would do what I had to do. I would do it my way, and she was not me. And maybe she would have to kill herself. Maybe that was her only way.

"I remember one time as I was driving back home after I'd visited her in the hospital. She couldn't contract her safety for one hour, let alone one day, and I was thinking, 'I may really lose her to this, not because I didn't do everything I could, but because she is who she is.' You can only do so much and be responsible for it so much. I can control my own life. I cannot control someone else's life. I used to think I was in control of whether she lived or died, and I'm not. I've come to terms with the fact that I am not. And if I lose her, it is not because I haven't tried. Of course, it's easier to say that because it hasn't happened, but I'm not in control of whether she takes her own life. I can't be. I can't feel bad. I'm not always physically there, not emotionally there."

Lisa's story is of an impossibly difficult illness, but also of remarkable strength. After a period in high school when she didn't talk to anyone, she had many friends in college, including several with whom she spoke about her mother. She remained very close to her siblings.

Her story illustrates a point that runs throughout the accounts of families. When one parent is impaired and the other steps forward, it makes a huge difference. Whatever happens, when children are cared for in a nonacrimonious way, it greatly enhances their ability to move on. Lisa said of her father: "He is the unsung hero. I don't know why anybody would stick with anyone through all of this. His love for her is really deep. I don't know why he stayed. He loves her so much. He made that commitment to her and to the kids. I remember he was always there for me: when I talked to him about the letter I found, I talked to him about all the times my mother was feeling suicidal. He is amazing to keep the communication open and to say, 'You can talk to me about everything.'"

Lisa also mentioned how important it was to have found a doctor, who happened to be me, she could rely on and the family could rely on, one that she and they could call night or day. Several times over the years, she or her parents called me when they were concerned that Lisa might be entering a period of depression, including one time after her grandfather died. Each time, I evaluated the situation and found that she wasn't depressed, but left the way open if they needed me again.

In the studies of resilience, many have commented that youngsters make it through and they're strong, but they pay a price. At twenty-five, Lisa struggled with how to get close to men. She said that she spent so much time taking care of others that it was very hard to open up and let herself be taken care of. These were issues she did eventually go on to confront. This too involved acknowledging what was lost, but also what could be understood in time.

Dealing with the Threat of Suicide

Because suicide is so often a threat in those who face depression, I want to give you some sense of how clinicians deal with this emergency, to try to help you recognize suicidal thoughts in yourself and in your family members, and to outline what kind of care is needed.[1]

In the older studies done before good treatment was available, 15 percent of people with severe depressions died by their own hand. Suicide remains one of the leading causes of death for adolescents, and prevention of suicide needs much greater attention.[2] The most common diagnosis of those attempting or committing suicide is mood disorders, although substance abuse, problems in controlling impulses, and profound interpersonal difficulty are also important.

Two eloquent books have appeared recently on suicide: Kay Redfield Jamison's remarkable *Night Falls Fast,* an intertwining of the best available knowledge of suicide with her own struggles as a young person with thoughts of suicide, and Alvin F. Poussaint and Amy Alexander's impassioned work on suicide and depression in minorities, *Lay My Burden Down.* Both provide important resources in understanding this problem.[3]

The assessment of suicide is different from that for depression, but both proceed along similar lines. Comprehensive medical and psychiatric assessment of all possible diagnoses must be a part of the assessment of suicidal thoughts. These are the questions clinicians ask:

- *Do you feel that life is not worth living?*

- *Have you felt that your life is meaningless?*

- *Have you considered ending your own life?*

- *Are you considering it now?*

- *Have you made any specific plans to do so, and if so, what are the means?*

- *Have you made any attempts to actually kill yourself, and what were they?*

- *Do you feel now, today, in this moment, that you wish to kill yourself?*

The questions increase in specificity, and the more a sufferer answers "yes," the more worried a clinician becomes and the more he or she must consider hospitalization. In extreme cases hospitalization is mandated by law, even against the person's will, when an individual states a clear intent to attempt suicide. The only other conditions that are mandated in the same way are when someone is at risk to do violence to others or, for children particularly, when someone is threatened with violence. These also require emergency evaluation.

It is important to emphasize that although less common than the threat of suicide, in cases of depression, the threat of family violence always constitutes an emergency as well. The clinician must ask whether anyone is at risk for physical abuse and/or other violence and, if so, by law action must be taken to protect children — even if it means removing them from their parents' care. Although this is relatively infrequent in homes with depression, it's sadly all too common in my work at the hospital, particularly in these times of family chaos.

Just as with depression, of course, the assessment of suicidal thoughts takes place in the context of the events in a person's life. How often have the suicidal thoughts occurred? How long-standing is the wish to die? What are the recent life events? What else is going on in the person's life? What mental illness is the person suffering from?

The assessment of the potential for suicide depends on the depth of the doctor's or other responsible caregiver's relationship with the patient in pain. The clinician must make a judgment about the accuracy of the information (for example, if someone is telling the truth) and the strength of the patient's commitment to staying alive. The patient will often be asked to agree to a contract in which he or she promises, "I will not attempt suicide no matter how bad I feel, and if I feel completely out of control, I will get in touch with you, or those who work with you, night or day." If such a contract can be negotiated with both the patient and with those around him or her, then the patient can often be cared for at home. If not, he or she cannot be.

Obviously, the evidence of forethought, a history of prior suicide attempts, or a wish to keep thoughts and plans for suicide secret all heighten the risk of someone dying by his or her own hand. Clearly, a clinician and a patient's family must make sure the common instruments of suicide — guns, lethal medications, even knives — are removed. Above all, the doctor or other caregiver must secure a commitment from the patient not to attempt to die, and from the family a similar commitment that they know the seriousness of the situation, will support the patient and the plan night and day, and will recontact the caregiver if anything changes for the worse.

It was rare for us to encounter an acutely suicidal parent or child in our work, but knowing how to deal with it competently was an essential part of interacting with families with depression.

Thirteen

Making Peace and Moving On

P art of depression's insidious effect is to undermine your sense of pride and accomplishment. But as we've seen often, the commitment of parents to raising children is so central that being able to see and acknowledge positive changes in the development of your children over time is a vital part of recovery. This means coming to believe that you can be, and are, a capable parent despite depression. Similarly, seeing depression for what it is — a serious illness that need not destroy the capacity to be a good parent — is essential. Dealing with depression means that it becomes possible once again to see yourself as part of larger groups: communities, religious traditions, and, of course, above all, your family.

Religious faith was sustaining for many parents wrestling with depression and for many children, as the stories of Peter and his family, Jesse, and Lisa Petrocelli have shown. Many families found that integrating the experience of depression into larger frameworks of meaning was a crucial part of making peace and moving on. In this sense, they reaffirmed their original commitments and faith despite the ravages of severe recurrent depression.[1]

Part of this was seeing the family history in a new way. Part of it was fitting the ongoing struggle with depression into the context of other vital shared beliefs. For some, depression challenged what was most dear to them about themselves. Also, families struggled to come to grips with the ways they were raised and came to understand that some elements could be maintained but many had to change.

In this chapter, I discuss these and other important elements that help in making peace with depression and moving on. I focus first on how several couples learned to understand each other, including one I have described before, Len and Clair Rothstein. I then describe the reflections of one woman, Meg Smith, who was thrown into a particular closeness with her son because of the loss of her marriage, her job, and her community all at once. Her family situation and her parenting had to be dramatically different than the way she was raised, but she also had to figure out her connection to the family she came from. Finally, I present the story of Liz and Henry as they and their son struggled with and made peace with her very difficult illness.

Ann and Rick Cartwright: Understanding the World of the Other

For Ann Cartwright, understanding depression came slowly, and her appreciation of what she'd come to accomplish even more gradually.

When we first talked to Ann, she was an upbeat and careful woman who kept various aspects of her life in neat compartments. Married and the mother of two sons, she worked in sales and was very reluctant to let others know about her depression. Even within herself, she had trouble acknowledging it. "Very few people know," she said. "I've not told my mother because it would be an additional worry to a lady in her seventies, even though she's been treated for depression herself. I could count on my ten fingers how many people I've told."

After her first family conversation to break the silence about her illness, she felt that the air had been cleared. But part of Ann's journey would be learning to talk with people outside that inner circle.

After a year, she initiated a conversation with her mother. "I wanted to share with her in a way that she could understand, but I didn't want to concern her or burden her. She actually surprised me.

She said, 'I'm glad you shared this with me. I'm glad you're feeling better and that there's something to help you.'" Ann went on to say, "I'm glad I did it, because I would have hated to have died or have her die without having shared that. There was a bond there. Now there is a door open. If she ever feels depressed, she can talk to me."

This positive experience led her to talk about it to others outside of her home. At work one day, a coworker said, "I wish I could go home. If I had some Prozac, I'd take it." She responded, "You know, Prozac is not Valium. If it works, it helps people to be able to cope with their lives and it lifts their depression." He countered by saying, "I'm sure there have been times in my life when I've been depressed," and she answered, "I'm sure you have. Everybody has had brief episodes of feeling down." But she was able to clarify the distinction. "It's when you don't have a reason and you can't function, then it's a clinical depression."

As for her coworker's comment about popping Prozac, she said, "I feel really irritated when people say things like that, because Prozac has gotten a lot of press. I feel more secure because my therapist has talked about some of these things, and I see it as an illness. The medication is just like insulin for a diabetic. I came to believe it, and my husband heard it and he accepted it too."

A part of understanding and moving on is having a clear sense of the past and how the present is different. Looking back over the seven years we had been working with her, she said, "I think I was shutting myself off from my husband rather than dealing with how I was feeling or talking to him. I just kind of hoped things would get better by themselves and that he wouldn't notice that everything was in disarray, and I thought, 'My God, what have I done this day?' Obviously, that didn't work very well.

"We did think about separating, and Rick said, 'I honestly believe if we didn't have the children we might just decide to separate right now. I feel that we have grown so far apart, and maybe we should never have gotten married.' That had a chilling effect on me, but it didn't surprise me, because I was feeling kind of the same way . . . although I hated to admit it.

"We lived in the same house, but not necessarily in the same room. There wasn't anything antagonistic or angry about it. Being left out made him feel worse in a way, because I was dealing with the depression. I couldn't even consider dealing with our relationship. I knew in part of my head it just wasn't going well. I just sort of figured it would somehow work itself out.

"Initially I felt very defensive because I perceived, and maybe incorrectly, that he wasn't going to understand what I was going to say to him. In the beginning, I thought there was no way I could make him understand what I was feeling without sounding foolish. As we began to talk about it, I think my husband thought way down deep, 'Well, if she really wanted to do this or that, she would get up and do it. She has more control over this than she's letting on.'"

Part of Ann believed the same thing — that she should have been more in control. As she came to believe that "lack of will power" was not an adequate explanation, so did Rick. "He believed what I was telling him. I wasn't so insistent upon hammering him with the information. I think he came to believe [my depression] was real. I felt better." She particularly appreciated working with us because having a third party in the room when she talked to her husband made it feel safer for her.

"It was a little shaky at first because, despite everything, there is still a tiny part of me that thinks, Could I be allowing myself to be more fatigued as an excuse? Would I rather stay in bed than deal with life because I'm being lazy? I knew that I wasn't feeling as good as I wanted to, so there was a little bit of walking on tiptoes. I think as time has gone by, he's seen some change because medication and therapy have helped.

"It was easier to relate rather than just saying, 'I couldn't get up this morning.' I could be more positive about it. Even through the depression, I continued maintaining a good rapport with our children. I suspect that Rick was feeling unloved and uncared for, but he saw me still attending our sons in the same way that I always had."

As their relationship got back on track, Ann learned to see the world through Rick's eyes. "I realized that he was unhappy. He didn't know what was going on. It was very discouraging for him to come home from work and find out that I had done almost nothing around the house. Dinner was something that was thrown together, I was still tired, and I had barely made a dent in any kind of work. That really got him down. By the time we were done saying what we had to say to each other, we kind of felt like we were back on the right track again and that we could go forward from there.

"One of the things I learned was that he didn't know how to react to the situation in terms of balancing or unbalancing me if I was being a little bit fragile. He probably felt a little bit in left field, not really knowing what was going on inside me. I think he has suffered a fair amount. I think learning to talk about it gives him a better understanding.

"The other thing that I do very well, as my therapist says, is bury my head in the sand. If I don't look at something, maybe it will go away. I know that I'm not quite right when I'm letting the house go. I know that I'm wasting a lot of time. I know that I'm playing too much solitaire. Now my therapist talks to me, and I know I have to talk about it. That's part of the resolution. Certainly, if it had persisted or gotten worse, I would have spoken to somebody, but [Rick and I] were able to talk about it."

Many of the families we worked with had the same experience that Ann did as first they mastered depression within the family, then talked about it outside of the family, and eventually found a whole new community of support. "The more I talked about it, the more I found out that there were many people who shared this same experience or knew someone who did. My best friend is being newly treated for depression and she's been very supportive of me over all these years."

Ann and her husband returned again and again to the ways of talking about depression that they had learned in the initial family meeting. "It's hard to imagine now what life would have been like if we'd not shared this," she said. "Talking about it is like riding a bicycle. It's something you don't forget. It's still there whether you use it or not. It helped me alleviate my concerns about my two sons — stepping into it and learning it together."

A New Understanding and a New Closeness

Like the Cartwrights, many families, through understanding depression, develop an unusual closeness. As one woman said about her husband some years after they'd begun to talk, "You know, I get pretty wrapped up in myself. I've been more sensitive in the last two years about how he's feeling. He got down for a reason and I realized that he didn't always have to be supporting me. He needed me too, and that was a good thing. When you're depressed, you're really into yourself. Everything is bad. When I started thinking that he needed me, that was a good thing. We talked about him being aware of me and suddenly I was aware of him. My husband understands it's a part of who I am — not like a cancer that can be cut out. Learning to talk together put the cards on the table for everyone to look at. When I was feeling very bad, learning to understand this, with your help, gave me hope that I would eventually get better."

Although for some families there are clear and dramatic awakenings, for many, if not most, there is a gradual awareness of the slow but real and important change.

In reflecting back, one man commented about his wife, "There's a depressive overlay that affects the way she looks at life. Everyone's had to deal with it. Talking about it helped me understand the subtle ways depression has affected our family. I think talking it through has increased my awareness and my sensitivity. Hopefully, my gestures of support are a little more consistent and I'm not as quick to withdraw from her when she withdraws. I'm aware that it's a symptom of depression and not just a rejection of me. We're more aware of each other's feelings."

Another part of gradually learning how to deal with depression is recognizing the limits that it imposes and then learning to live with them. In this sense, it is like learning to live with any other chronic illness. A part of this process is putting those limits into words. As one mother told us, "I need to accept my diagnosis as not all or nothing. I can do something about it — set realistic goals, work with what I have. I feel less guilty about how I am. Talking is better than not talking, just like arthroscopic surgery is better than having general surgery."

This was also true in couples. As one woman put it, "It made me realize that my husband had an illness, but I didn't cause his illness and there was only so much help I could give him. I have to take care of myself. I can't really change things for him, but I certainly try to be as helpful as I can."

Part of healing for many families was no longer seeing depression as the central part of their lives, but as just one of the many things they had to deal with. Also, it was important that families, informed by their success in the past, had some confidence that they could deal with whatever would come in the future. "The longer time when he doesn't have an episode, I think about it less and I'm less concerned about the effects on my family," one mother explained.

Another, in thinking about the fears of illness in her child, said, "If my daughter became depressed, I think I'd have some background about what's going on and be able to talk to her about it. What I remember is that it is an illness that may not be cured but is aided by medication, communication, and therapy, and that it's not my fault."

Summing up, she said this of learning to talk in the family: "Communication increases. We've learned some things about each other we wouldn't have known. To me, this was always like some dark secret you can't talk about so much, but then, if you didn't talk about depression, so much had to be hidden about what someone was feeling. I don't feel like I have this cloth over my mouth. You can say what you need to say and it's not a problem."

She also emphasized the value of strategies, saying that they "gave me the ability to get help from my own children. Without learning to talk, I wouldn't have trusted my judgment. Meeting together as a family gave us some structure in which to talk about it. We're more open now because we put depression into a bigger picture. It's less frightening. I also learned how helpless the bottomless pit felt for me."

Integrations

For many, making peace with the disruptions wrought by depression involves integrating the catastrophe of depression into their most deeply held religious and cultural beliefs. Depression profoundly threatens such frameworks for many sufferers, precisely because it is inexplicable and because it taxes the very processes that allow one to be part of such traditions — a sense of self, of choice, of being able to relate to others, and seeing a continuity across generations, having an awareness of something larger than oneself. Part of this reintegration is seeing one's family history in a new way.

The Rothsteins helped us understand this when we went back to them a number of years after they had successfully broken the silence and asked them for their reflections. Len emphasized that he and Clair had to learn to be very different parents from their own. "Talking about things," he said, "is not the way I was raised."

Clair concurred. "I didn't get much guidance at all. Dad gave me some, but Mom was pretty much checked out the whole time."

Clair's experience was to try to get away from the way her mother had done things, but fear brought her back in line with her mother's approach. Clair developed a new feeling of compassion for her mother. "I think she may have been scared for a long, long time," she said. "She probably was scared about her health for years." Clair commented that she was raised in a very strict home, that she had a difficult time in high school, and that this was the time during which both her parents had died. Her way of grieving was to withdraw from the world. She began to get therapy in college because, as she said, "I can't look at the future without seeing black."

For his part, Len said that he didn't want to be the kind of father his father was — that he wanted to listen to his kids. Len's father was a minister, very different at home than in public, revered and beloved in the world, while at home tyrannical and controlling. Len remembered clearly an incident from childhood when they were playing Ping-Pong, and for the first time he beat his father, and his father became angry, as if this were a personal affront. At the time, Len remembered thinking, "This is not appropriate. I hope I can take pride in my kids' being better than me at something." Len acknowledged, however, that he shared some tendencies with his father, like a tendency to bottle things up and blow off steam over trivial issues.

When Len struggled with where to find himself in a religious context, he found meditation and walking in the woods to be very helpful. "Just simply me," he said, "the night and the woods, and the moon. I tried to become aware of something beyond me and ask for strength. It was a very healing moment, separating myself from everything else in my life, and the rest, and connecting with nature and my basic humanity."

Later on, Clair would get frightened when he went out without a light after dark, so he stopped doing it.

"Instead of being this ultrarational guy," Len said, "I was trying to open myself up to a different world. I had to go through a wholesale rejection of my childhood religion. I call myself a religious agnostic in the sense that, rationally, there's no reason to believe or disbelieve, but emotionally, I have religious needs that I can't rationalize away. I need those kinds of experiences — spiritual experiences. There's part of me that's powerfully affected by these situations, and I think that kind of praying to the spirit was part of it.

"I still get angry in church," Len went on, "when there's a situation when someone tells me what I should believe. My childhood anger and atheism roll back in full force." And yet, he married a very religious woman.

"My sister died three years ago," Clair told us. "That really knocked me faith-wise, because it just never occurred to me that something like that would happen. I guess I've come around to a little different understanding of God than I had before. I guess I really assumed that God was protecting us much more, and our families. After my sister died, it was just such a shock, and it's taken me two or three years to get back to the point of feeling even like I wasn't still mad at God for it happening. I do believe that God can be personally involved with your life, and I do believe that so-called coincidences can be more than coincidences. The church I believed in most allowed me to question a lot and still have faith. I don't call myself a Christian. I call myself a person on a journey following Christ. There are always struggles. I've gone through many different things with my faith. What I've come to is I really do believe it's an important part of my life, and I need some sense of comfort from feeling God as a part of my life."

Len's accommodation was very similar. "The skepticism grew as a result of seeing the disconnect between the message my dad was presenting in church on love, peace, and caring for everyone, and what I was experiencing at home — a man who was sometimes out of control, who brought his work, his feelings, and anger home and imposed them on his family, who wasn't reliable. There were some good experiences, but he was definitely inconsistent."

Like many others too, Len recognized that he could not do it alone, that raising children was a shared endeavor and even now, he needed a different perspective. "At a certain point, I realized that spirituality had to be a part of my life. I needed to have someone who did have a faith in my life, like my wife. I needed some balance in my life. I knew it was something I would never find on my own."

Meg Smith: Making Peace
When Everything Goes Wrong All at Once

Meg Smith endured the breakup of her marriage, her husband's alcoholism, dealing with his continued assaults against her in court, his trying to turn their son against her, and the loss of economic status. Gradually, through breaking the silence with her son, through therapy for a serious depression, which she had resisted recognizing, through disentangling herself from the constant harassment of her husband, and with our help, she made it through. After a series of false starts, she found a job, though she had to learn to live with much less money.

The first thing she was able to focus on was insuring that her son, Mario, age eight, was able to go on with his own pursuits. She experienced setbacks because her former husband constantly undermined her. In fact, at every turn he tried to thwart her, battling her in court, not showing up when he promised, not providing economic support, and generally harassing her. But at least she was given full legal control of the raising of her son, and as she and Mario together negotiated his entry into adolescence, she came to some peace.

Her initial fears were that given all the stresses she was under, she would fail. As she put it, "If Mario is not doing things to take care of himself, it all reflects on me. What's wrong with me as a mother? I'm not doing something right." She was able to see that her constant self-criticism was neither accurate nor effective; in fact, it might have had the opposite result of what she intended.

Meg had terrible self-doubt about her competence due to the sudden failure of the life she had created with her husband and what she and her high-achieving family expected of her. Poignantly, she said she depended even more on her son's doing well because so many other things had gone wrong. She wanted clear and demonstrable proof that he was all right. She even confessed that it was very scary to be responsible for him and said, "I failed him and have no one to blame but myself." But as she gradually let him be independent, she became more confident.

Meg gradually recognized that much of the roughness and uneasiness that Mario conveyed was not a direct result of her failure, but just part of the physical awkwardness and uneven development of a normal boy. Knowing that, she could both acknowledge his resources and begin to see him as separate. "For the first time," she said, "I had a new concept. I began to think of him as going on his own path, not because of me." And this too involved acknowledging the positive development toward independence in him.

Meg came to believe that she had learned a set of behaviors from her mother that included putting herself down and remaining silent when she should speak up. Meg's father was violent, and her mother saw her job as keeping the peace. Meg took on this role in her marriage, smoothing things over and making life as predictable as possible for her husband.

As she said, "You learn behaviors from your family, and when you love your family, it's hard to admit that the behaviors you're learning from them are not positive ones. I learned a lot about being a mother and a wife and a woman from my mother. You know, when my dad would yell, she'd run around the house and close the windows so the neighbors wouldn't hear. You learn that, and you just assume that everybody in the world is that way. She was loving, but she didn't think enough of herself to stand up to him. And you have trouble decoupling those behaviors."

Meg's memories of her parents, in her view, had led her into the marriage, a bad choice for her, one in which she was trying to fulfill family expectations, not look for what she needed. "I went into the marriage from the upbringing that says emotional problems can be controlled if you are strong, but I realize now it's not just a matter of mind." After she separated from her husband, she had to learn a whole new way to be as a parent, and her life and her raising her son were very different than she had expected. But it became all the more important that she could see the positives and take some pride in what she had struggled so much to accomplish.

As Mario moved into the early teen years, some five years after they began to talk together, she realized that her self-image had changed. "I was so afraid that all my weaknesses would show up in this kid. I came to see that I really was a good parent despite the depression. And I came to believe in my ability to communicate with Mario and to give him the guidance he needs at the time he needs it, and to feel in control a little bit of our household and how it operates."

She said that it made a huge difference to realize, after conversations with one of us, "You are a good mother. You have suffered an incredible loss. Everything that could go wrong went wrong. And you are still standing and you love your kid.

"I thought I had to be superwoman, and that he had suffered so much my job was to do it all and keep this stone face. And somebody said to me, 'If you live that way, you teach him to be that way,' which I didn't want to do.

"The fact that I can say that Mario is not depressed is evidence of what I have learned. I was always worried if he didn't want to play with someone — it meant something terrible was happening. I realize now that that is different from kids who never want to go out and see anyone. He's come to me occasionally and said, 'I don't want to go to church. I'm not sure I believe in God.' Before I started this project, that would really freak me out, but now I realize that is quite different from Mario feeling a sense of futility. It's just a reaction to one day. Another example is the way he reacts when something bad happens with his father. He is quiet and he doesn't want to talk about it. But it is very short-lived. An hour later, he's Mario. So I think I know some of the signs.

"But I think you caught it just in time. His age, my behavior. I felt I was such a loser as a mother, a loser as a woman. I hated where we lived. I hated our life. It was awful. We almost went down the tubes. And getting help and understanding each other made the difference.

"In the beginning, my whole shtick as a parent was that I should put my best face forward. He shouldn't know that I am hurting, and I thought I should cover it up. That was the way my mother tried to be. He would often say to me, 'Mom, why are you so sad? You seem so sad.' And finally I told him. I used to worry about whether I should tell Mario. I thought he didn't know. But being able to talk about it has made a huge difference. I had to address it because of the large impact it was having on my relationship with my son."

She also felt a greater empathy for others. "I tend not to look down my nose at anyone anymore, because I realize that your life is oftentimes kind of the luck of the draw."

Liz and Henry: Finding Faith Again

Liz and Henry struggled for years with Liz's depressions and her rarer episodes of mania. Once, when her son was young, she stood up in a school meeting in a neighboring town. She singled out a person from another country, an immigrant man who looked and spoke differently, and began to rant about the differences. Everyone present became quite upset, but no one, including the leader of the meeting, stopped her.

For the rest of that day and evening, she continued to be confused. The next day, she was hospitalized and eventually she was diagnosed as being in an episode of mania.

For years thereafter, she found it very difficult to go to school meetings. In fact, she stopped going to meetings of any kind. Sunday mornings were the worst mornings of the week. She'd stay in bed while her husband and son vainly struggled to get her up.

She was a thoughtful and intelligent woman who was aware of the toll her illness had taken on her. Because of the humiliation she'd suffered, because of the times when she had been completely overwhelmed by the mania and the longer intervals of depression, and because of the chronic fatigue associated with the side effects of the medications, she was fearful she wouldn't be able to do the usual things parents do.

"I am always either hypomanic or slightly depressed, at best," she observed. "I don't have any plateau between those two things. I'm either up or down. It's really continuous. The depression is the worst problem, and it gets worse in the winter without the sunlight, but that doesn't mean there aren't things, like if there is a big project at work, that will trigger me off to go into a hypomanic state. Maybe when it was more handicapping in the past, I tended to think of it as being this all-encompassing thing. But as I've broken away from it, I have it more in control. I start thinking, 'Okay, this is something I have to deal with, but I can put it in a compartment. I have gastroesophageal reflux disease, I have manic depression, I have high blood pressure; but that is not what defines me.'"

Making sense of her depression involved not just talking about what had happened at the school meeting or in front of her son and her husband, but also, as it turned out, confronting a long legacy of hiding illnesses in the family, inextricably intertwined with religion and her family's story. Her first episode of being really out of control and hearing voices occurred in her early twenties, when she was in college. It was misunderstood by her health care providers and not diagnosed as an episode of mania. The university health services at her prestigious college prescribed Valium — a mild antianxiety drug inappropriate for what she was experiencing, which was erratic behavior and visions. Her parents checked on her, and this led her to feel paranoid. After an intense struggle to regain control, she gradually recovered.

Liz took an impossibly difficult job after college working with disabled adults, in part because of her strong ethical conviction that she should help others. This demanding job, compounded by depression, led her to return to her parents' home. This homecoming led in turn to further conflicts with her parents, so after she regained her strength, she went back out on her own. The sequence of unrecognized depression and mania returned, however, and eventually she was hospitalized in a psychiatric unit, where her symptoms were recognized as a serious illness.

As so often happens, there was a family history of mania and depression, but no one had let on. This delayed the recognition of her true condition. Inadvertently, during her first hospitalization her grandmother told her that her father had experienced episodes of mania shortly after he graduated from college. Previously, she had been told he had been hospitalized for "a nervous breakdown," but no details had been provided. How long her father was in the hospital remained unknown, and the details of his treatment were unclear.

Liz's father was a well-regarded public figure, active in church, and led a very regimented life. In her view, this structure and rigidity were a part of how he had managed against the possibility of losing control and becoming ill again. As she tried to make sense of her childhood with him, she couldn't remember anything she would have called an episode of mania. She did remember that he had outbursts of temper — that he would get angry and then be unable to talk about anything for the rest of the day.

Her husband, Henry, had a similar story about hidden illness. When he was two and his twin brothers were four, his father ran away from the family and was never seen again. He also had an uncle who had returned from the Second World War only to spend the remainder of his life in a VA hospital. With the aid of hindsight, one suspects that both these cases were very likely serious mood disorders. Thus, Henry and Liz struggled against a complicated backdrop. They had to overcome the family biases against talking while dealing with their own recognition that a number of close relatives probably had struggled with the same illness.

As they began with our help to try to make sense of the illness for their twelve-year-old son, Jamie, their immediate focus was the marital battles he had witnessed. Liz described herself as a screamer when she was ill. Much to her shame, she knew she could become verbally abusive to her husband and her son. Sometimes she even threw or broke things. The violent talk and erratic behavior were very frightening to all of them. She wanted to be loving and caring toward her son, but her illness made her the opposite. The episodes threatened the very core of who she was and what she held most dear.

As they began to explain things to their son, Liz and Henry simultaneously planned ways to avoid further verbal confrontations. Like many couples, they found common ground in seeking a different kind of family experience, a future different from their past. Following the same sequence as the families described before, they gradually made progress. The immediate focus on avoiding confrontations provided some relief to Jamie. Henry was able to connect Liz's illness to erratic behaviors, like losing his temper, that Jamie had seen in his grandfather, and to explain both as biological illnesses. Both Liz and Henry worked to enhance Jamie's resilience, in particular recognizing the importance of outside activities and relationships. In part, perhaps because their own childhoods had been so devoid of attempts to build friendships, they made special efforts. Although she didn't like sports, Liz attended virtually all of Jamie's baseball games.

They and their son gradually developed strategies that helped them deal with the recurrent bouts of illness. Fights continued, but they didn't last as long. Episodes of illness recurred, but were quickly recognized. Sunday mornings were a particularly difficult time. Liz stayed in bed, perhaps understandably, and the family learned to make plans and work around this. Henry helped by making Sunday a planned and organized day, and Jamie began inviting other children over to play regardless of whether or not Liz was up and dressed.

Jamie challenged them during his adolescence. "Occasionally, he tries to get to me," Liz said. "He is so defiant and says, 'I'm not going to bed,' and, 'I'm going to hit you in the head.' We've gotten to the point of shoving each other. But I leave it alone. I say, 'Do what you want,' and he goes to bed." And, of course, for Liz it was particularly difficult that he manifested the aggressive symptoms she feared most in herself. At another point, Jamie struggled with depression and got treatment.

Henry was able to help resolve these confrontations. He felt that the tensions came because although the two loved each other very much, they couldn't figure out a way to deal with their anxiety that Liz might become ill again.

During his teens, Jamie, like so many children, required a different kind of explanation about depression. He asked more and deeper questions. He began to ask about his grandfather's hospitalizations and wondered why more wasn't talked about or why his grandfather didn't do more. Through these difficult years, Liz's involvement in Jamie's social life and in his sports continued to provide the visible means for him to know that she cared.

As she looked back, Liz spoke of the benefits of their learning to talk and work together. "Before, my husband and son would yell, 'Get out of bed!' and I would yell, 'Leave me alone!' Now we understand it better." As the fighting in the family gradually cleared, their relationship improved. But as in all the families profiled here, progress was made over a period of years.

It was an important benchmark for Liz when Jamie completed high school and went on to college. This was proof that she had accomplished something. Undeniably, she had been a good enough parent despite the illness. Acknowledging the positives — including the resilience that she'd been able to develop in her son — became an important part of her outlook.

Still, certain troubling moments lingered in her mind. "When I think of my illness, it's the manic episode that occurred in the school meeting, and the fear that something like that might overtake me in other meetings. I still cannot go to public meetings. I'm still trying to sort this out, why I can't go. There are so many things wrapped up with that incident, it's hard to sort out."

Another crucial part of making sense of the illness for Liz was acknowledging it as a part of her, but only a part. "I've been doing a lot of looking back at my life over the past year. I used to feel that I got kicked out of a career progression and I felt very bad about it. I work with twenty-year-olds around me, so I am very out of place." But, as she put it, "I think at this point the illness and I are getting along pretty well. It doesn't have me."

She also acknowledged that there had been a great risk to her marriage. "I decided to treat the manic depression because my husband would not have put up with my being in the hospital a second time. I knew that would have [meant] divorce at that point. He's long-suffering, but not that long-suffering." So she acknowledged the cause, the risks, the losses, but also that not all had been lost by any means. Much of what was essential had survived.

Liz summed it up: "About now, I can look back and say, 'Okay, I'm in the job I'm in and not in a more high-powered job so that I can manage the disease and my life together, and have more time for my family. If I had wanted to continue with the career, I would have undoubtedly lost the family. I could have decided to do that, but I didn't.'"

Henry had his own reflections about sticking it out in the marriage. "When I was two years old," he said, "my father left me and walked out the door. There is not much chance that I would do that, regardless of my situation. That's part of what keeps me going at times . . . as well as I really do believe in my marriage."

Henry acknowledged that the marriage had improved because they were able to talk about things, and that he was able to stand up to Liz even in the midst of her anger and not accept being a scapegoat. He had learned that he and Liz "could deal with anything we have to."

Liz also reflected that as they learned to talk with Jamie, something sustaining had been transmitted to their son that would help him prevail against future adversities. She had hope that he would be different, and this hope was now anchored in concrete experience of his resilience. Liz put it this way: "In fact, I want to say thank you, because I think the biggest thing that I got out of learning to talk was the idea of getting him involved and participating in the community and other activities. He is now doing that and it's become a part of his life. He does not have any social difficulties. He has friends. He has those things that are going to get you through a bout of depression."

It also was essential for Liz to try to make sense of what she'd been through in the context of the religious framework in which she'd been raised. "In Christianity, there is a very strong belief in miracles and that if you pray, that some of the time, God will intervene in your life. Basically, also, if you are Christian, you believe that God is kind of looking out for you. A lot of people take experiences like this and once they get to a certain point, they can say, 'Oh, this was a great learning experience I was given so that I would be a richer kind of person than I would have been if things had just gone smoothly,' and maybe at some point I will do the same. But, initially and for a long time, I had extreme anger at God that he let this happen. At this point, I think I'd say I'm a deist, like the founding fathers of the country were. They believed there was a higher power, but they did not believe that he intervened in history. That is sort of my way of making peace with God. I don't have to be angry at him anymore, because that's not how he functions."

Liz was a spiritual and moral person, and she could not abandon her religious and ethical framework even though the illness profoundly threatened it. For others, there was a profound reconnection with their religious faith, faith that sustained them through episodes of depression. For still others, there was a struggle to discover faith for the first time. But the common ground they found was in caring for their offspring and for their spouses and themselves, and in coming to see that they were able to do these things well.

Fourteen

Facing the Future
Reflections for Families

Benjamin Spock begins his book for parents with the admonition, "Relax. You're doing better than you think you are." Dr. Spock's encouragement applies even more to families wrestling with depression. Most families have the resources they need to deal with depression. They simply don't know that they do.

You, as a parent, have the resources to cope with and deal with this illness, as long as you recognize your depression and as long as you can find the help you need to raise your children. In fact, you have the capacity to do a wonderful job with your children despite the illness. Again and again, depressed parents torture themselves with recriminations, guilt, and blame when in fact they are doing just fine.

There are many opportunities to help your children, not just one chance. Many conversations are possible, and if your child doesn't want to talk at one point, he or she may well do so later. Often, trying to talk simply introduces the idea that it is okay to talk, even though actual back-and-forth interchanges do not take place. Also, children hear and think about what's been said to them even if they don't always acknowledge it. Again and again, families had simple exchanges with a child, maybe even just saying, "You are not to blame." They did not hear much back, but this nonetheless laid the groundwork for much deeper conversations over the months and years that followed.

Being able to plan is essential. If you're in the middle of the throes of a depression, the plan may be how to make it through the day, how to make it to the next doctor's appointment, or how to get someone to take care of the children because you have to go to bed for the day. As you recover your strength, planning is also essential in talking to children and in doing all the myriad things required to take care of them. Plans are more effective when stated ahead of time and then carried through. Reestablishing routines, hearing that something will happen and then having it happen, is very comforting for children. It can also be comforting for you if you are struggling to put your life back together.

Habits of Self-Reflection

Habits of self-reflection are vital. This includes keeping track of what happens, especially what works well for your family. There's nothing abstract about self-reflection. It means figuring out what does and doesn't work for you and for your children, and then acting on it. Then it means remembering what worked. It may even mean writing it down or setting up a time in the week to review things. Reflecting is questioning and figuring out whether you're getting the right treatment, or communicating to your partner about a strategy, or talking over something that is a conflict. But it also means having fun, planning a vacation, or making sure to celebrate a positive anniversary.

These also require having time to think about a day's or a week's event or an anniversary, about what was stirred up and the feelings that were evoked. Just as with planning, putting the self-reflections into words is very important. Keeping a journal, writing things down, and talking about things with others help. It takes time to recognize your place in the larger picture of the history of your family and what you stand for. Changing and thinking in a new way also require time, and finding the positives when you feel down and blue, even longer.

Starting Again

Don't hesitate to go back and start again in thinking how to talk to your children. That is, go back over the six stages, review information, and plan a conversation. Each time you get depressed involves starting again in a way, perhaps even going over what worked before or just reviewing the straightforward information about depression and resilience.

Each time you need help, you may have to rediscover how to get it. Recognize that the illness turns you back on yourself and conspires to keep you from getting help. Also, there are many setbacks in long-term depression, and with each of these, it is possible to be overwhelmed. Then it is important to start back on the first steps of getting into treatment, and to recognize too that circumstances as they change require different and new conversations with kids. As your children grow older, they will require new conversations and ask new questions. It is not a failure if a conversation has to be had again, or simply serves as a way of figuring out what works at one stage and not at another.

Reconnecting and Communicating

Breaking the silence, changing lifelong patterns of communication — these are not easy tasks. Kids will always be kids: irreverent, self-absorbed, with minds of their own. And parents are not therapists. Family life does not take place in a structured setting but happens on the fly. Communication with children happens most often while you are looking for your car keys or brushing your teeth. But as we've seen, open, ongoing communication is the foundation of the resilience we all want for our kids. Family meaning and continuity, enhanced by open channels of communication, are the strong, protective arms in which we can care for them.

Above all, dealing with depression means finding and connecting with many resources at different times — community, religious faith, caregivers, friends, and family. Depression does disrupt your usual connections to all of these, and the resources you and your family need will be different at different times in your life and your children's lives. But just as depression can be understood, those bonds can be reassembled. Learning to deal with depression is learning to reconnect to others and to resources.

I have spent the past twenty-five years trying to use open communication to provide the same safe haven for my own children, but lest you think conversations go easily in my family, let me share a story with you.

In the introduction, I alluded to my sister's severe depression and subsequent suicide. I wondered for years whether my sister had both pushed herself and been pushed too hard to meet the high standards of our family. Our father had a Ph.D. and a ministerial degree, and was deeply revered at the university where he taught. Our mother was a college graduate and a graduate of the Yale School of Nursing. Our grandfather ran a seminary and our great-grandfather was also a man of the cloth, as were two of my father's brothers. I'd had my own struggles about following in that tradition and had broken away, as had my father, but I always worried that these pressures had led my sister to madness. Hence, I always questioned how hard I pushed my children.

One spring day, our second daughter came in. She moves like sunshine through a room: bright, effervescent, and impossible to contain. I thought it was an auspicious moment to talk. She looked expectant. I told her about my sister and about her suicide. I told her my greatest fear was that I would push her too hard. It was a dilemma because it was best for her to strive academically, but at the same time, it was hard for me to urge her on because of what had happened with my sister. Drawing on a lifetime of experience and, I thought, beautifully combining insight and linking it directly to her life experience, I suggested that in addition to her wonderful social presence and great interest in her friends, perhaps slightly more emphasis on the pursuit of scholarship would be in order. I openly indicated my own conflicts about this, obviously with the hope that my openness would reinforce the desired results.

She smiled, lighting up the room, and said, "Dad, thank you for sharing your issues with me. Can I have the car now?"

Epilogue
Personal Reflections: Overcoming
Depression in All Families

Working with these families has been a great privilege for me. The families' stories stay with me and have profoundly changed the way I practice. When I began, I was steeped in the idea of diagnosis and in the view of the physician as expert. But as our work with families has evolved, it showed me how limited and narrow the categories of diagnosis are. Rather than thinking of expert and patient, over time I saw that the families became our partners. Not only did they help us learn what care was needed, they helped us understand their stories and thereby helped us learn what all families with depression need. And the young people too became partners.

Diagnosis is essential in rendering the correct empirically validated treatment, but recovery from depression draws on all the resources you, I, or anyone can muster: family, friends, community, religious faith, ethical convictions, economic resources, self-help and advocacy organizations, and even new friends. None of this is captured by the use of a narrow diagnosis. In fact, trying to help families prevent illness in their children was very freeing because it required thinking in new ways.

My work with families caused me to rethink my notions of identity. We began our work by trying to align resources with the concerns of the family. For the vast majority of parents, the single dominant fact of our mental existence is taking care of our children. It is central to who we are. And through this work, I came to see that raising a child has the capacity to transform parents for the better. It does lead to a new identity. Yet there is very little in the professional literature about how raising children can positively change us as adults.

I was struck again and again as families dealt with depression — as parents understood it and as children gradually came to understand it — how that too became a part of who they were. Depression emerged as something they had mastered, and they looked at it with a sense of accomplishment that they carried within them from that point on.

For families, there is no single answer about what depression is, but rather the development of a process of understanding, a set of strategies that can help them again and again. The stories of these families and the children in them are still being written and they will continue to evolve.

But their stories move forward because families have hope. And they have hope both because they understand differently and because resources are available to help them.

Just as self-understanding is important for families, so it is for those taking care of them — healers like myself. This means constantly questioning, seeing what works and what doesn't work, revising and changing. And part of this understanding is learning from the families we work with about what all families need from their caregivers and their care systems when they face depression. Such self-understanding means not only looking at what families face in the present, but also considering the risk factors that families faced in the past: exposure to violence, poverty, lack of access. It means looking forward to the resources that families need in the future.

It has been a great opportunity to design a prevention strategy and then actually have the resources to implement and study it — to offer it to families and then follow them over time and see what happened. Because ours was a new strategy, we as a staff had the opportunity to try and institute what's called "best practices," that is, to draw on the best empirical evidence in the field and the best clinical approaches we were aware of. Yet, above all, we were try-ing to meet both the needs and the expressed concerns of families where they were when we saw them, so constantly inquiring about their concerns was an essential part of what we did.

The Care Families Need for Depression

When I interviewed the Petrocellis some years after first working with them, they emphasized a key element of care that defied my preconceived notions of what they would say. In those days, in the mid-eighties, I had recently completed my training in psycho-analysis. Mrs. Petrocelli was being treated by two outstanding prac-titioners in the Boston area, one a psychopharmacologist and the other a clinician who worked from a psychoanalytic perspective, and her treatment involved combining the two points of view. I had worked hard with the Petrocellis to be empathic and thought-ful, and to formulate clearly for them what was going on. As they looked back on what meant the most to them, I thought they would mention my insight and empathy. Instead they said, "You gave us your home phone number. We knew we could call you whenever we needed you. You were available for us in a crisis."

Those who suffer from depression need to have available an array of services to get through a life crisis: the illness itself, a divorce, the loss of a child, marital breakup, or economic downturn. Families need rapid access to caregivers in the early stages of illness, access not determined by whether they meet diagnostic criteria but by concern built upon their prior experience of depression and their worries about a family member.

That care cannot focus only on a single illness like depression; it must also involve care for all illnesses, so that if another problem occurs, alcoholism in an adult or attention deficit in a child, that problem can be treated effectively. Moreover, to be successful, care must be of high quality, it must be evidence based, and those providing it must be experienced in treating depression.

And the care needs to be coordinated and made simple for families. They need one person to deal with who can follow them over time. Again and again, families talked about the value of their long-term relationship with us. Care systems and caregivers themselves need to recognize such a long-term responsibility. Depression is a chronic illness, and care must be rendered and available over the long term once it is recognized. Put more positively, such a recognition will provide better outcomes for families and greater rewards for clinicians.

Of vital importance to all the families we worked with was the need for time to figure things out. We in turn took the position that we needed to be flexible. Flexibility meant making sure we had the time to do what families needed — to meet in their homes, to reschedule appointments, and to serve as advocates to help them get the services they needed. Our flexibility, being available when needed, made a large difference. I think all high-quality care must involve flexibility.

We went back to see how families were doing every nine to twelve months when we were working with them clinically, and also went back as a team of assessors whose job it was to evaluate the effects of our program. Families found both types of follow-up useful, saying that following up helped them remember and construct their histories. It also helped them acknowledge their progress. These follow-ups were not driven by the need for clinical care, and often came when families were not in crisis. Accordingly, we recommend that all care for depression involve regular and predictable meetings, and not just be driven by emergency requirements.

We also found as a staff that we needed time to talk together and to draw on one another's experience in order to figure out what was best for each family. This allowed the family to get the benefit of several people's perspectives and allowed us to share the particularly difficult times that are inevitable in working with those who face adversity and even tragedy. Caregivers need time and space to work together and a structure that supports such endeavor.

Equally important was the awareness that getting care represented an active partnership, and that families have both the right and the need to question their care, to understand it fully, to participate in a dialogue about it over time, to question treatments if they don't understand them, and to know the plan for treatment and how to evaluate it. Also, as different treatments worked for different individuals, and as both talking therapies and medications have been supported by empirical evidence, choice in treatments is an important part of any successful partnership.

Not only do families need choice, but care has to be rendered in a manner, in a location, and even in a community that fits the family. Care for depression works only when it can be understood in the culture and language of those who are receiving the care, and we as a society are becoming increasingly diverse.

The fact that we were able to go to families' homes and communities and help them made an enormous difference, particularly in the instances of those initially reluctant to engage, such as adolescent children. This is even more true with regard to the two central concerns of this work: how people with depression can be cared for and the long-term futures of their children. These inevitably require a great deal of sensitivity to the language, culture, and customs from which families come. As we took our work into Dorchester, a multicultural and economically distressed part of Boston, we were again and again struck by the way a different cultural and economic center completely changed how even the word *depression* was understood.[1]

But as we talked with families about what they needed, we were also inevitably drawn into seeing the stark inadequacies in our health care system. When we started, we thought that many families were so experienced with depression that giving them information about treatment or even information about health care plans wouldn't be necessary. Again and again, even those receiving treatment said that they did not understand their coverage or even how to get the help they needed and deserved.

At times, when there was an acute family crisis, much of our work meant serving as guides, interpreters, coaches, and advocates for families to get the care they needed. This work specifically involved ascertaining what the insurance coverage was, which clinicians — psychologists, social workers, and psychiatrists — were paid for by which coverage, and what kinds of services families required. Then there was a series of calls, first to find clinicians that would match up with the families' needs, and then to figure out the appropriate strategies to get the care authorized by insurance companies. Sometimes it meant working with families over time to help them evaluate whether they were getting the right care or not.

Some families found good care easily; others did not. Three problems emerged in our attempts to care for families suffering from the effects of depression, and they reflect larger issues in medicine and mental health care. They were: lack of access, lack of understanding of how the available systems worked, and, for some, lack of adequate coverage or even lack of health insurance altogether.

The level of frustration with the health care system is such that many families of means, worried about confidentiality or about the inadequacy of their coverage, simply go outside the system and pay for care out of pocket rather than through their insurance company. As one mother put it, "Thank God we could afford this illness."

This is not a solution available to most families, and it is not acceptable as a solution for a system of health care, certainly not in the wealthiest democracy in the world.

The Need for Reform of Care Systems

The fact that we ended up putting resources into dealing with the complications in health care was a reflection of the time and place in which we live and work. While our system perhaps provides the best care in the world for some, and adequate care for most, it is not readily clear to families that they have access when they need it — even when they have health insurance — and our system unfortunately does not cover all of our citizens. This must change.

I became drawn into thinking about prevention originally in the late 1970s, after seeing emergency after emergency at Children's Hospital in Boston. I came to believe that we had to do more for parents and their children earlier. The youngsters we see now in our emergency room come from even worse situations than when I started this work twenty years ago. Homes are more chaotic and disorganized, and the children appear to be suffering from more powerfully disruptive mental illnesses and living through a worse set of adversities — being abused, not being able to understand the dominant culture, having the family break down, and often being victimized by violence. There is now compelling evidence that rates of depression among young people are increasing significantly — both within this country and abroad.

At Children's, where I proudly work because we have never refused care to any child because of inability to pay, the psychiatric inpatient unit runs at 100 percent occupancy. The number of psychiatric emergencies seen in our emergency room and on our wards has tripled over the last five years as more and more children come in with serious psychiatric illness, often after suicide attempts.

Compared to the 1970s, when I began the work, an increasingly large percentage of my time or any other clinician's time is spent dealing with the climate of overregulation. This is perhaps most apparent with hospitalized children, for whom there is an almost daily negotiation with insurance companies over the number of days-in-hospital allowed.

Outrageously, real spending on children's mental health has declined from 1990 until now, while spending on physical health has remained constant.[2] We are not close to achieving parity in care for physical and mental illness, despite new legislation.[3] Yet, for the first time in our history, we have a set of studies that show valid treatments for major afflictions of childhood such as attention deficit disorder, anxiety disorders, and — yes — depression, so we have the knowledge base from which to help children.

All my work, both with families with depression and at Children's, has led me to a set of core principles that characterize good care and should, I believe, be the core principles for changing our care system.

Core Principles for Change

First, the only outcomes that we as a society, a group of health care providers, or as family members should concern ourselves with are those that are sustained over time, and the only programs we should support are those that are engineered to sustain changes over time in children and families. The more evidence we have about what works, the better, but the primary point is that short-term solutions will not work for children.

Second, the care of children and their parents or those who serve in place of parents are inseparable. Care systems for families must be integrated and coordinated. The health of the child is inseparable from the health of the parent. Care must be available for both.[4]

Third, mental health care and physical health care are inseparable.

Fourth, we must strengthen and improve our focus on prevention and intervention early in the course of illness, and not wait until children and their parents are in dire straits.

And fifth, we must have universal access and universal coverage for both mental and physical illness, for all adults and children.

As we think about what is needed, I believe it is the families who should be the judges. Are they getting the care they need in a timely and effective manner? Similarly, practitioners on the front lines also need to be able to evaluate the systems to see whether they meet their and the families' needs.

Above all, we must respond to the immense burden of suffering depression causes for children, for parents, and for the larger community. It is simply immoral not to take action.

The fundamental commitments to equity, justice, and fairness that bind us as a country should be reflected in the way we care for illness. No one should be excluded. Our legal system, in principle, applies the same laws to all — rich and poor, black and white, Latino and Native American. There are many ways in which we show that we are committed to a shared future, including the policy that every child has the right to a comprehensive education. We show this commitment in education; we should show it in health care as well.

Forcing parents to make impossible choices — mental health care versus physical health care versus other basic necessities — places an impossible burden on them, and in some ways, those who need health care the most, that is, those with the fewest resources, are most likely to be denied it. The costs of paying out of pocket for an unknown and frightening illness of indefinite duration are overwhelming, and families cannot nurture their children properly with such worries hanging over their heads. We need to remove the fear.

We are at a time in our history when prosperity gives us more resources than ever before to provide the same kind of safety net of care for all children and their caregivers that we do for all those over sixty-five. What is all this money for if we cannot care for the children of this country? What good does it do and how can it possibly be wisely spent if we continue to neglect them?

Who would not forgo those few dollars for a guarantee that all of our children, all of our grandchildren, would never be without health care? Removing the fear that plagues so many parents about their own health and that of their children could not help but vastly improve our society.

We are concerned about costs, and rightly so. But there is compelling evidence that the cost of *not* treating depression in families and *not* attempting to prevent it is far too high.

It is also important to recognize that other countries that rank far ahead of the United States in the health and longevity of their citizens spend a far smaller percentage of their gross national product on health care.[5] They have somewhat different priorities than we do and, not surprisingly, emphasize primary care and rapid response to illnesses as they emerge. They have care for all and a strong investment in prevention.[6]

Thinking about prevention means we must think not only about treating an illness when it occurs, but we must also learn from the histories of those who have wrestled with depression. Their lives reflect at least four risk factors that occur again and again: exposure to violence, discrimination and prejudice, social isolation, and poverty. We must reduce these factors as part of a comprehensive preventive approach to depression and many other afflictions.

There are many sound reasons to confront violence, and we must do so. We can take steps to diminish the amount of violence. Listening to the families' stories emphasizes that one long-term cost of violence is that it is imprinted on the memories and experiences of many of those who are depressed, and its effects extend for decades.

Bias, prejudice, and stigma run throughout the accounts of those who wrestle with mental illness in this book and in the world at large. Sadly, such prejudice has a cumulative effect. Many opportunities are lost, many roads not taken.[7] Thus, we must continue the battle and remove the barriers that have hindered those with mental illness from being recognized. At the same time, we must remove the barriers of stigma that keep families and children from getting the care they need.

We must also acknowledge that there is a direct relationship between mental illness and poverty, particularly in association with other difficulties, including poor physical health. This does not mean that many children in families who are poor cannot grow up healthy and prosper. But the combination of poverty and other risk factors, such as being different, not speaking English well, or being the victim of violence, is a particularly devastating one. The clustering of these risk factors together in neighborhoods without support or resources, which then become overwhelmed and unsafe, creates an almost impossibly difficult combination.[8]

It is important to remember that in any one life, depression will strike at the time we are most vulnerable and without resources. To overcome this, we need to address the risk factors. Everything we know about how risk is distributed tells us that families are more likely to have youngsters with depression when there are three or more risk factors. It is important, then, to recognize that many of these are not going to be randomly distributed, but clustered together; that is, those who lose their jobs are more likely to be poor, and those who live in difficult neighborhoods are more likely to be exposed to violence.[9] And they may also look or act differently than those in the mainstream, so prejudice, stigma, and even racism may further complicate the picture. And the very nature of these adversities also makes it harder for the individuals to be understood and to get the care they need. We must therefore make certain that high-quality care is readily available to all when they are most in need and, paradoxically, perhaps, least able to reach out on their own behalf.

Beyond the definition of risk, we know much more about a set of positive strategies that will in the long run preserve and even expand the capacities of children and their parents: adequate nutrition and protection from harm for both mother and fetus during pregnancy; support in the early years for parenting; high-quality day care; nurse home visitation; neighborhoods that are knit together and fully integrated; and good schools.[10] More and more, we know that we need to strengthen systems — schools, neighborhoods, communities — and not just intervene on behalf of individuals alone. We must make special efforts to care for and provide preventive services for those at highest risk, especially children and minorities. We need to address increasing disparities between us — disparities that have widened alarmingly in the last thirty years and contribute to our poor health record.[11] We need to develop social and human capital to build for the future.[12]

As I look to the future, I am hopeful, but as one of the civil rights workers I talked to the first time I truly encountered resilience, Charlie Sherrod in southwest Georgia, said, "I do have hope, but it is a troubled hope."

More and more parents and others who have had profound personal experience with mental illness are coming forward as advocates. Also, parents and other advocates have an increasing and important role in the governance of mental health systems, and their concerns are being heard and responded to more fully. Substantial empirical research provides the basis for mounting effective treatments for many of the afflictions that have traditionally been called mental illnesses in both children and adults. This did not exist ten years ago. Moreover, there is every evidence that the knowledge base will expand in terms of fundamental understandings of the brain and how it develops.[13] If we are able to continue these scientific advances and have a measured, nonideological approach, new knowledge can substantially help us. This must, of course, move forward with a parallel recognition and expansion of the ways we use this knowledge to help people of different cultures, different backgrounds, different neighborhoods. This is particularly true for depression.[14]

And finally, we are privileged to live in a time of great plenty. Thus, it is possible to achieve the goal of health care for all children and all of their caregivers without an undue burden or without cutting other essential services.

The hope is troubled, though, because we seem to fail so often in this country to act on our knowledge and implement the programs we need. Hence, we have failed thus far to realize the promise of either the resourcefulness of parents or what we know about fostering the development of children. Knowledge conveys responsibility. We know much more about what all children need and we know much more about how the assembly of adversities can affect children, and if we do not provide care for all and do not address depression and the risk factors now, we run the risk of perpetuating inequity for generations to come. Those least able to combat it will be victimized again and again.

My fear is that in this country, we will hold parents solely responsible for the long-term futures of their children. And parents alone cannot provide all that is necessary. Instead, we all must come together and put into place the resources needed. They involve schools, communities, neighborhoods, food, housing, and equal access and equal opportunity for all children.

I sometimes imagine a future dialogue with my children or other children I have met. That is, I wonder what our children will say to us. How will they view us as guardians of the future? I think our children will look at us and wonder why we did not do more to recognize that all futures are shared, and that the only principles that make sense in a democracy are justice and equality. Why did we not act on the knowledge we have with the immense resources we possess?

In our work with families, we found our greatest common ground with them in thinking about the future of the children. Whatever our creeds, faiths, or cultures, children are our best hope for the future. They are the light in the midst of darkness.

No parent can provide all the resources children need alone. I think we as a society can and must come together around the shared futures of all our children. We can do so by finding the will to provide the basic necessities to all children and their parents.

Acknowledgments

W*hen a Parent Is Depressed* results from a collaborative effort of many individuals over more than twenty years. Our empirical studies of the risks and resilience in families facing depression (1979–1985) and in evaluating different forms of preventive intervention (1989–2000) were funded with grants from the W. T. Grant Foundation, the National Institute of Mental Health, the Overseas Shipbuilding Group, and, more recently, the Klingenstein Foundation. I also had the support of a Faculty Scholar Award of the W. T. Grant Foundation. Within the NIMH, Dr. Doreen Kouretz, Ms. Vicki Levin, MSW, and Dr. Kimberly Hoagwood have provided invaluable support, as have Dr. Robert Haggerty and Dr. Betty Hamburg of the Grant Foundation. Much of our research was conducted in collaboration with the Harvard Community Health Plan. Dr. Thomas Kreilkamp played a vital role as our coinvestigator in that effort.

The staff of these projects has made major contributions both in the empirical investigations and in understanding family stories. Dr. Pat Salt has ably served as a coinvestigator on the project to evaluate different forms of preventive intervention, now in its tenth year. Ms. Ellen Wright, MA, has been the project director for the same period. Clinicians who worked with the families (many for five or ten years) include Ms. Polly van der Veldt, LICSW, Dr. Beth Hoke, Dr. Donna Podorefsky, Ms. Lynn Focht, LICSW, and Ms. Susan Swatling, LICSW. In terms of assessment of families, Ms. Phyllis Rothberg, MSW, Ms. Ellen Wright, MA, Ms. Eve Versage, MS, Ms. Carol Tee, and Ms. Ellen Murachver, MSW, have conducted literally hundreds of interviews with families. The work itself has been enhanced by four consultants who have been with the project since the mid-eighties: Dr. Leon Eisenberg, Dr. Julius Richmond, Dr. Robert Selman, and Dr. Felton Earls. I have had generous support from the two institutions in which I work: Children's Hospital Boston and the Judge Baker Children's Center. We explored the usefulness of a preventive intervention approach with a group of inner-city families in Dorchester in collaboration with a community action organization, Dorchester Cares. Dr. Donna Podorefsky led the effort, ably assisted by Ms. Kina Thomas, Ms. Marjorie McDonald, LICSW, and Dr. Phyllis Curtis-Tweed.

Two close friends and colleagues, Dr. Robert Selman, Harvard Graduate School of Education, and Dr. Susan Linn, the Media Center at Judge Baker Children's Center, writers themselves, have read many different iterations of the manuscript and have made major contributions. My father also read several drafts with great care. I have drawn from accounts we wrote for research journals and clinical audiences in trying to frame this work and, in particular, my collaborations on papers with Ms. Lynn Focht, Ms. Eve Versage, Dr. Harriet McMillan, and Dr. Tracy Gladstone have proved essential. I have also incorporated much of the work that we have presented as a team in scientific journals and have provided references to those.

I have had help from several editors along the way, in particular, in early phases, Ms. Lucie Prinz, Ms. Virginia LaPlante, and Ms. Barbara Rifkind. My editor extraordinaire, Mr. Bill Patrick, has guided this process at every step of the way and without his support, it would not have been possible. My editor at Little, Brown and Company, Ms. Deborah Baker, provided extraordinary help. I am also deeply grateful to my agent, Ms. Helen Rees.

My wife, Barbara, and our four children stood by me throughout the process and lent invaluable support.

Above all, I want to acknowledge the contributions of the extraordinary families with whom we had the privilege of working. They generously helped us just as we were trying to help them in their struggles with depression, in learning how families can and do deal with this terrible affliction and move on.

Our understanding of how families dealt with illness are based on what families told us in assessment or intervention sessions during the course of our project to evaluate different forms of preventive intervention or study risks to families. In order to protect the families' confidentiality, no family's story is used with real names, and other details have been changed. Sometimes I have combined accounts while trying to remain true to the essence of the families' experience. Thus, no one account corresponds to the life of any one family. For the long accounts of families in the book, their explicit permission was sought and obtained in addition to the human studies permission used with all of our research subjects.

Resources for Families

Books About Depression

Two beautifully written overall perspectives on families' struggles with mental illness are available:

Carter, Rosalynn. *Helping Someone with Mental Illness: A Compassionate Guide for Family, Friends, and Caregivers.* New York: Random House, Inc., 1998.

Thorne, Julia. *You Are Not Alone: Words of Experience and Hope for the Journey Through Depression.* New York: Harper Perennial, 1993.

Guides that parents have found helpful around specific questions about mood disorders in children or adults are:

American Academy of Child and Adolescent Psychiatry. *Your Child: What Every Parent Needs to Know: What's Normal, What's Not, and When to Seek Help.* New York: HarperCollins Publishers, Inc., 1998.

Burns, David D. *Feeling Good: The New Mood Therapy.* New York: William Morrow and Co., 1999.

Cytryn, Leon, and Donald McKnew. *Growing Up Sad: Childhood Depression and Its Treatment.* New York: W. W. Norton and Company, 1996.

Fassler, David G., and Lynne S. Dumas. *Help Me, I'm Sad: Recognizing, Treating, and Preventing Childhood and Adolescent Depression.* New York: Penguin Putnam, Inc., 1997.

Lewinsohn, Peter M., Rebecca Forster, and Mary A. Youngsen. *Control Your Depression.* New York: Prentice Hall Press, 1986.

Miller, Jeffrey A. *The Childhood Depression Sourcebook.* Chicago: Lowell House, 1999.

Morrison, Andrew L. *The Antidepressant Sourcebook: A User's Guide for Patients and Families.* New York: Main Street Books, 1999.

Nicholson, Joanne, Alexis D. Henry, Jonathan C. Clayfield, and Susan M. Phillips. *Parenting Well When You're Depressed: A Complete Resource for Maintaining a Healthy Family.* Oakland: New Harbinger Publications, Inc., 2001.

Real, Terrence. *I Don't Want to Talk About It: Overcoming the Secret Legacy of Male Depression.* New York: Scribner, 1997.

Waltz, Mitzi. *Bipolar Disorders: A Guide to Helping Children and Adolescents.* Cambridge: O'Reilly & Associates, 2000.

Wemhoff, Richard Theodore, and Rich Wemhoff, eds. *Anxiety and Depression: The Best Resources to Help You Cope.* Seattle: Resource Pathways, 1999.

Many families have found these personal accounts of those who have wrestled with depression of use:

Duke, Patty, and Kenneth Turan. *Call Me Anna.* New York: Bantam Books, 1988.

Jamison, Kay Redfield. *An Unquiet Mind: A Memoir of Moods and Madness.* New York: Random House, 1997.

Styron, William. *Darkness Visible: A Memoir of Madness.* New York: Vintage Books, 1992.

Thompson, Tracy. *The Beast: A Journey Through Depression.* New York: Penguin USA, 1996.

Two authors who write from the perspective of having a family member with manic-depressive illness are:

Gibbons, Kaye. *Sights Unseen.* New York. Avon Books, 1996. (A fictionalized account of a family struggling with depressive illness)

Lyden, Jacki. *Daughter of the Queen of Sheba: A Memoir.* Boston: Houghton Mifflin Company, 1997.

Straightforward Facts About Depression:

National Institute of Mental Health. *Reference List: Science on Our Minds.* Washington, D.C.: United States Government Printing Office, 2001. NIH Publication No. 01-4930.

National Institute of Mental Health. (2001). *The Invisible Disease: Depression.* Washington, D.C.: United States Government Printing Office [Fact Sheet].

National Institute of Mental Health. *In Harm's Way: Suicide in America.* Washington, D.C.: United States Government Printing Office [Fact Sheet].

Web Sites:

Professional associations offer a wide array of valuable resources for families and often also provide direct assistance in locating therapists. I identify them by their Web sites, but they are also accessible by mail and telephone. The major reports from the Institute of Medicine, the Surgeon General, and the National Institute of Mental Health are available online through their Web sites.

American Academy of Child and Adolescent Psychiatry. 1997. AACAP Abramson Fund. <http://www.aacap.org>.

A link to "Facts for Families" includes questions and answers on child and adolescent psychiatry, symptoms and illnesses affecting teenagers, and a catalog of publications on these areas.

American Psychiatric Association. 2001. <http://www.psych.org>.

Health information for patients is found in the section titled "Medem" on the home page. This source includes a medical library and a physician finder by geographic area.

American Psychological Association. <http://www.apa.org>.

The "Public" branch of the site includes information on health care, depression, and other illnesses.

National Association of Social Workers Online. 14 May 2001. National Association of Social Workers, Inc. <http://www.naswdc.org>.

Other important resources include:

Institute of Medicine. 2001. National Academy of Sciences. <http://www.iom.edu>.

Provides invaluable reports on general issues in medical care.

National Institute of Mental Health. 27 April 2001. <http://www.nimh.nih.gov>.

"For the Public" section contains a vast amount of information on mental health and illnesses including depression, manic depression, and others, with a section on child and adolescent mental health.

Substance Abuse and Mental Health Services Administration, especially the *Center for Mental Health Services.* <http://www.mentalhealth.org>.

The Virtual Office of the Surgeon General. <http://www.surgeongeneral.gov>.

The most comprehensive directory of Web sites about psychiatric and psychological issues is:

Slavney, P. R., and E. Meyer, eds. *Psychiatry 2000: An Internet Resource Guide.* Princeton, New Jersey: eMedguides.com, Inc. <http://www.eMed guides.com>.

This guide can be accessed online by visiting "Psychiatry" at the above Web site.

A good overall source for empirical evaluations of various kinds of medical and psychiatric treatments, including depression, is:

Clinical Evidence. 16 November 2000. BMJ Publishing Group. <http://www.clinicalevidence.org>.

WorcesterResources.org. <http://www.worcesterresources.org>.

This site details the steps involved in applying for state benefits such as food stamps, cash assistance, SSI, and Section 8 Rental Assistance. Although the eligibility criteria given are specifically relevant to residents of Massachusetts, this Web site offers a relatively accurate description of the criteria that one will encounter in other states. Further, the Web site serves to highlight a range of issues and needs that low-income individuals and families experience.

Advocacy organizations that families have found particularly helpful include:

Family Forum. Institute for Family-Centered Care. <http://www.family centeredcare.org/parental-illness.html>.

A resource for families wrestling with any medical or psychiatric parental illness.

Federation of Families for Children's Mental Health. <http://www.ffcmh. org>.

A national organization with many resources for families.

Manic-Depressive and Depressive Association of Boston. <http://www. mddaboston.org>.

Included is a list of Boston-area resources such as hotlines, advocacy, medication, government agencies, health insurance, rehabilitation and employment, legal information, therapy services and referrals, and information on research and educational programs.

National Alliance for the Mentally Ill. 2001. <http://www.nami.org>.

This site contains information on education, advocacy, and research for mental illnesses, as well as links to related sites.

National Depressive and Manic-Depressive Association. <http://www. ndmda.org>.

Information on depression including symptoms, detection, and different types of depressive illness, as well as ways to become involved in advocacy about mental illness.

National Mental Health Association. <http://www.nmha.org>.

The "Children and Families" section is valuable and includes a link named "Childhood Depression Awareness Day" that details the symptoms of depression and the warning signs of suicide in children and adolescents.

Parent Professional Advocacy League. Massachusetts State Chapter, Federation of Families for Children's Mental Health. <http://www.ppal.net>.

This site provides resources for families in Massachusetts struggling with illness in their kids and serves as an example of how local chapters of the Federation of Families for Children's Mental Health provide specific local resources.

Notes and References

Introduction

1. Byrne, C., G. Browne, J. Roberts, B. Ewart, M. Schuster, J. Underwood, S. Flynn-Kingston, K. Rennick, B. Bell, A. Gafni, S. Watt, Y. Ashford, and E. Jamieson. "Surviving Social Assistance: 12-Month Prevalence of Depression in Sole-Support Parents Receiving Social Assistance." *Canadian Medical Association Journal* 158 (1998): 888.

Fombonne, E. "Increased Rates of Psychosocial Disorders in Youth." *European Archives of Psychiatry and Clinical Neuroscience* 248 (1998): 14–21.

Frasure-Smith, N., F. Lesperance, and M. Talajic. "Depression and 18-Month Prognosis After Myocardial Infarction." *Circulation* 91 (1995): 999–1005.

Greenberg, P. E., L. E. Stiglin, S. N. Finkelstein, and E. R. Berndt. "The Economic Burden of Depression in 1990." *Journal of Clinical Psychiatry* 54 (1993): 405–418.

Kessler, R. C., and R. G. Frank. "The Impact of Psychiatric Disorders on Work Loss Days." *Psychological Medicine* 27 (1997): 861–873.

Kessler, R. C., K. A. Mcgonagle, S. Zhao, C. B. Nelson, M. Hughes, S. Eshleman, H. U. Wittchen, and K. S. Kendler. "Lifetime and 12-Month Prevalence of DSM-III-R Psychiatric Disorders in the United States." *Archives of General Psychiatry* 51 (1994): 8–19.

Lavori, P. W., G. L. Klerman, M. B. Keller, T. Reich, J. P. Rice, and J. Endicott. "Age-Period-Cohort Analysis of Secular Trends in Onset of Major Depression: Findings in Siblings of Patients with Major Affective Disorder." *Journal of Psychiatric Research* 21 (1987): 23–35.

Murray, C. J., and A. D. Lopez. "Mortality by Cause for Eight Regions of the World: Global Burden of Disease Study." *The Lancet* 349 (1997): 1269–1276.

Siefert, K., P. J. Bowman, C. M. Heflin, S. Danziger, and D. R. Williams. "Social and Environmental Predictors of Maternal Depression in Current and Recent Welfare Recipients." *American Journal of Orthopsychiatry* 70 (2000): 510–522.

2. Dohrenwend, B. P., I. Levav, P. E. Shrout, S. Schwartz, G. Naveh, B. G. Link, A. E. Skodil, and A. Stueve. "Socioeconomic Status and Psychiatric Disorders: The Causation-Selection Issues." *Science* 255 (1992): 946–951.

Shaffer, D., M. S. Gould, P. Fisher, P. Trautman, D. Moreau, M. Kleinman, and M. Flory. "Psychiatric Diagnosis in Child and Adolescent Suicide." *Archives of General Psychiatry* 53 (1996): 339–348.

3. Frank, R. G., T. G. McGuire, S. T. Normand, and H. H. Goldman. "The Value of Mental Health Care at the System Level: The Case of Treating Depression: Contrary to Popular Belief, Mental Health Benefits in Private Health Insurance Represent Solid Value for the Money Spent." *Health Affairs* 18 (September–October 1999): 71–88.

4. Hirschfeld, R. M., M. B. Keller, S. Panico, B. S. Arons, D. Barlow, F. Davidoff, J. Endicott, J. Froom, M. Goldstein, J. M. Gorman, D. Guthrie, R. G. Marek, T. A. Maurer, R. Meyer, K. Phillips, J. Ross, T. L. Schwent, S. S. Sharfstein, M. E. Thase, and R. J. Wyatt. "The National Depressive and Manic-Depressive Association Consensus Statement on the Undertreatment of Depression." *Journal of the American Medical Association* 277 (1997): 333–340.

Keller, M. B., and R. J. Boland. "Implications of Failing to Achieve Successful Long-Term Maintenance Treatment of Recurrent Unipolar Major Depression." *Biological Psychiatry* 44 (1998): 348–360.

Keller, M. B., P. W. Lavori, W. R. Beardslee, J. Wunder, and N. Ryan. "Depression in Children and Adolescents: New Data on 'Undertreatment' and a Literature Review on the Efficacy of Available Treatments." *Journal of Affective Disorders* 21 (1991): 163–171.

Wang, P. S., P. Berglund, and R. C. Kessler. "Recent Care of Common Mental Disorders in the United States: Prevalence and Conformance with Evidence-Based Recommendations." *Journal of General and Internal Medicine* 15 (2000): 284–292.

5. Recognizing difficulties in children, their parents, and families, and rendering effective empirically based treatments have only become common in the last two decades. There are four fundamental facts about mental illness in children that must be reiterated:

1) Mental illness in youngsters is common. The Surgeon General estimates that close to 20 percent of children will have a mental illness in childhood.

2) Good treatments exist, and children suffering from depression or other problems need good treatment as early in the course of the illness as possible. Some of the empirical evidence for the treatment of depression is presented in chapter 4.

3) Most youngsters with depression in the country do not get the treatment they need; in fact, the majority get no treatment at all.

4) At the present time, many families with good health insurance have access to good care. Nonetheless, there are great disparities in the way care is rendered, both to those without health insurance or with inadequate or difficult to access coverage, and to those who do not understand mental illness or how to get care.

These same difficulties also apply to adults. These difficulties are evident in my work at Children's Hospital and in many other mental health systems. I discuss them briefly in the epilogue.

The best overall summary for the problems posed by mental illness is the recent Surgeon General's report.

Department of Health and Human Services. *Mental Health: A Report of the Surgeon General.* Washington, D.C.: Author, 2000.

The plight of minorities struggling with mental health has been clearly portrayed in the recent Surgeon General's Supplement to the Mental Health Report.

United States Department of Health and Human Services. *Mental Health: Culture, Race, and Ethnicity — A Supplement to Mental Health: A Report of the Surgeon General.* Rockville, MD: Author, 2001.

They are also discussed more fully in the Surgeon General's report on a national agenda for child mental health based on a conference that I had the privilege of attending. I also address these issues in "Prevention and the Clinical Encounter."

Beardslee, W. R. "Prevention and the Clinical Encounter." *American Journal of Orthopsychiatry* 68 (1998): 521–533.

United States Public Health Service. *Report of the Surgeon General's Conference on Children's Mental Health: A National Action Agenda.* Washington, D.C.: Author, 2000.

6. The last two decades witnessed a remarkable expansion in the knowledge base on how to understand and treat depression in adults, adolescents, and children, and on how to mount prevention efforts. Prevention science rests first on recognizing risks and resiliencies and the mechanisms by which they take effect, then conducting pilot studies to explore how best to intervene, next conducting efficacy studies to compare different forms of intervention, and finally implementing findings into larger-scale programs.

Coie, J. D., N. F. Watt, S. G. West, J. D. Hawkins, J. R. Asarnow, H. J. Markman, S. L. Ramey, M. B. Shure, and B. Long. "The Science of Prevention: A Conceptual Framework and Some Directions for a National Research Program." *American Psychologist* 48 (1993): 1013–1022.

Institute of Medicine. *Reducing Risks for Mental Disorders: Frontiers for Preventive Intervention Research.* Washington, D.C.: National Academy Press, 1994.

7. In general, our empirical work compared two forms of psychoeducational preventive intervention for depressed families over time: lectures and clinician-centered contacts. Empirical evaluation has demonstrated that both approaches are safe, and that families find that the interventions are helpful and lead families to make substantial positive changes that are sustained over time. In general, there is more change in the clinician intervention. We are continuing to study the long-term effects. I draw on families' accounts from both intervention groups to illustrate how families can cope effectively.

Beardslee, W. R., E. M. Versage, P. Salt, and E. Wright. "The Development and Evaluation of Two Preventive Intervention Strategies for Children of Depressed Parents." In *Rochester Symposium on Developmental Psychopathology, Volume IX, Developmental Approaches to Prevention and Intervention,* edited by D. Cicchetti and S. L. Toth. Rochester: University of Rochester Press, 1999.

Beardslee, W. R., E. Wright, P. C. Rothberg, P. Salt, and E. Versage. "Response of Families to Two Preventive Intervention Strategies: Long-term Differences in Behavior and Attitude Change." *Journal of the American Academy of Child and Adolescent Psychiatry* 35 (1996): 774–782.

8. My father's essay on narrative within the biblical tradition has helped me a great deal in understanding the value of narrative in families' lives, and in particular in understanding how important it is that individual narratives connect with the larger narratives within our cultures and religious faiths. His work on hope also influenced me.

Beardslee, W. A. *A House for Hope: A Study in Process and Biblical Thought.* Philadelphia: The Westminster Press, 1972.

———. "Vital Ruins: Biblical Narrative in the Post-Modern World." In *Margins of Belonging.* Atlanta: Scholars Press, 1991. First published in *Southern Humanities Review* 24 (1990): 101–116.

My understanding of rituals and continuity was enhanced by an early paper by Wolin and Bennett on family rituals and alcoholism.

Wolin, S. J., and L. A. Bennett. "Family Rituals." *Family Process* 23 (1984): 401–420.

9. Beardslee, W. R. "Commitment and Endurance: Common Themes in the Life Histories of Civil Rights Workers Who Stayed." *American Journal of Orthopsychiatry* 53 (1983): 34–42.

———. *The Way Out Must Lead In: Life Histories in the Civil Rights Movement.* 1977. Reprinted in an expanded second edition, Westport: Lawrence Hill and Co., 1983.

———. "The Role of Self-Understanding in Resilient Individuals: The Development of a Perspective." *American Journal of Orthopsychiatry* 59 (1989): 266–278.

Chapter One

1. Dr. Harriet MacMillan and I described a different perspective on a similar family in:

Beardslee, W. R., and H. MacMillan. "Preventive Intervention with the Children of Depressed Parents: A Case Study." *Psychoanalytic Study of the Child* 48 (1993) 249–276.

2. Most of the families described in this book were families who started with us by receiving one of the two forms of preventive intervention we developed and evaluated in a research program to meet families' needs when facing depression. We provided many resources for families but did not undertake the treatment of the depression in the adults. We did, however, work very closely with the families to get them good care, and often, in fact, became advocates for them to get the care they needed, as I describe in the Epilogue. As described in the Acknowledgments, the families in this book are portrayed with their real names changed and other details of their lives altered to protect their privacy and confidentiality.

Chapter Two

1. American Psychiatric Association. *Diagnostic and Statistical Manual of Mental Disorders (4th ed.).* Washington, D.C.: Author, 1994.

2. Keitner, G. I., and I. W. Miller. "Family Functioning and Major Depression: An Overview." *American Journal of Psychiatry* 147 (1990): 1128–1137.
Sholevar, G. P. *The Transmission of Depression in Families and Children: Assessment and Intervention.* Northvale: Jason Aronson, Inc., 1994.

3. Coyne, J. C., R. C. Kessler, M. Tal, J. Turnbull, C. B. Wortman, and J. F. Greden. "Living with a Depressed Person." *Journal of Consulting and Clinical Psychology* 55 (1987): 347–352.

Chapter Three

1. Gorman, C. "Anatomy of Melancholy: Scientists Take a Picture of Depression and Discover That It Actually Changes the Shape of the Brain." *Time* 8 (May 1997): 78.
Steingard, R. J., C. Schmidt, and J. T. Coyle. "Basic Neuroscience: Critical Issues for Understanding Psychiatric Disorders." *Adolescent Medicine* 9 (1998): 205–215.
Thase, M. E., and R. H. Howland. "Biological Processes in Depression: An Updated Review." In *Handbook of Depression,* 2nd ed., edited by E. E. Beckham and W. R. Leber, 213–279. New York: The Guilford Press, 1995. This overall handbook provides an excellent introduction to the issues.

2. Nemeroff, C. B. "The Neurobiology of Depression." *Scientific American* (1998): 42–49.

3. Many of these risk factors were identified in the Institute of Medicine's report. I am using the list with permission from the Institute of Medicine.
Institute of Medicine. "Risk and Protective Factors for the Onset of Mental Disorders: Depressive Disorders." In *Reducing Risks for Mental Disorders: Frontiers for Preventive Intervention Research,* 163–171. Washington, D.C.: National Academy Press, 1994. (Previously cited.)

Each of the factors was identified through empirical studies.

Anthony, J. C., and K. R. Petronis. "Suspected Risk Factors for Depression Among Adults 18–44 Years Old." *Epidemiology* 2 (1991): 123–132.

Bruce, M. L., D. T. Takeuchi, and P. J. Leaf. "Poverty and Psychiatric Status: Longitudinal Evidence from the New Haven Epidemiologic Catchment Area Study." *Archives of General Psychiatry* 48 (1991): 470–474.

Kaplan, G. A., R. E. Roberts, T. C. Camacho, and J. C. Coyne. "Psychosocial Predictors of Depression: Prospective Evidence from the Human Population Laboratory Studies." *American Journal of Epidemiology* 125 (1987): 206–220.

Reinherz, H. Z., R. M. Giaconia, M. S. Wasserman, A. B. Silverman, and L. Burton. "Coming of Age in the 1990s: Influences of Contemporary Stressors on Major Depression in Young Adults." In *Historical and Geographical Influences on Psychopathology*, edited by P. Cohen, C. Slomkowski, and L. H. Robins, 141–161. Mahwah, New Jersey: Lawrence Erlbaum Associates, 1999.

4. Recent work on exposure to abuse and violence emphasize how it is a risk factor for many poor outcomes, including depression.

Cooley-Quille, M. R., S. M. Turner, and D. C. Beidel. "Emotional Impact of Children's Exposure to Community Violence: A Preliminary Study." *Journal of the American Academy of Child and Adolescent Psychiatry* 34 (1995): 1362–1368.

Felitti, V. J., R. F. Anda, D. Nordenberg, D. F. Williamson, A. M. Spitz, V. Edwards, M. P. Koss, and J. S. Marks. "Relationship of Childhood Abuse and Household Dysfunction to Many of the Leading Causes of Death in Adults." *American Journal of Preventive Medicine* 14 (1998): 245–258.

MacMillan, H. L. "Child Sexual Abuse: An Overview (Part II)." *Canadian Child Psychiatric Bulletin* 5 (1997): 90–94.

MacMillan, H. L., J. E. Fleming, D. L. Streiner, E. Lin, M. H. Boyle, E. Jamieson, E. K. Duku, C. A. Walsh, M. Y.-Y. Wong, and W. R. Beardslee. "Childhood Abuse and Lifetime Psychiatric Disorder in a Community Sample of Ontario Residents." *American Journal of Psychiatry* (2001). In press.

McAlister-Groves, B. M., B. Zuckerman, S. Marans, and D. J. Cohen. "Silent Victims: Children Who Witness Violence." *Journal of the American Medical Association* 269 (1993): 262–264.

Prothrow-Stith, D. *Deadly Consequences: How Violence Is Destroying our Teenage Population and a Plan to Begin Solving the Problem.* New York: HarperCollins Publishers, 1991.

Straus, M. A. *Beating the Devil Out of Them: Corporal Punishment in American Families and Its Effects on Children,* 2nd ed. New Brunswick: Transaction Publishers, 2000.

Turner, J., and D. A. Lloyd. "The Stress Process and the Social Distribution of Depression." *Journal of Health and Social Behavior* 40 (1999): 374–404.

United States Department of Health and Human Services. *Youth and Violence: A Report of the Surgeon General.* Washington, D.C.: Author, 2001.

5. The struggle for women living in poverty who face multiple demands is described in:

Belle, D. *Lives in Stress: Women and Depression.* Beverly Hills: SAGE Publications, Inc., 1982.

Lennon, M. C., J. Blome, and K. English. "Depression and Low-Income Women: Challenges for TANF and Welfare-to-Work Policies and Programs." Research Forum on Children, Families and the New Federalism, National Center for Children in Poverty, Joseph L. Mailman School of Public Health, Columbia University, 2001.

Podorefsky, D. L., M. McDonald-Dowdell, and W. R. Beardslee. "Adaptation of Preventive Interventions for a Low-Income, Culturally Diverse Community." *Journal of the American Academy of Child and Adolescent Psychiatry* 40 (2001): 879–886.

Schwartz, A., J. Eilenberg, and M. T. Fullilove. "Gloria's Despair: Struggling Against the Odds." *American Journal of Psychiatry* 153 (1996): 1334–1338.

6. Faraone, S. V., M. T. Tsuang, and D. W. Tsuang. *Genetics of Mental Disorders: A Guide for Students, Clinicians, and Researchers.* New York: The Guilford Press, 1999.

Tsuang, M. T., and S. V. Faraone. *The Genetics of Mood Disorders.* Baltimore, MD: The Johns Hopkins University Press, 1990.

Earlier genetic models primarily described single genes, and more recent ones have emphasized patterns of genes. Recent studies in behavioral genetics have emphasized that some patterns of parenting also run in families. As one of the experts, Dr. David Reiss, continues to emphasize, however, findings of the more recent investigations do not take away the importance of either environmental factors or parental efforts.

Reiss, D. "Mechanisms Linking Genetic and Social Influences in Adolescent Development: Beginning a Collaborative Search." *Current Directions in Psychological Science* 6 (1997): 100–105.

Reiss, D., J. M. Neiderhiser, E. Mavis Hetherington, and R. Plomin. *The Relationship Code: Deciphering Genetic and Social Influences on Adolescent Development.* Cambridge: Harvard University Press, 2000.

7. Kendler's work showed that roughly half of depression's liability can be predicted. There is undoubtedly an interaction between various kinds of vulnerabilities (including genetic), protective resources, and stressors or traumas that lead to the expression of depression. Further work by Kendler has emphasized that the two main classes of influence on a depressive episode are familial/genetic vulnerability and severe negative life events. There is also an interaction between the life event and the vulnerabilities, i.e., depressed individuals respond differently than non-depressed individuals to the same negative events.

Kendler, K. S., L. M. Karkowski, and C. A. Prescott. "Causal Relationship Between Stressful Life Events and the Onset of Major Depression." *American Journal of Psychiatry* 156 (1993): 837–841.

Kendler, K. S., R. C. Kessler, M. C. Neale, A. C. Heath, and L. J. Eaves. "The Prediction of Major Depression in Women: Toward an Integrated Etiological Model." *The American Journal of Psychiatry* 150 (1993): 1139–1148.

The mapping of the human genome offers great promise for many disorders. Its effect on understanding the etiology of major depression remains less clear, because major depression is a heterogeneous condition with many different causes, and, when genetic influences occur, they are likely to involve multiple different genes.

My colleague David Mrazek has suggested that as the full import of the human genome becomes known, we will need a whole new class of genetic counselors to help families make sense of this. His concern that the possibility of misunderstanding and, indeed, making everything appear to be due to genetic causes is large. This would be a profound misinterpretation of what we know about the interplay between genes and the environment.

Collins, F. S., and K. G. Jegalian. "Deciphering the Code of Life." *Scientific American* (December 1999): 86–91.

Mrazek, D. A. "Genetic Medicine and Genetic Psychiatry." *American Academy of Child and Adolescent Psychiatry News* 31 (2000): 16–17.

8. Berkman, L. F., and T. Glass. "Social Integration, Social Networks, Social Support, and Health." In *Social Epidemiology,* edited by L. F. Berkman and I. Kawachi, 137–173. In press.

9. Dr. Brown's model was based on a detailed study of women of working-class origins. He examined the influence of a specific risk factor, death of a parent before age eleven, on whether or not they became depressed later in life. He found that the risk factor resulted in depression only when the context of protective resources and vulnerabilities was taken into account. Specifically, being socially isolated was a vulnerability, as was having a large number of children or working in a job that was unsatisfying, while the presence of a close, confiding, intimate relationship was a protective factor against becoming depressed. Depression occurred in the face of a life stressor when someone had current vulnerabilities and lacked protective resources. Brown later replicated this study on an island in the Outer Hebrides, finding that closeness to community and doing work that involved social contact with others were also protective against becoming depressed, again emphasizing how important good relationships are in protecting against depression. He then developed an intervention for depressed women using volunteers from their communities who befriended them. In a randomized trial, he and his colleagues showed that volunteer befriending promoted remission of chronic depression in these women and significantly helped them. This provides another confirmation of the importance of Brown's observations about how vital close, intimate relationships are.

Brown, G. W. "Stress, Risk, and Resilience in Children and Adolescents: Processes, Mechanisms, and Interventions." *Journal of Child Psychology and Psychiatry and Allied Disciplines* 37 (1996): 237.

Brown, G. W., and T. Harris. *Social Origins of Depression: A Study of Psychiatric Disorder in Women.* London: Tavistock, 1978.

Harris, T., G. W. Brown and R. Robinson. "Befriending As an Intervention for Chronic Depression Among Women in an Inner City: 1: Randomized Controlled Trial." *The British Journal of Psychiatry* 174 (1999): 219–224.

Discussion of the social and cultural contexts of depression is found in:

Jenkins, J. H., A. Kleinman, and B. J. Good. "Cross-Cultural Studies of Depression." In *Psychosocial Aspects of Depression,* edited by J. Becker and A. Kleinman, 67–99. Hillsdale: Lawrence Erlbaum Associates, Publishers, 1991.

10. Post, R. M. "Transduction of Psychosocial Stress into the Neurobiology of Recurrent Affective Disorder." *American Journal of Psychiatry* 149 (1992): 999–1010.

11. To summarize, at the extremes of the large group of people who become depressed are, at one end, those who have many, many family members with depression and who can become depressed without severe adverse life experiences, and at the other, those who suffer from severe adverse life experiences and become depressed solely because of that. Many depressions are a combination of the two and many remain of unknown cause.

What we know about cause is that risk factors increase the likelihood of depression, so, for example, having a depressed relative increases the likelihood that others in the family will be depressed, but we don't know the mechanism by which this occurs. We suspect that there are underlying proclivities or patterns in children and adults that predispose them to respond to stress in certain ways. Some people become depressed; others respond in other ways. Some of these proclivities may well have in part a genetic determination, just like temperament or body type. When someone with the proclivity to depression encounters severe stress, he or she becomes depressed.

Also, because a clear-cut family history of depression is difficult and sometimes impossible to ascertain, and as depression has only recently been recognized, it is very difficult to be conclusive about the role of family history in most depressions.

Whatever the cause or mechanism, once the process starts and becomes a depression, it consists of both the constellation of psychological symptoms and the underlying biological rearrangements at the same time.

Chapter Four

1. For recent summaries of the best available treatments for mood disorders, see:

Gabbard, G., ed. *Treatment of Psychiatric Disorders*. Washington, D.C.: American Psychiatric Association Press, 2001.

Gotlib, I. H., and C. L. Hammen, eds. *Handbook of Depression and Its Treatment*. New York: Guilford, 2001.

2. Keller, M. B., and R. J. Boland. "Implications of Failing to Achieve Successful Long-Term Maintenance Treatment of Recurrent Unipolar Major Depression." *Biological Psychiatry* 44 (1998): 348–360.

Keller, M. B., J. P. McCullough, D. N. Klein, B. Arnow, D. L. Dunner, A. J. Gelenberg, J. C. Markowitz, C. B. Nemeroff, J. M. Russell, M. E. Thase, M. H. Trivedi, and J. Zajecka. "A Comparison of Nefazodone, the Cognitive-Behavioral Analysis System of Psychotherapy, and Their Combination for the Treatment of Chronic Depression." *New England Journal of Medicine* 342 (2000): 1462–1470.

Pava, J. A., M. Fava, and J. A. Levenson. "Integrating Cognitive Therapy and Pharmacotherapy in the Treatment and Prophylaxis of Depression: A Novel Approach." *Psychotherapy and Psychosomatics* 61 (1994): 211–219.

3. Keller, M. B., and R. W. Shapiro. "Double Depression: Superimposition of Acute Depressive Episodes on Chronic Depressive Disorders." *American Journal of Psychiatry* 139 (1982): 438–442.

4. Birmaher, R., N. Ryan, D. Williamson, D. Brent, J. Kaufman, R. Dahl, J. Penel, and B. Nelson. "Childhood and Adolescent Depression: A Review of the Past Ten Years, Part 1." *Journal of the American Academy of Child and Adolescent Psychiatry* 35 (1996): 1427–1439.

Cicchetti, D., and S. L. Toth. "Developmental Psychopathology and Disorders of Affect." In *Developmental Psychopathology, Vol. 2: Risk, Disorder, and Adaptation,* edited by D. Cicchetti and D. J. Cohen, 369–420. New York: John Wiley and Sons, Inc., 1995.

Shaffer, D. "Depression, Mania, and Suicidal Acts." In *Child and Adolescent Psychiatry: Modern Approaches,* 2nd ed., edited by M. Rutter and L. Hersov, 698–719. Boston: Blackwell Scientific Publications, 1985.

Weller, E. B., and R. A. Weller. "Mood Disorders." In *Child and Adolescent Psychiatry: A Comprehensive Textbook,* edited by M. Lewis, 646–664. Baltimore: Williams and Wilkins, 1991.

The entire volume of the *Journal of Biological Psychiatry* (June 2001) is concerned with the topic of childhood depression. It provides a summary of current knowledge and treatments.
Journal of Biological Psychiatry 49, no. 12 (2001): 959–1159.

5. Beck, A. T. *Depression: Causes and Treatments*. Philadelphia: University of Pennsylvania Press, 1967.

DeRubeis, R. J., M. D. Evans, S. D. Hollon, M. J. Garvey, W. M. Grove, and V. B. Tuason. "How Does Cognitive Therapy Work? Cognitive Change and Symptom Change in Cognitive Therapy and Pharmacotherapy for Depression." *Journal of Consulting and Clinical Psychology* 58 (1990): 862–869.

Hollon, S. D., R. J. DeRubeis, and M. D. Evans. "Cognitive Therapy in the Treatment and Prevention of Depression." In *Frontiers of Cognitive Therapy*, edited by P. Salkovskis, 293–317. New York: Guilford Press, 1996.

6. Lewinsohn, P. M., and I. H. Gotlib. "Behavior Theory and Treatment of Depression." In *Handbook of Depression*, edited by E. E. Beckham and W. R. Leber, 352–375. New York: The Guilford Press, 1995.

Rush, A. J., ed. *Short-Term Psychotherapies for Depression*. New York: Guilford Press, 1987.

7. Klerman, G. L., M. Weissman, B. J. Rounsaville, and E. S. Chevron. *Interpersonal Psychotherapy of Depression*. New York: Basic Books, 1984.

8. Hyman, S. E., and E. J. Nestler. "Initiation and Adaptation: A Paradigm for Understanding Psychotropic Drug Action." *American Journal of Psychiatry* 153 (1996): 151–162.

9. American Psychiatric Association. "Practice Guideline for the Treatment of Patients with Major Depressive Disorder (revision)." *American Journal of Psychiatry* 157 suppl. (2000): 1–45.

10. Coulehan, J. L., H. C. Schulberg, M. R. Block, M. J. Madonia, and E. Rodriguez. "Treating Depressed Primary Care Patients Improves Their Physical, Mental, and Social Functioning." *Archives of Internal Medicine* 157 (1997): 1113–1120.

Department of Health and Human Services. *Depression in Primary Care: Volume 2. Treatment of Major Depression*. Rockville: Author, 1993. Rep. No. 93–0551.

Merriam, A. E., and T. B. Karasu. "The Role of Psychotherapy in the Treatment of Depression: Review of Two Practice Guidelines: A Commentary." *Archives of General Psychiatry* 53 (1996): 301–302.

Munoz, R. F., S. D. Hollon, E. McGrath, L. P. Rehm, and G. R. Vanden-Bos. "On the AHCPR Depression in Primary Care Guidelines: Further Considerations for Practitioners." *American Psychologist* 49 (1994): 42–61.

Wells, K. B., C. Sherbourne, M. Schoenbaum, N. Duan, L. Meredith, J. Unutzer, J. Miranda, M. F. Carney, and L. V. Rubenstein. "Impact of Disseminating Quality Improvement Programs for Depression in Managed Primary Care: A Randomized Controlled Trial." *Journal of the American Medical Association* 283 (2000): 212–220.

11. Blacker, D. "Maintenance Treatment of Major Depression: A Review of the Literature." *Harvard Review of Psychiatry* 4 (1996): 1–9.

Frank, E., D. J. Kupfer, E. F. Wagner, A. B. McEachran, and C. Cornes. "Efficacy of Interpersonal Psychotherapy as a Maintenance Treatment of Recurrent Depression: Contributing Factors." *Archives of General Psychiatry* 48 (1991): 1053–1059.

Shea, M. T., I. Elkin, S. D. Imber, S. M. Sotsky, J. T. Watkins, J. F. Collins, P. A. Pilkonis, E. Beckham, D. R. Glass, R. T. Dolan, and M. B. Parloff. "Course of Depressive Symptoms over Follow-Up: Findings from the National Institute of Mental Health Treatment of Depression Collaborative Research Program." *Archives of General Psychiatry* 49 (1992): 782–787.

12. The following provides the most recent useful guide for clinicians treating childhood depressive disorders. Similar practice parameters are available for other disorders from the American Academy of Child and Adolescent Psychiatry.

Birmaher, B., D. Brent, and Work Group on Quality Issues. "Practice Parameters for the Assessment and Treatment of Children and Adolescents with Depressive Disorders." *Journal of the American Academy of Child Adolescent Psychiatry* 37 (1998): 63S–83S.

See also:

Brent, D. A., D. Holder, D. Kolko, B. Birmaher, M. Baugher, C. Roth, S. Iyengar, and B. A. Johnson. "A Clinical Psychotherapy Trial for Adolescent Depression Comparing Cognitive, Family, and Supportive Therapy." *Archives of General Psychiatry* 54 (1997): 877–885.

Emslie, G. J., A. J. Rush, W. A. Weinberg, R. A. Kowatch, C. W. Hughes, T. Carmody, and J. Rintelmann. "A Double-Blind, Randomized,

Placebo-Controlled Trial of Fluoxetine in Children and Adolescents with Depression." *Archives of General Psychiatry* 54 (1997): 1031–1037.

Kaslow, N. J., E. B. McClure, and A. M. Connell. "Treatment of Depression in Children and Adolescents." In *Handbook of Depression and Its Treatment,* edited by I. H. Gotlib and C. L. Hammen. New York: Guilford. In press.

Lewinsohn, P. M., G. N. Clarke, and P. Rhode. "Psychological Approaches to the Treatment of Depression in Adolescents." In *Handbook of Depression in Children and Adolescents,* edited by W. M. Reynolds and H. E. Johnston, 309–344. New York: Plenum Press, 1994.

Szigethy, E. M., P. Ruiz, D. R. DeMaso, R. Shapiro, and W. R. Beardslee. "Cutting-Edge Consultation Liaison Psychiatry: The Importance of a Longitudinal and Integrative Perspective." *The American Journal of Psychiatry.* In press.

Weisz, J., C. Thurber, L. Sweeney, V. Proffitt, and G. LeGagnoux. "Brief Treatment of Mild to Moderate Child Depression Using Primary and Secondary Control Enhancement Training." *Journal of Consulting and Clinical Psychology* 65 (1997): 703–707.

Recommendations of treatment for children with depression are part of a new knowledge base of empirical evaluation of treatments for children in general, summarized in:

Burns, B. J., K. Hoagwood, and P. J. Mrazek. "Effective Treatment for Mental Disorders in Children and Adolescents." *Clinical Child and Family Psychology Review* 2 (1999): 199–254.

Hibbs, E. D., and P. S. Jense. *Psychosocial Treatments for Child and Adolescent Disorders: Empirically Based Strategies for Clinical Practice.* Washington, D.C.: American Psychological Association, 1996.

The challenges for developing more effective treatments for children in the future are discussed in:

Kazdin, A. E. "Developing a Research Agenda for Child and Adolescent Psychotherapy." *Archives of General Psychiatry* 57 (2000): 829–835.

Weisz, J. R., S. S. Han, D. A. Granger, B. Weiss, and T. Morton. "Effects of Psychotherapy with Children and Adolescents Revisited: A Meta-Analysis of Treatment Outcome Studies." *Psychological Bulletin* 117 (1995): 450–468.

Weisz, J. R., and P. S. Jensen. "Efficacy and Effectiveness of Child and Adolescent Psychotherapy and Pharmacotherapy." *Mental Health Services Research* 1 (1999): 125–157.

Weisz, J. R., and V. R. Weersing. "Psychotherapy with Children and Adolescents: Efficacy, Effectiveness, and Developmental Concerns." In *Rochester Symposium on Developmental Psychopathology, Volume X: Developmental Approaches to Prevention and Intervention,* draft ed., edited by D. Cicchetti and S. L. Toth. Rochester: University of Rochester Press, 1997.

For recent reviews of prevention of depression in childhood, see:

Beardslee, W. R., and T. R. G. Gladstone. "Prevention of Childhood Depression: Recent Findings and Future Prospects." *Biological Psychiatry* 49, no. 12 (2001): 1101–1110.

Clarke, G. N., M. Hornbrook, F. Lynch, M. Polen, J. Gale, W. R. Beardslee, E. O'Conner, and J. Seeley. "A Randomized Trial of a Group Cognitive Intervention for Preventing Depression in Adolescent Offspring of Depressed Parents." *Archives of General Psychiatry.* In press.

Gillham, J. E., A. J. Shatte, and D. R. Freres. "Preventing Depression: A Review of Cognitive-Behavioral and Family Interventions." *Applied and Preventive Psychology* 9 (2000): 63–88.

Rather sadly, the history of health care in this country is fraught with stories of quackery and false claims. One of the most recent experiences was with laetrile for cancer. We need to be very careful to fully evaluate any treatments before they are widely used, to avoid false claims, and to understand what the risks of treatment are for children.

Young, J. H. *American Health Quackery: Collected Essays by James Harvey Young.* Princeton, New Jersey: Princeton University Press, 1992.

Chapter Five

1. A recent overall summary of work on resilience that emphasizes that the emergence of resilience is the result of underlying positive developmental processes is:

Luthar, S. S., D. Cicchetti, and B. Becker. "The Construct of Resilience: A Critical Evaluation and Guidelines for Future Work." *Child Development* 71 (2000): 543–562.

Other important resources are:

Cicchetti, D., and N. Garmezy. "Prospects and Promises in the Study of Resilience." *Development and Psychopathology* 5 (1993): 497–502.

Egeland, B., E. Carlson, and L. A. Sroufe. "Resilience As Process." *Development and Psychopathology* 5 (1993): 517–528.

Haggerty, R. J., L. R. Sherrod, N. Garmezy, and M. Rutter. *Stress, Risk, and Resilience in Children and Adolescents.* New York: Cambridge University Press, 1994.

Masten, A. S., and J. D. Coatsworth. "The Development of Competence in Favorable and Unfavorable Environments: Lessons from Research on Successful Children." *American Psychologist* 53 (1998): 205–220.

2. Our work on resilience and on the role of understanding is best described in:

Beardslee, W. R. "The Role of Self-Understanding in Resilient Individuals: The Development of a Perspective." *American Journal of Orthopsychiatry* 59 (1989): 266–278.

Beardslee, W. R., and D. Podorefsky. "Resilient Adolescents Whose Parents Have Serious Affective and Other Psychiatric Disorders: The Importance of Self-Understanding and Relationships." *The American Journal of Psychiatry* 145 (1988): 63–69.

The writings of Dr. Robert Coles, in particular the first volume of his Children of Crisis series, profoundly influenced me when I was working in the civil rights movement, as did the subsequent volumes in this series later.

Coles, R. *Children of Crisis: A Study of Courage and Fear.* Boston: Atlantic Little, Brown, and Company, 1967.

For an overview of how young people form their enduring identities, see:

Erikson, Erik H. *Childhood and Society.* 2d. ed. New York: W. W. Norton and Company, Inc., 1963.

3. Dr. Robert Selman and I collaborated on understanding the importance of youngsters' being able to enter the world of others in children of depressed parents in several studies. His work combines the developmental-stage sequential perspective of Piaget with an emphasis on moral and interpersonal development following Harry Stack Sullivan and Lawrence Kohlberg.

Beardslee, W. R., L. H. Schultz, and R. L. Selman. "Level of Social-Cognitive Development, Adaptive Functioning, and DSM-III Diagnosis in Adolescent Offspring of Parents with Affective Disorders: Implications of the Development of the Capacity for Mutuality." *Developmental Psychology* 23 (1987): 807–815.

Selman, R. L. *The Growth of Interpersonal Understanding: Developmental and Clinical Analyses*. New York: Academic Press, 1980.

Selman, R. L., and S. Adalbjarnardottir. "A Developmental Method to Analyze the Personal Meaning Adolescents Make of Risk and Relationship: The Case of 'Drinking.'" *Applied Developmental Science* 4 (2000): 47–65.

Selman, R. L., W. R. Beardslee, L. H. Schultz, M. Krupa, and D. Podorefsky. "Assessing Adolescent Interpersonal Negotiation Strategies: Toward the Integration of Structural and Functional Models." *Developmental Psychology* 22 (1986): 450–459.

Selman, R. L., C. L. Watts, and L. H. Schultz. *Fostering Friendship: Pair Therapy for Treatment and Prevention*. New York: Walter de Gruyter, Inc., 1997.

Chapter Six

1. Throughout the work, I have emphasized that the overall scientific findings provide important guidance and hope. It is, however, very difficult to apply those findings directly to one's life because they inevitably describe statistical averages on large groups of people. Also, any study is limited to a sample of individuals, and thus cannot be representative of all families or of your family. Hence, caution needs to be exercised in drawing conclusions for any one family. This is true for estimating genetic risk in families for adults. Even more caution is needed in trying to determine such risk for any individual child.

2. The best overall perspective on the interplay between biological givens and environment is provided by Eisenberg.

Eisenberg, L. "The Social Construction of the Human Brain." *American Journal of Psychiatry* 152 (1995): 1563–1575.

See also:

Kandel, E. R. "A New Intellectual Framework for Psychiatry." *American Journal of Psychiatry* 155 (1998): 457–469.

Miller, N. E. "Clinical-Experimental Interactions in the Development of Neuroscience: A Primer for Nonspecialists and Lessons for Young Scientists." *American Psychologist* 50 (1995): 901–911.

National Institute of Mental Health. *Advancing Research on Developmental Plasticity: Integrating the Behavioral Science and Neuroscience of Mental Health*. Washington, D.C.: NIMH, 1998.

A valuable perspective on how these approaches can be incorporated in pre-
vention programs is:
Earls, F., and M. Carlson. "The Social Ecology of Child Health and Well-
Being." *Annual Review of Public Health* 22 (2001): 143–146.

3. Bronfenbrenner, U. *The Ecology of Human Development.* Cambridge:
Harvard University Press, 1979.

4. Werner, E. E. "Risk, Resilience, and Recovery: Perspectives from the Kauai
Longitudinal Study." *Development and Psychopathology* 5 (1993): 503–515.
Werner, E. E., and R. S. Smith. *Vulnerable but Invincible: A Study of Resilient
Children.* New York: McGraw Hill, 1982.

5. Davis, N. J. "Resilience: Status of the Research and Research-Based Pro-
grams." Substance Abuse and Mental Health Services Administration,
Center for Mental Health Services, Division of Program Development,
Special Populations and Projects, Special Programs Development Branch.
Rockville, Maryland, 1999.

6. Robins, L. *Deviant Children Grown Up: A Sociological and Psychiatric
Study of Sociopathic Personality.* Melbourne: Krieger Publishing Company, 1975.

7. Aarons, B., K. Kumpfer, J. Johnson, M. Windle, W. Beardslee, B. Flynn,
M. J. English, A. Masten, and J. Rolf. "Resilience Working Group Pro-
ceedings." *Proceedings of the Center for Mental Health Services* (1999):
1–38.
Baumrind, A. "Rearing Competent Children." In *Child Development Today
and Tomorrow,* edited by W. Damon, 349–378. San Francisco: Jossey
Bass, 1989.
Cohler, B. J. "The Life Story and the Study of Resilience and Response to
Adversity." *Journal of Narrative and Life History* 1 (1991): 69–99.
Glantz, M. D., and J. L. Johnson. *Resilience and Development: Positive Life
Adaptations.* Boston: Kluwer Academic/Plenum Publishers, 1999.
Hamburg, D. A. "Toward a Strategy for Healthy Adolescent Development."
The American Journal of Psychiatry 154 (1997): 7–12.
Hauser, S. T. "Understanding Resilient Outcomes: Adolescent Lives Across
Time and Generations." *Journal of Research on Adolescence* 9 (1999):
1–24.

Institute for Mental Health Initiatives. "Resilience: How People Overcome." *Dialogue* 7 (1999): 1–4.

Knitzer, J. *Promoting Resilience: Helping Young Children and Parents Affected by Substance Abuse, Domestic Violence, and Depression in the Context of Welfare Reform.* New York: National Center for Children in Poverty, 2000. Rep. No. Issue Brief 8.

Kumpfer, K., and J. DeMarsh. "Family, Environmental, and Genetic Influences on Children's Future Chemical Dependency." In *Childhood and Chemical Abuse: Prevention and Intervention,* edited by S. Ezekoye, K. Kumpfer, and W. Bukoski. New York: Hayworth Press, 1985.

Masten, A. S., K. M. Best, and N. Garmezy. "Resilience and Development: Contributions from the Study of Children Who Overcome Adversity." *Development and Psychopathology* 2 (1990): 425–444.

Radke-Yarrow, M., and E. Brown. "Resilience and Vulnerability in Children of Multiple-Risk Families." *Development and Psychopathology* 5 (1993): 581–592.

Rae-Grant, N. I., B. H. Thomas, D. R. Offord, and M. H. Boyle. "Risk, Protective Factors and the Prevalence of Behavioral and Emotional Disorders in Children and Adolescents." *Journal of the American Academy of Child and Adolescent Psychiatry* 28 (1989): 262–268.

Steinhauer, P. D. "The Effect of Growing up in Poverty on Developmental Outcomes in Children: Some Implications of the Revision of the Social Security System." *Canadian Child Psychiatry Bulletin* 4 (1995a): 32–39.

Walsh, Froma. *Strengthening Family Resilience.* New York: Guilford Press, 1998.

Yoshikawa, H. "Prevention As a Cumulative Protection: Effects of Early Support and Education on Chronic Delinquency and Its Risks." *Psychological Bulletin* 115 (1994): 28–54.

8. The six factors in Rutter's Adversity Index were parental discord or divorce, psychiatric disorder in the mother, paternal criminality, single-parent family, overcrowding or large family size, probably related to low socioeconomic status, and parental loss. When only one risk factor was present, the risk to children was small, but as the number of factors increased, the corresponding risk to children increased dramatically.

Rutter also addressed the question of the difficulty of urban neighborhoods by examining the difference between the island community on the Isle of Wight and a working-class London borough. The difference was primarily explained by a greater number of the identified risk factors in the urban setting; the risk factors themselves were the same in both areas.

Rutter, M., A. Cox, C. Tupling, M. Berger, and W. Yule. "Attainment and Adjustment in Two Geographical Areas: I. The Prevalence of Psychiatric Disorder." *British Journal of Psychiatry* 126 (1975): 493–509.

Rutter, M., B. Yule, D. Quinton, O. Rowlands, W. Yule, and M. Berger. "Attainment and Adjustment in Two Geographical Areas: III. Some Factors Accounting for Area Differences." *British Journal of Psychiatry* 125 (1975): 520–533.

9. Sameroff's initial work examined a set of factors in groups of women who had severe mental illness including schizophrenia, depression, and anxiety disorder. The factors were chronicity of maternal mental illness, maternal anxiety, parental perspectives, maternal interactive behaviors, maternal education, occupation of head of household, minority group social status, family social support, stressful life events, and family size. As in Rutter's studies, the presence of one risk factor alone led to very little increased risk. As the number of factors increased, so did the likelihood that the children would become ill. Also, environment had a large influence. Many of the youngsters who were rated as doing poorly in middle-class environments were still functioning much better than youngsters who looked resilient in the inner city. He attributed this to environmental influence.

Sameroff, A. J., R. Seifer, M. Zax, and R. Barocas. "Early Indicators of Developmental Risk: Rochester Longitudinal Study." *Schizophrenia Bulletin* 13 (1987): 383–394.

Sameroff, A. J., and M. J. Chandler. "Reproductive Risk and the Continuum of Caretaking Casualty." In *Review of Child Development Research*. 4th ed., edited by F. D. Horowitz, M. N. Hetherington, and S. Scarr-Salopatek, 187–244. Chicago: University of Chicago Press, 1975.

In later studies, Sameroff and colleagues examined similar factors in schoolchildren in Philadelphia but enlarged the domains and found that factors including individual, family, neighborhood, and school had influence. As the number of risk factors increased, so did the likelihood that children would do badly. As in the previous study, the context or environment of the child was very important in determining what happened.

Sameroff, A. J., W. T. Bartko, A. Baldwin, C. Baldwin, and R. Seifer. "Family and Social Influences on the Development of Child Competence." In

Families, Risk, and Competence, edited by M. Lewis and C. Feiring, 161–185. Mahwah, New Jersey: Lawrence Erlbaum Associates, 1998.

In general, the cumulative impact of numerous negative influences in multiple domains, or risk factors, on children's lives is well-documented to lead to poor outcome.

Foege, W. H. "Adverse Childhood Experiences: A Public Health Perspective." *American Journal of Preventive Medicine* 14 (1998): 354–355.

Lynch, J. W., G. A. Kaplan, and S. J. Shema. "Cumulative Impact of Sustained Economic Hardship on Physical, Cognitive, Psychological, and Social Functioning." *New England Journal of Medicine* 337 (1997): 1889–1895.

McLoyd, V. C. "Socioeconomic Disadvantage and Child Development." *American Psychologist* 53 (1998): 185–204.

The best recent summary of the genetic influence in childhood depression is:

Silberg, J., and M. Rutter. "Nature-Nurture Interplay in the Risks Associated with Parental Depression." In *Children of Depressed Parents: Alternative Pathways to Risk for Psychopathology,* edited by S. H. Goodman and I. H. Gotlieb. Washington, D.C.: American Psychological Association. In press.

This entire volume provides a good overall recent summary of research on children of depressed parents.

10. Rutter, M. "Meyerian Psychobiology, Personality Development and the Role of Life Experiences." *American Journal of Psychiatry* 143 (1986): 1077–1087.

Rutter, M. L. "Psychosocial Adversity and Child Psychopathology." *British Journal of Psychiatry* 174 (1999): 480–493.

11. Beardslee, W. R., M. B. Keller, R. Seifer, P. W. Lavori, J. Staley, D. Podorefsky, and D. Shera. "Prediction of Adolescent Affective Disorder: Effects of Prior Parental Affective Disorders and Child Psychopathology." *Journal of the American Academy of Child and Adolescent Psychiatry* 35 (1996): 279–288.

My understanding of risk and resilience in our sample of children at risk because of parental depression was greatly enhanced by working with this sample with two young psychologists, both of whom completed their doctoral dissertations using information from these families: Dr. Donna Podorefsky and Dr. Ann Boese.

My understanding of the connection between poor health, poverty, and depression has been enhanced by working on the literature review with a research assistant, Ms. Becky Pettingill. Ms. Marcy Burstein has helped in organizing the final references.

12. Beardslee, W. R., and T. R. G. Gladstone. "Children of Affectively Ill Parents: A Review of the Past Ten Years." *Journal of the American Academy of Child and Adolescent Psychiatry* 37 (1998): 1134–1141.

Garber, J., and N. C. Martin. "Negative Cognitions in Offspring of Depressed Parents: Mechanisms of Risk." In *Children of Depressed Parents: Alternative Pathways to Risk for Psychopathology,* edited by S. H. Goodman and I. H. Gotlieb. Washington, D.C.: American Psychological Association. In press.

Garber, J., B. Weiss, and N. Shanley. "Cognitions, Depressive Symptoms, and Development in Adolescents." *Journal of Abnormal Psychology* 102 (1993): 47–57.

Hammen, C., D. Burge, E. Burney, and C. Adrian. "Longitudinal Study of Diagnoses in Children of Women with Unipolar and Bipolar Affective Disorder." *Archives of General Psychiatry* 47 (1990): 1112–1117.

Weissman, M. M., V. Warner, P. Wickramaratne, D. Moreau, and M. Olfson. "Offspring of Depressed Parents." *Archives of General Psychiatry* 54 (1997): 932–940.

13. Lewinsohn, P. M., R. E. Roberts, J. R. Seeley, P. Rohde, I. H. Gotlieb, and H. Hops. "Adolescent Psychopathology: II. Psychosocial Risk Factors for Depression." *Journal of Abnormal Psychology* 103 (1994): 302–315.

Nolen-Hoeksema, S., and J. S. Girgus. "The Emergence of Gender Difference in Depression During Adolescence." *Psychological Bulletin* 115 (1994): 424–443.

Reinherz, H. Z., R. M. Giaconia, A. M. Carmola-Hauf, M. S. Wasserman, and A. B. Silverman. "Major Depression in the Transition to Adulthood: Risks and Impairments." *Journal of Abnormal Psychology* 108 (1999): 500–510.

14. Petersen, A. C., P. A. Sarigiani, and R. E. Kennedy. "Adolescent Depression: Why More Girls?" *Journal of Youth and Adolescence* 20 (1991): 247–271.

15. Rutter, M. "Some Research Considerations on Intergenerational Conti-
nuities and Discontinuities: Comment on the Special Section." *Developmental Psychology* 34 (1998): 1269–1273.

Rutter, M. "Commentary: Some Focus and Process Considerations Regarding Effects of Parental Depression on Children." *Developmental Psychology* 26 (1990): 60–67.

16. Beardslee, W. R., E. M. Versage, P. Salt, and E. Wright. "The Development and Evaluation of Two Preventive Intervention Strategies for Children of Depressed Parents." In *Rochester Symposium on Developmental Psychopathology, Volume IX: Developmental Approaches to Prevention and Intervention,* edited by D. Cicchetti and S. L. Toth. Rochester: University of Rochester Press, 1999.

17. Beardslee, W. R., and G. Vaillant. "Adult Development." In *Psychiatry,* edited by A. Tasman, J. Kay, and J. A. Lieberman, 145–155. Philadelphia: W. B. Saunders, 1997.

Chapter Seven

1. Ms. Lynn Focht-Birkerts, Ms. E. Versage, Ms. Phyllis Rothberg, and I collaborated on the study of family narratives. As much of the information from families was collected in interviews that kept the accounts separate for different family members, one member of our team read all of the accounts and tried to put together a story or narrative of the family's experience as a whole over time. We often also went back and asked family members whether what we thought happened in fact had happened.

Ms. Focht-Birkerts deserves credit for the awareness of the need for children to eventually be able to acknowledge the pain they have undergone and to talk it over. Some of the stories were originally formulated by her for clinical audiences. She also led me to see the connection between our work and the emerging traditions in narrative and family therapy. The journal *Family Process* has generously given us permission to use these accounts, although I am presenting them here from a somewhat different perspective.

Focht, L., and W. R. Beardslee. "Speech After Long Silence: The Use of Narrative Therapy in a Preventive Intervention for Children of Parents with Affective Disorder." *Family Process* 35 (1996): 407–422.

Focht-Birkerts, L., and W. R. Beardslee. "A Child's Experience of Paternal Depression: Encouraging Relational Resilience in Families with Affective Illness." *Family Processes* 39 (2000): 417–434.

There is increasing evidence that talking and writing about difficult illness can help in mastering such illness.

Pennebaker, J. W. "Putting Stress into Words: Health, Linguistic, and Therapeutic Implications." *Behavioral Research Therapy* 31 (1993): 539–548.

Pennebaker, J. W. "Writing about Emotional Experiences as a Therapeutic Process." *Psychological Science* 8 (1997): 162–169.

This also applies in cases of abuse and other related experiences.

Daniel, J. H. "The Courage to Hear: African-American Women's Memories of Racial Trauma." In *Psychotherapy with African American Women*, edited by L. C. Jackson and B. Greene, 126–144. New York: Guilford Publications, Inc., 2000.

Grossman, F. K. *With the Phoenix Rising: Lessons from Ten Resilient Women Who Overcame the Trauma of Childhood Sexual Abuse*. San Francisco: Jossey-Bass, 1999.

Weingarten, K. "Witnessing, Wonder, and Hope." *Family Process* 39 (2000): 389–402.

For a perspective on the healing principles that we saw in working with families, see:

Beardslee, W. R., S. Swatling, L. Hoke, P. C. Rothberg, P. Van de Velde, L. Focht, and D. Podorefsky. "From Cognitive Information to Shared Meaning: Healing Principles in Preventive Intervention." *Psychiatry* 61 (1998): 112–129.

Beardslee, W. R., E. Versage, E. Wright, P. Salt, P. Rothberg, K. Drezner, and T. Gladstone. "Examination of Preventive Interventions for Families with Depression: Evidence of Change." *Development and Psychopathology* 9 (1997): 109–130.

Overall perspectives that also helped guide me were provided by:

Kleinman, A. *The Illness Narratives: Suffering, Healing, and the Human Condition*. New York: Basic Books, 1989.

Reiss, D. "The Represented and Practicing Family: Contrasting Visions of Family Continuity." In *Relationship Disturbances in Early Childhood: A*

Developmental Approach, edited by A. J. Sameroff and R. N. Emde. New York: Basic Books, Inc., 1989.

Sameroff, A. J. "Principles of Development and Psychopathology." In *Relationship Disturbances in Early Childhood: A Developmental Approach,* edited by A. J. Sameroff and R. N. Emde. New York: Basic Books, 1989.

Chapter Eight

1. The phrase I use, "time to heal," comes from the title of Kenneth Ludmerer's history of medical education. Ludmerer argues that the current problems in health care do not allow medical students time to learn or take care of patients. This is another powerful reason to consider the need for systems reform (see Epilogue).

Ludmerer, K. M. *Time to Heal: American Medical Education from the Turn of the Century to the Era of Managed Care.* New York: Oxford University Press, 1999.

Chapter Twelve

1. Goldman, S., and W. R. Beardslee. "Suicide in Children and Adolescents." In *The Harvard Medical School Guide to Suicide Assessment and Intervention,* edited by D. Jacobs. San Francisco: Jossey-Bass, 1998. This entire volume is a fine overall resource on what is known about suicide.

Gould, M. S., D. Shaffer, P. Fisher, and R. Garfinkel. "Separation/Divorce and Child Adolescent Completed Suicide." *Journal of the American Academy of Child and Adolescent Psychiatry* 37 (1998): 155–162.

Pfeffer, C. R. *The Suicidal Child.* New York: Guilford Press, 1986.

Shaffer, D., C. R. Pfeffer, and Work Group on Quality Issues. "Practice Parameter for the Assessment and Treatment of Children and Adolescents with Suicidal Behavior." *Journal of the American Academy of Child and Adolescent Psychiatry* 40, No. 7 suppl. (2001): 24S–51S.

2. The prevention of suicide is a pressing public health concern. Brent's commentary emphasizes that the presence of guns in a home increases the risk for suicide among adolescents, demonstrating that the prevention of suicide must involve comprehensive consideration of all factors.

Brent, D. A. "Risk Factors for Adolescent Suicide and Suicidal Behavior: Mental and Substance Abuse Disorders, Family Environmental Factors, and Life Stress." *Suicide and Life-Threatening Behavior* 25 (1995): 52–63.

The Surgeon General's report describes the urgent need to address the problem of suicide.

U.S. Public Health Service. *The Surgeon General's Call to Action to Prevent Suicide.* Washington, D.C.: 1999.

3. Jamison, K. R. *Night Falls Fast: Understanding Suicide.* New York: Alfred A. Knopf, 1999.

Poussaint, A. F., and A. Alexander. *Lay My Burden Down.* Boston: Beacon Press, 2000.

Chapter Thirteen

1. I was again and again struck by the power of faith to help families deal with depression. There is a substantial amount of research in this area that supports this observation, including a large set of investigations of how important faith is in coping with illness.

Fricchione, G. L. "Religious Issues in the Context of Medical Illness." In *Psychiatric Care of the Medical Patient,* edited by A. Stoudemire, B. Fogel, and D. Greenberg. New York: Oxford University Press, 2000.

Kendler, K. S., C. O. Gardner, and C. A. Prescott. "Religion, Psychopathology, and Substance Use and Abuse: A Multimeasure, Genetic-Epidemiologic Study." *American Journal of Psychiatry* 154 (1997): 322–329.

Koenig, H. G., et al. "Religious Coping and Depression among Elderly, Hospitalized Medically Ill Men." *American Journal of Psychiatry* 149 (1992): 1693–1700.

Larson, D. B., J. P. Swyers, and M. E. McCullough, eds. *Scientific Research on Spirituality and Health: A Consensus Report.* Rockville, MD: National Institute for Healthcare Research, 1998.

Miller, L., M. Davies, and S. Greenwald. "Religiosity and Substance Use and Abuse among Adolescents in the National Comorbidity Survey." *Journal of the American Academy of Child and Adolescent Psychiatry* 39 (2000): 1190–1197.

Epilogue

1. Belfer, M. L., ed. *Cultural Influences in Child Psychiatry: Child and Adolescent Clinics of North America.* St. Louis: Harcourt/WB Saunders, 2001.

Canino, I. A., and J. Spurlock. *Culturally Diverse Children and Adolescents: Assessment, Diagnosis, and Treatment.* New York: The Guilford Press, 1994.

Podorefsky, D. L., M. McDonald-Dowdell, and W. R. Beardslee. "Adaptation of a Depression Prevention Program for Use in a Low-Income Culturally Diverse Community." *Journal of the American Academy of Child and Adolescent Psychiatry* (2001). In press.

Powell, G. J. *The Psychosocial Development of Minority Group Children.* New York: Brunner/Mazel, Inc., 1983.

The manuals for the conduct of our Preventive Intervention Program and its adaptation to new settings are available to any clinician who wants them by writing directly to us at Children's Hospital Boston.

We have also learned about the great importance of cultural effects in families from working with colleagues in Canada, Finland, and the Netherlands in adapting our prevention approach for use in those countries. My colleague Dr. Tytti Solantaus of STAKES, Federal Ministry for Health Policy in Finland, has been particularly helpful.

2. Hay Group. "Health Care Plan Design and Cost Trends: 1988 through 1998." *Report Prepared for the National Association of Psychiatric Health Systems and the Association of Behavioral Group Practices.* Arlington, VA: Author, 1999.

3. Frank, R. G., C. Koyanagi, T. G. McGuire. "The Politics and Economics of Mental Health 'Parity' Laws." *Health Affairs* 16 (1997): 108–119.

4. The need to include caretakers as well as children is presented from a different perspective by:

Chavkin, W., V. Breitbart, and P. H. Wise. "Finding Common Ground: The Necessity of an Integrated Agenda for Women's and Children's Health." *The Journal of Law, Medicine, and Ethics* 22 (1994): 262–269.

5. Anderson, G. F., and J. Poullier. "Health Spending, Access, and Outcomes: Trends in Industrialized Countries." *Health Affairs* 18 (1999): 178–192.

Marmot, M. G. "Improvement of Social and Environment to Improve Health." *Lancet* 351 (1998): 57–60.

Starfield, B. "Is United States Health Really the Best in the World?" *Journal of the American Medical Association* 284 (2000): 483–485.

6. A useful summary of how we might approach systems reform is provided in:

Institute of Medicine. *Crossing the Quality Chasm: A New Health System for the 21st Century.* Washington, D.C.: United States Government Printing Office, 2001.

7. Hinshaw and Cicchetti's remarkable work on stigma provides a good overview of this issue.

Hinshaw, S. P., and D. Cicchetti. "Stigma and Mental Disorder: Conceptions of Illness, Public Attitudes, Personal Disclosure, and Social Policy." *Development and Psychopathology* 12 (2000): 555–598.

8. The work of Earls and Sampson has demonstrated the effects communities can have on mental health.

Earls, F. "A Developmental Approach to Understanding and Controlling Violence." In *Theory and Research in Behavioral Pediatrics,* edited by H. E. Fitzgerald, 61–88. New York: Plenum Press, 1991.

Sampson, R. J., J. D. Morenoff, and F. Earls. "Beyond Social Capital: Spatial Dynamics of Collective Efficacy for Children." *American Sociological Review* 64 (1999): 633–660.

9. Unfortunately, the link between poverty and poor health is well established.

Aber, J. L., N. G. Bernett, D. C. Conley, and J. Li. "The Effects of Poverty on Child Health and Development." *Annual Review of Public Health* 18 (1997): 463–483.

Brunner, E. "Socioeconomic Determinants of Health: Stress and the Biology of Inequality." *British Medical Journal* 314 (1997): 1472–1476.

Call, K. T., and J. Nonnemaker. "Socioeconomic Disparities in Adolescent Health: Contributing Factors." *Annals of NY Academy of Science* 896 (1999): 352–355.

Link, B. G. and J. Phelan. "Social Conditions As Fundamental Causes of Disease." *Journal of Health and Social Behavior* (Extra Issue 2000): 80–94.

Turner, J., and D. A. Lloyd. "The Stress Process and the Social Distribution of Depression." *Journal of Health and Social Behavior* 40 (1999): 374–404.

10. In the past, those concerned about mental illness in adults often have not taken into account factors early in infancy and childhood that build resources to protect against future adversities, including mental illness in adulthood. For example, there is now definitive evidence that both high-quality day care and nurse home visitation have major positive

effects on mental health in adolescence and young adulthood, in particular in preventing child abuse and smoking, and fostering educational development in young mothers and their offspring. To consider the long-term prevention of depression inevitably involves recognizing the need to provide the resources for healthy development across the span of childhood, long before the age when depression begins to appear.

Berrueta-Clement, J. R., L. J. Schwienhart, W. S. Barnett, A. S. Epstein, and D. P. Weikart. *Changed Lives: The Effects of the Perry Preschool Program on Youths Through Age 19.* Ypsilanti: High/Scope Press, 1984.

Knitzer, J. "Early Childhood Mental Health Services Through a Policy and Systems Development Perspective." In *Handbook of Early Childhood Intervention, 2nd ed.,* edited by J. P. Shonkoff and S. J. Meisels. New York: Cambridge University Press, 2000.

Olds, D. L., C. R. Henderson, R. W. Chamberlin, and R. Tatelbaum. "Preventing Child Abuse and Neglect: A Randomized Trial of Nurse Home Visitation." *Pediatrics* 78 (1986): 65–78.

Vega, W. A., and J. Murphy. "Projecto Bienestar: An Example of a Community-Based Intervention." In *Culture and the Restructuring of Community Mental Health,* edited by J. Murphy, 103–122. Westport: Greenwood Press, 1990. Contributions in Psychology, ser. no. 16.

Yoshikawa, H., and J. Knitzer. *Lessons from the Field: Head Start Mental Health Strategies to Meet Changing Needs.* New York: National Center for Children of Poverty, Joseph L. Mailman School of Public Health, Columbia University, 1997.

Prevention of depression may occur when another important preventive initiative occurs. Thus, Kellam found a strong reduction in depressive symptomatology when reading scores for children improved. In adults, Vinokur and Price have demonstrated that a high-quality job retraining program given to those who were recently unemployed led to significantly reduced depression over time compared to those who did not receive it.

Kellam, S. G., L. Werthamer-Larsson, L. J. Dolan, C. H. Brown, L. S. Mayer, G. W. Rebok, J. C. Anthony, J. Laudolff, G. Edelsohn, and L. Wheeler. "Developmental Epidemiologically Based Preventive Trials: Baseline Modeling of Early Target Behaviors and Depressive Symptoms." *American Journal of Community Psychology* 19 (1991): 563–584.

Vinokur, A. D., and R. H. Price. "Impact of the JOBS Intervention on Unemployed Workers Varying in Risk for Depression." *American Journal of Community Psychology* 23 (1995): 39–74.

11. Evidence that a large disparity in the distribution of wealth within a country leads to poor health outcomes is provided by:

Kawachi, I., B. P. Kennedy, and R. G. Wilkinson. Introduction to *The Society and Population Health Reader,* edited by I. Kawachi et al. Volume 1. New York: The New Press, 1999.

Massey, D. S. "The Age of Extremes: Concentrated Affluence and Poverty in the Twenty-first Century." *Demography* 33 (1996): 395–412.

Rogler, L. M. "Increasing Socioeconomic Inequalities and the Mental Health of the Poor." *Nervous and Mental Disease* 184 (1996): 719–722.

Wilkinson, R. G. "Socioeconomic Determinants of Health: Health Inequalities: Relative or Absolute Material Standards?" *British Medical Journal* 314 (1997): 591–595.

12. One of the most useful volumes in understanding how to make social programs effective is Lee Schorr's *Common Purpose.*

Schorr, L. B. *Common Purpose: Strengthening Families and Neighborhoods to Rebuild America.* New York: Doubleday Dell Publishing Group, Inc., 1997.

The following publication provides a good overview of how resilience-enhancing approaches similar to ours can be incorporated into public policy.

Maton, K., C. Schellenbach, B. Leadbeater, and A. Solarz. *Investing in Children, Youth, Families, and Communities: Strengths-Based Research and Policy.* Washington: American Psychological Association. In press.

A fine review of what we know about what young children need is:

Institute of Medicine and Board on Children, Health, and Families. *From Neurons to Neighborhoods: The Science of Early Childhood Development.* Edited by Jack P. Shonkoff and Deborah A. Phillips. Washington, D.C.: National Academy Press, 2000.

For a useful perspective on neighborhoods, see the following:

Sampson, R. J., S. W. Raudenbush, and F. Earls. "Neighborhoods and Violent Crime: A Multilevel Study of Collective Efficacy." *Science* 277 (1997): 918–924.

Weissbourd provides a good overview of the factors placing children at risk.

Weissbourd, R. *The Vulnerable Child: What Really Hurts America's Children and What We Can Do About it.* Reading: Addison-Wesley Publishing Company, 1996.

13. The promise and direction of new research on children was recently summarized in a report of the National Institute of Mental Health Child Care Workgroup, of which I was a member.

The National Advisory Mental Health Council Workgroup on Child and Adolescent Mental Health Intervention Development and Deployment. "Blueprint for Change: Research on Child and Adolescent Mental Health." Washington, D.C.: 2001.

A similar plan for research on recent findings and future research directions in depression in both adults and children has been presented in:

Hollon, S. D., R. Munoz, D. Barlow, W. Beardslee, C. C. Bell, G. Bernal, G. Clarke, L. P. Franciosi, A. Kazdin, L. Kohn, M. Linehan, J. Markowitz, D. Miklowitz, J. Persons, K. Hoagwood, E. Nottelman, D. Sommers, R. Desimone, and L. Colpe. "Psychosocial Interventions for the Prevention and Treatment of Depression: Promoting Innovation and Increasing Access — A Report of the Psychosocial Intervention Development Workgroup." *Biological Psychiatry.* In press.

Some of the most promising future research directions for depression include combining theories from different domains, both in neuroscience and in developmental psychology, and understanding how to deliver high-quality evidence-based treatments to all who need them through finding new culturally sensitive delivery systems and perhaps even new means to deliver services, such as the Internet.

Because depression is heterogeneous both in how it presents and in what causes it, the identification of subtypes of depression will assist both in understanding how certain depressions come to be and in mounting effective treatments. As the application of the sequencing of the human genome proceeds, it may be possible to better tailor medications for individuals through the evolving field of pharmacogenetics.

Also, investigations into underlying processes such as emotion regulation (see Munoz and Dahl below) or the overall phenomenon of behavioral inhibition (see Kagan below) will provide important new perspectives that will help in understanding depression.

Dahl, R. E. "Affect Regulation, Brain Development, and Behavioral/Emotional Health in Adolescence." *The International Journal of Neuropsychiatric Medicine* 6 (2001): 60–72.

Goodman, S. H., and I. H. Gotlieb. "Risk for Psychopathology in the Children of Depressed Mothers: A Developmental Model for Understanding Mechanisms of Transmission." *Psychological Review* 106 (1999): 458–490.

Kagan, Jerome. *Galen's Prophecy.* New York: Basic Books, 1994.

Munoz, R. F. "On the Road to a World Without Depression." *The Journal of Primary Prevention* 21 (2001): 325–338.

Rudolph, K. D., C. Hammen, D. Burge, N. Lindberg, D. Herzberg, and S. E. Daley. "Toward an Interpersonal Life-Stress Model of Depression: The Developmental Context of Stress Generation." *Development and Psychopathology* 12 (2000): 215–234.

World Health Organization. *The World Health Report: 2001: Mental Health: New Understanding, New Hope.* Geneva World Health Organization, 2001.

14. Dr. Julius Richmond, Surgeon General under President Carter, described a model of how new knowledge can eventually be translated into successful large-scale programs. There are three components: the knowledge base to know what to do; an implementation strategy that allows such approaches to be widely used and remain of high quality; and the political will to bring about change, including the appropriation of necessary resources. Head Start is perhaps the best example of a program that has successfully gone through these stages.

The scientific and research progress over the last two decades has provided the knowledge base both to effectively treat children for psychiatric illness and to mount successful prevention programs for children and families. The challenge in the future will be to implement such programs widely and, above all, to find the political will to make this happen.

Richmond, J. B., and M. Kotelchuck. "Commentary on Changed Lives." In *Changed Lives: The Effects of the Perry Preschool Program on Youths Through Age 19,* edited by J. R. Berrueta-Clement, L. J. Schweinhart, W. S. Barnett, A. S. Epstein, and D. P. Weikart, 204–210. Ypsilanti: High/Scope Press, 1995.

Index